MANAGING HIGH RELIABILITY SYSTEMS

SAFE HIGH RELIABILITY SYSTEMS

DR PATRICK S MAHER

Dedicated to the memory of Allan

For Mary, Tamara and Damien

With eternal gratitude to Rosemary

Contact the author at:

Dr Patrick Maher
PO Box 1646
Booragoon WA 6954
Australia

Set in Crimson Text

Created with Vellum

ACKNOWLEDGMENTS

The front cover was designed with Canva.

CONTENTS

INTRODUCTION

WHAT THIS BOOK IS ABOUT.

This book inspires people to ask: 'Can I do something in my own job, right now, to save lives?'

Professor Barbara Hinton from the University of Arkansas describes it as *'exquisitely crafted...excellent, it can contribute to managerial training, especially in the arena of accidents, where management is reactive rather than proactive. Dr Maher's work could change the thinking of management.'*

Associate Professor Katherine Dixon (Curtin University) says, *'This book reads like a detective novel. It has important implications for industry... the sweep of the literature is associated with ethics, leadership, decision-making models, organisational perspectives, socio-technical perspectives...a careful examination of the factors impacting upon effective managerial decision-making prior to, during and after an accident. Dr Maher has exercised precision, clarity and restraint.'*

Professor Athanasou UTS (Sydney) says it is a *'comprehensive study... and makes a substantial contribution to a topic of major importance and the approach is unique...it documents major oversights, incompetence, negligence and failures to learn under conditions of complexity and uncertainty that might reasonably have been foreseen. It has profound implications for educa-*

tion and training, human resource development and occupational safety and health, human error, judgement and decision making. The five cases studied represent excellent examples of human error and are vital for our understanding and "learning".'

Why this book is valuable

Dr Maher sets out a critical set of competencies to put the reader in control of disasters caused by management greed and negligence. He shows the reader how to expose psychopathic and dangerous behaviour in the early stages of an unfolding disaster.

The eleven critical competencies set out in this book can be mastered by any intelligent person.

Suppose you are in a hazardous front-line situation. In that case, this book will help you save lives and back your decisions with reason and facts in the face of line management resistance where the professional advice you give is met with intimidation and the old 'saw', "That's just your opinion."

If you are a middle-level manager, this book will provide you with the language and arguments that you need to avoid dangerous incidents and to manage safety upwards to senior decision-makers in the face of demands to meet deadlines and cut costs.

If you are a senior manager or member of a board of directors, this book will reveal rational ways of persuading key stakeholders to support responsible investment in safety and minimise the risk resulting from corporate greed.

The book is essential reading for those engaged in coronial inquests and inquiries into preventable corporate accidents. It shows that hiding behind the 'corporate veil' is no longer a tool senior executives can use to defend personal negligence and bad decision-making.

The facile blame shifting argument from the phantom in the machine used by lawyers and public relations, known as 'systemic failure', is deftly moved aside by Dr Maher's insights to establish that responsibility for preventable fatal accidents in high reliability organisations lies solely with senior executives who make decisions. It reveals how an accident cascade is set in train from the bad decision to the accident.

The book provides a powerful arc of reasoning showing how certain critical management competencies build on one another. It directly confronts the problem of corporate greed and the underlying psychopathologies that give rise to it. It shows how it is important to identify and master the core managerial competencies. Acquiring the competencies is possible through training, especially when a strict regulatory and compliance framework is in place.

High reliability organisations governed by statutory regulations are required to comply with safety guidelines and specifications. When fatalities or serious injuries occur in otherwise preventable accidents, these organisations are routinely exonerated from any responsibility by claiming to have '*systemic management problems* and their senior managing coalitions are legally able to hide behind the 'corporate veil'.

Other than 'acts of God', most accidents resulting in fatalities and serious injury, occur in organisations where prior knowledge of a potential accident existed, and this knowledge was not applied.

Most accidents in high reliability organisations might have been prevented if the cascade of events leading to the accidents could have been interrupted.

The competencies described in this book are not usually taught in orthodox management studies programs in higher education institutions. However, when these competencies fail, they not only result in accidents but also cause orthodox management problems such as production delays and losses, costly litigation, increasing indemnity insurance and erosion of an organisation's credibility in the marketplace.

Who should buy this book

This book fits into the current managerial domains of organisational development and management psychology, occupational health and safety, organisational leadership and change, innovation and development, technology policy, regulation of safety at the government level, and managing safety compliance at an organisational level.

The competencies identified in this book apply to senior coalitions and the organisations they govern and manage. It will appeal to managers, organisation development consultants, and management training specialists. Academics teaching and studying financial management, policy, organisational behaviour, management and other social/behavioural sciences should also find it relevant. Its prime interest should be to members of the dominant coalitions of high-reliability organisations and their principal stakeholders.

Its Peers

This book sits on the same shelves as *The Corporation, Outfoxed,* and Charles Perrow's *Normal Accidents* and it resonates with the views of Arundhati Roy and Michael Moore. The book distinguishes itself from its peers by revealing specific examples of preventable accidents and their drivers. It describes a detailed set of critical competencies and locates the issues in the critical areas of corporate governance. The work focuses on the skills needed by managers of high-reliability corporations to prevent such accidents in the future. It is much more than an expose. It is a handbook to save lives.

The book takes a fresh and accessible approach to the problem of the power that is vested in the hands of corporate psychopaths who run many high-reliability organisations.

There is little other material that so adroitly spans the management-psychology gap and explains it so well. While the author acknowledges his debt to the work of scholars who have taken somewhat different approaches to management negligence and corporate greed, this book stands apart from theirs because it can be readily adapted to organisations, TAFE and university teaching and learning. It can also be used as a personal handbook and text to support management and safety courses in the emerging fields of Organisational Development and Organisational Psychology.

The problems, the reasons, and the situations that prompted this book.

Accidents occur because incompetent, responsible personnel managing organisations ignore available safety-critical information and signals even though the organisations concerned reassure the public that they comply with current safety regulations and standards. In the Seaview case, for example, the manuals were on the shelves of the CAA but turned out to be nothing more than shelf decorations and were used to 'Buck Pass' and obfuscate CAA systemic management failings.

This book identifies management competencies repeatedly shown to arise as issues of concern by Commissions of Enquiry and Coronial reports. These reports show that dominant coalitions of directors and managers in organisations fail in relation to their *Competencies for Safety-Conscious Practice.*

The evidence suggests that these competencies are not properly understood even though they are significant enablers of organisational safety in high-reliability organisations. When they fail, people die and organisations experience catastrophic losses and reputational damage.

Principal Question

What significant underpinning capacities, organisational factors, and performance capacities are revealed in accident reports, and what competencies flow from these to enable dominant coalitions in high-reliability organisations to engage in accident prevention effectively?

Subsidiary Question

What significant factors in accident reports and key literature are required by dominant coalitions in high-reliability organisations to enable compliance with accident prevention regulations and appropriate intervention strategies in unfolding accident scenarios?

What makes this book unique?

This book draws on direct evidence from Commissions of Inquiry and Coronial Inquest Reports into preventable fatal accidents.

High Reliability Culture

All the people in an organisation, like fish in a fish tank, swim in and breathe the organisation's culture and adopt its values. It is the water all around people and it is mostly invisible.

If safety is not valued in the water the organisation swims in, then it will not be there when it is needed. You have a safety culture, or you do not.

The guiding investigation discipline confined the research to identical system failures in each of five exemplar cases. The research revealed examples of failings that were repeated over again. The forensic grounded investigation of the five cases guided the author to identify the essential accident prevention competencies that should have been in place in each culture but were not.

Summary: The project investigated what management skills are needed to keep people safe in high-risk organisations like power plants or air traffic control, aiming to create a guide for better leadership and fewer accidents.

Explanation: The research explores how managers in high-risk environments can prevent accidents. It looks at existing research on organisations that operate safely in hazardous settings (High Reliability Organisations or HROs). The research uses data from accident reports and other sources to pinpoint crucial management skills. These skills are then organised into a structured system (a taxonomy) to help understand and teach them. The project also looks at existing theories to explore how personality, social factors, and individual strengths affect how managers behave and create a safe working culture. Ultimately, the research aims to build a better understanding of what makes a good manager in a high-risk environment to improve safety and prevent future accidents.

Some Key terms:

- **High-Reliability Organisations (HROs)**: Organisations that operate in hazardous environments but maintain very high safety records. Examples include air traffic control, nuclear power plants, and aircraft carriers.
- **Competency**: A specific skill, knowledge, or behaviour that contributes to successful performance in a particular role.
- **Taxonomy**: A structured classification system used to organise and categorize information, in this case, managerial competencies.
- **Grounded Theory**: A research method that uses data (like interviews or observations) to develop theories.
- **Habitus**: Deeply ingrained habits, skills, and dispositions that we possess due to our life experiences. These shape our perceptions and actions within the social world.

Here is one of the best handbooks of accident prevention on the market for thousands of management readers and front-line operators who are regularly placed in almost impossible positions where their moment-to-moment decisions can either prevent or cause fatal accidents.

This book gives readers many practical tools needed to help save lives. It shares a common essential language all organisational cultures can understand, and it reveals approaches to safety that front-line workers can master to defend their decisions to act responsibly. It is an invitation for readers to read more widely and to do their own research and in-house investigations.

For senior executives in high-reliability corporations, it shows that the corporate veil is nothing more than legal vapour and can easily be blown away to reveal those hiding behind it. It clearly shows that justice is now firmly on the side of the victim, not the narcissists and psychopaths who run corporations that purport to protect their victims from avoidable harm but fail to.

For those involved in Commissions of Enquiry, it provides clear, step-by-step arguments and references based on prior cases that identified failures of specific managerial competencies. The failure of a particular competency is now set down in context so that each incidence of failure can be easily identified and appropriately named and described as part of a comprehensive set of essential competencies. Naming the problems this way is the first step to eliminating them.

Dr Maher's analysis focuses on ten core managerial competencies identified as crucial for maintaining safety in high-reliability organisations (HROs).

Central Argument: Dr Maher argues that despite operating in high-risk environments, certain organisations fail to cultivate a "high-reliability habitus" – a culture that prioritises safety and learns from past mistakes. He attributes this failure to managerial incompetence, particularly in relation to the ten core competencies.

Methodology: Dr Maher adopted a modified grounded theory approach to the foundational research, drawing upon diverse sources, including formal accident reports, legal proceedings, psychological literature, and philosophical concepts. This multidisciplinary approach enabled a comprehensive analysis of factors influencing HRO safety.

Key Themes and Concepts:

1. Ten Core Competencies:

The book identifies ten core managerial competencies essential for high-reliability management, which can be categorised as follows:

Underpinning Capacities:

•Ethics: Aligning individual and organisational values with ethical decision-making in safety matters.

•Foresight: Adopting a proactive stance and anticipating potential hazards through scenario planning and risk assessment.

•Vigilance: Maintaining a heightened awareness of risk, actively seeking out potential hazards, and effectively interpreting warning signals.

•Judgement: Carefully weighing trade-offs, considering diverse factors, and making well-informed decisions, particularly in ambiguous situations.

•Balance: Cultivating a psychologically balanced approach to decision-making, avoiding neurotic or psychopathic tendencies.

Capacities to Perform:

•Salience and Context: Understanding the unique characteristics of each situation and tailoring safety measures to the specific context.

•Performance in a Particular Situation: Effectively applying skills and knowledge in real-time, adapting to changing circumstances, and utilising intuition when necessary.

•Multidisciplinary Performance: Drawing upon expertise from

diverse fields and collaborating effectively with specialists to address complex challenges.

•Error Modelling: Accurately identifying and analysing potential errors, understanding their root causes, and implementing preventative measures.

•Compliance: Ensuring strict adherence to regulatory regimes and proactively engaging with relevant authorities.

2. The High-Reliability Habitus:

Inspired by Bourdieu's concept of "habitus," Dr Maher emphasises the importance of cultivating a safety-oriented culture within HROs. This involves instilling values, practices, and systems that prioritise safety and facilitate continuous learning from past incidents.

Quote: "Habitus informs this book as a principle of sociation and individuation: sociation because our categories of judgment and action, coming from society, are shared by all those who were subjected to similar social conditions and conditionings (thus one can speak of a high-reliability habitus)."

3. The Role of Psychopathy:

Dr Maher expresses concern regarding the presence of individuals with psychopathic tendencies in management positions within HROs. He argues that their manipulative, remorseless, and self-serving behaviours can undermine safety efforts and create hazardous conditions.

Quote: "Perhaps most frightening, [psychopaths] often seem completely normal to unsuspecting targets. Babiak and Hare (2000) argue that the corporate psychopath's cold-blooded ability to manipulate others without remorse, coupled with a veneer of charm and high energy, can make them successful in many walks of life."

4. The Importance of Salience:

Dr Maher stresses the need for managers to understand the specific context of each situation and tailor their actions accordingly. He criticises the generic, "off-the-shelf" approach often adopted in risk management, arguing that it fails to account for the unique nuances of each situation.

Quote: "Salience is a psychological way of seeing a 'particular' situation and the events that pertain to it. It is necessary, therefore, for managers cultivate the skill to manage the 'salient' psychological space. This leads to a requirement for a capacity to manage the 'particular' background and the 'salient' physical factors."

5. Systemic Failures and Compliance:

Dr Maher argues that systemic failures often contribute to accidents in HROs. He highlights the importance of robust compliance regimes, holding both individuals and organisations accountable for safety breaches.

Quote: "The Westralia incident was another example of how several factors can work together to subvert vigilance. What should have been a vigilance - foresight building opportunity was contaminated by Navy ethos issues."

6. Practical Implications:

Dr Maher's work offers practical guidance for enhancing safety in HROs. He recommends:

•Implementing competency-based training programs for managers, focusing on the ten core competencies.

•Establishing clear ethical guidelines and fostering a culture of accountability.

•Developing robust risk assessment and scenario planning processes.

•Encouraging multidisciplinary collaboration and knowledge sharing.

•Implementing rigorous compliance and auditing systems.

•Screening potential employees for psychopathic tendencies.

*NOTE:** The British 'Enquiry' and the American 'Inquiry' have been used as close as possible to the way they are used in the source literature and case reports.

WHY THIS BOOK WAS WRITTEN

A Nutshell look inside the Book

Dr Maher's research provides valuable insights into the complexities of high-reliability management. His emphasis on managerial competencies, the cultivation of a "high-reliability habitus," and the need for robust compliance regimes offers a practical framework for improving safety in organisations operating in high-risk environments.

This is a compelling and readable book about managing risks in organisational systems.

High-reliability organisations must comply with safety guidelines and specifications.

All organisations are governed by laws that demand that staff safety and health policies protect workers.

When fatalities or serious injuries occur due to otherwise preventable accidents, the senior managers governing these entities are exonerated from any responsibility by claiming that the organisation has experienced *'systemic management problems'*. These dysfunctional senior managing coalitions can hide behind the corporate veil and only suffer a minor inconvenience. They paper over their failures with fatuous, meaningless, silly comments such as, 'We value our customers,' or 'We put safety first,' following a fatal, preventable accident.

If fines or censure are imposed, the organisation meets the impost. This means that shareholders pay the fines, and the perpetrators go about their business as if nothing had happened and remain incompetent until the next disaster. The cycle is repeated over and over.

The book examines cases of such incompetence and suggests ways to break this cycle and bring about competent management through insight, training, and strong compliance regimes.

Clear and understandable core management competencies are needed to prevent 'preventable' accidents. These competencies can be identified and mastered if a strong regulatory and compliance regime mandates them.

Other than 'Acts of God' (a dubious theological expediency used by insurance companies to avoid paying out on policies, such as acts of blowing up, sinking, crashing into, etc.), most accidents that result in fatalities and serious injury occur in organisations where prior knowledge of a potential accident existed. This knowledge was trivialised, ignored, or rejected as inconvenient.

Most accidents in high-reliability organisations can be prevented if the cascade of events leading to the accidents can be interrupted. The essential competencies needed to intervene in preventable accidents could and should be taught in orthodox management studies programs in higher education institutions. When these core managerial competencies are lacking, preventable fatal accidents occur.

An organisational accident triggers a cascade of subsequent orthodox management problems, such as production delays and losses, costly litigation, increasing indemnity insurance and erosion of an organisation's credibility in the marketplace.

The central concern of this book sprang from the unnecessary and preventable death of the author's brother-in-law. He was a father to a little girl and a new baby boy. They grew up not knowing their father. Further injustice was metered out when the compensation case saw the mining company influence the magistrate and persuade him that their mother would marry again. It led to the magistrate deciding on reduced compensation. The magistrate focused on that rather than on the harm caused by the mining company. Therefore, the mining company learned nothing useful about its negligence or the cascade of system failures that caused the fatality. The apparent class of system errors the company was prone to were again hidden behind a veil of corporate greed and smugness at their win in court, and there were similar fatalities both before and after the accident.

The mother never married again, and those children now have their own children. They spent their entire lives under a financial cloud and were left struggling and denying their necessities. They were robbed of a father and many of the simple, normal joys of life.

Remediation was a fatuous recommendation that the company 'hold an enquiry'.

The author would direct readers to go to this site.

https://en.wikipedia.org/wiki/Fatality_statistics_in_the_West
ern_Australian_mining_industry

With some irony, the author's grandfather was killed in a gold mine smelting accident when the author's father was eleven years old.

Both accidents were preventable. Both accidents resulted from poor systems management.

These post-hoc inquiries are inclined to drift away in the billowing smoke of industry as it grinds on regardless of a trail of preventable fatalities and accidents.

The work for this book rests on the exemplary research of the late Dr Barry Turner of Exeter University. Dr Turner established that a lack of foresight, together with misinformation, was high on the list of key factors leading to preventable fatal accidents. Dr Turner's work suggests that accidents occur in organisations where prior organisational knowledge of an unfolding accident exists—as it did with the author's brother-in-law. This book takes up the idea of management ignoring signals and prior knowledge of unfolding conditions for an accident to occur.

While Dr Turner's work was central to the research behind this book, it also stands on the shoulders of other respected scholars in the field and honours their work: Nick Pidgeon, Charles Perrow, James Reason, Neil Gunningham & Richard Johnstone, Ian Mitroff, Andrew Hopkins, and Dan Petersen.

The work finds a natural alignment with several organisational psychology and management disciplines, including management studies in organisational development and management psychology, occupational health and safety, organisational leadership and change, innovation and growth, technology policy, regulation of safety at the government and policy level, and managing.

When senior management values and nurtures the ten competencies, it enables applying well-developed 'multidisciplinary organisational and managerial expertise' in unforeseen, perilous, and tumultuous circumstances. The work may also be relevant in hospital, medical, military and security settings.

With diligence by senior management, the ten competencies can be embedded in an organisation's operational heuristics and managerial thinking patterns so that when extraordinary circumstances arise, the skills are available as a natural part of an organisation's responses. If the ten competencies are valued and fostered by senior management, then well-developed 'multidisciplinary organisational and managerial expertise' can be brought to bear in unexpected situations to eliminate or mitigate dangerous and chaotic situations.

The ten core competencies could also supplement (not replace) orthodox managerial training in universities, technical and Further Education programs, and Training and Development options for organisational consultants and management psychologists working in the Management of High-Reliability Organisations.

The project goes several layers deeper than most accident reports and shows how responsibility for preventable accidents rests with key managerial figures, such as the Board of Directors and Senior Management, rather than frontline personnel.

PART I

PART 1. HIGH-RELIABILITY MANAGEMENT: FUNDAMENTAL COMPETENCIES

1. CHAPTER 1. INTRODUCTION TO HIGH RELIABILITY SYSTEMS

THIS CHAPTER INTRODUCES THE CONCEPT OF HIGH-RELIABILITY organisations (HROs) and their importance in managing hazardous environments. It sets the stage for exploring the key competencies required for effective leadership in these organisations, emphasising the need for a deeper understanding of human factors and organisational dynamics in accident prevention.

And Eeyore whispered back: 'I'm not saying there won't be an accident now, mind you. They're funny things, accidents. You never have them till you're having them.'

A. A. Milne, The House at Pooh Corner.

Introduction

For those interested in understanding how the research for this book was done, this chapter examines the 'preventable accident' argument and introduces the research method that was adopted. This insight might prove useful to others thinking about doing academic or in-house research along the same lines.

The research began with the premise that accidents and disasters are all unintended. They are all events that surprise and violate expectations, and they result from failures of foresight and judgement for the individuals or organisations involved in them. The research investigated the idea that *accidents occur because incompetent, responsible management ignores available safety-critical information, even though the organisations concerned may espouse compliance with current safety regulations and standards.*

The author first examined the literature to determine if it 'confirms', or 'dis-confirms', or refutes the 'prior knowledge' proposition. The literature review and analysis were deep and extensive, but the detail is inappropriate for a working handbook of skills such as this. A decision had to be made to address only the most significant research.

For example, when reports from Commissions of Enquiry were examined, some fundamental directional questions arose. Why do dominant management coalitions with access to information about unfolding conditions for an accident and the power to intervene in its development don't?

Reports of accidents reveal that the information needed to prevent them was available and known to organisational personnel and others before the accident. Most of these people sustained an official mental model of safety management and claimed to have a good understanding of the responsibilities they said they practiced.

The official understanding that suggests that individuals at the work-face (front line) cause accidents while appealing to intuition is often prone to significant error and can lead to organisations creating and maintaining pathological assumptions that shape decision-making concerning safety, making matters worse. This suggests that managers in these organisations do not exercise essential pro-active management competencies.

The management competencies of concern are vigilance, foresight, judgment and balance, sufficient to plan for and avoid predictable accidents and other devastating events, such as corporate fraud. It also throws into relief values distorted by double standards and a broken ethical compass to guide the organisation. It illustrates what happens when there is a failure to comply with compliance guidelines and specific corporate and safety regulations and often occurs in organisations lacking an appropriate ethos of safety.

There has been a significant shift in accident analysis over the last few decades. The trend has been away from blaming individual front-line workers for accidents, toward identifying system failures and defeating them using the tools of systems analysis.

The literature pointing to 'prior knowledge' found during the incubation period of an impending accident, show that both erroneous assumptions and the minimisation of emergent danger by those involved are characteristic of 'man-made' accidents. For example, persistent alarms and other signals warning of a systems failure are often ignored and dismissed with comments such as, "Ignore that alarm. It's been going for ages." Or, "She'll be right, mate."

One overweening conclusion can be drawn: Individuals are less to blame for accidents than the systems that allow them to occur. Instead, we see in a close analysis of cases determined efforts by dominant coalitions, such as Corporate Directors and Managers, to shift the blame away from themselves to others. We often see in cases of failure of fiduciary responsibility that the blame for financial disaster is attributed to low-level staff. In each case, the power to make changes and respond with authority to signals was not in the responsibility of frontline staff who are blamed for accidents but resided with managing coalitions.

The relationship between accidents and failures of competencies and compliance is still under-researched.

It is also well established that regulation and compliance requirements in high-reliability organisations are backward-looking and develop from the lessons learned from previous incidents. This means they are 'system-based' and 'evolutionary'.

The cases examined in this book confirmed that compliance issues are often backward focused and did not account for emerging theories or the dramatic development of technologies and complex systems. Dunphy (1981, 1992, 1998) also confirmed these technology-related concerns in Australia.

Looking back to previous accidents may predict future accidents because the phenomena that trigger accidents are particular to that accident and industry. However, management needs to learn that there is little point in trying to prevent the *last* incident when it is at the expense of habituating to and failing to sensitise the organisation to the *next* incident.

This book examined several cases heard by Commissions of Enquiry or published Coronial Inquests. It distils ten critical managerial competencies and accountability procedures from these disasters that can act as system enablers to help build an ethos of safety in high-reliability organisations.

Stable management systems that are management-proofed from interference are needed to respond to an accident or systems failure with rapid and targeted interventions. These interventions help high-reliability organisations reach a level of safety beyond fundamental compliance, but ten critical competencies are needed to sustain such an organisation and its systems.

2. EXAMINING INCIDENTS OF FAILURE: THE RESEARCH QUESTION

THIS CHAPTER DELVES INTO THE CENTRAL RESEARCH QUESTION: "WHAT are the key managerial competencies required to ensure safety in high-reliability organisations?". It discusses the importance of identifying and developing these competencies to minimise the risk of accidents and foster a culture of safety.

"Any fact facing us is not as important as our attitude toward it, for that determines our success or failure. The way you think about a fact may defeat you before you ever do anything about it."

Norman Vincent Peale

Examining the questions arising from narratives of reported incidents of failure

Good managerial judgement is developed through a thorough theoretical and practical education in management. This knowledge should then be synthesised and brought to bear on individual experiences. These experiences can be narratively constructed and deconstructed (Denzin, 2000). The discourse revealing *failure* of managerial judgement is also revealed in similar narratives of preventable accidents that have been attributed to managerial failure.

This book is bounded by an interpretive approach to narratives and analyses of actual case reports (*texts*) of core competencies failing that resulted in fatal accidents. Turner and Pidgeon (1997: xvii) suggest this is a useful approach to examining a little-explored area and using the examination to build up a vocabulary, a set of concepts, and a theory of the phenomena of interest.

Sit down for the next paragraph!

The methodology (literature review, data gathering, research method and analysis) adopted in this book is *grounded* in the data. It relies on a modified (*elaborated*, grounded theory) hermeneutic cycle suggested by William Dilthey (1972) as a way of understanding texts.

The research method adapted Dilthey's principle of reasoning from the part to the whole to the part again through *coding* and *interpretation* of overt and covert managerial competencies and compliance issues that failed in five actual incidents and which, if they had been prevented from failing, might have prevented the incidents displayed in the book. The incident texts exist as Coronial Inquests and Commission of Enquiry reports any researchers may also investigate.

There! That was too easy.

Easy version: the author researched five accidents which were all very different. They all pointed to some simple but lifesaving conclusions:

The research showed that prior knowledge of conditions that could cause a serious accident existed within organisations, and management ignored the signals. That connection between potential accidents and managerial competencies does not appear to have been made before.

If these recommendations sound like 'aspirational motherhood statements,' then look again in detail at the statistics for mining alone.

https://en.wikipedia.org/wiki/Fatality_statistics_in_the_Western_Australian_mining_industry

This book suggests that managers (the dominant coalition - supervisors, managers, directors) who purport to be responsible should be held responsible for the adequacy of safety systems in place in their organisations and for the consequences of ignoring information available prior to accidents happening.

While the research focused on pathologies revealed in Coronial Inquests and Royal Commission Enquiry reports, its aim was diagnostic and prognostic. It seeks to discover ways of avoiding these pathologies, in effect, going beyond systemic causes to return with a new perspective to Turner's theory. The chapters, taken together, argue the case that there are critical competencies that can be identified and acquired and imposed and mandated by regulation.

A vision of perfect safety.

Factors such as the culture of the organisation, the personality and psychological stability of managers, the effects of power, greed, and self-protection, and the effectiveness of regulations and compliance all appear in the case reports. From a management training perspective these factors form part of the complex but identifiable background to most accidents.

Therefore, the approach must be cross-disciplinary (using information from education, ethics, philosophy, law and management and behavioural psychology). The research attempted to do this while taking as few risky inferential leaps as possible, but one that an examination of this nature requires. For example, Ackoff (1981), Emery and

Trist (1981), Ozbekham (1973-74) and Hamel and Prahalad (1994) have all emphasised the importance of taking the future as a starting point for analysing iterations towards an idealised state (in high-reliability organisations an idealised future state would be zero accidents).

These authors all agree that while scenario building and forecasting start with what *is* and then project *forward* to what might happen. The quest for foresight should begin with scenario after scenario to what could be and then work back to what triggers might hide in the organisation that will lead to that future. This activity has also been referred to as "vision building".

A clear, specified and well-communicated desired future will impact organisational focus, motivation, cohesion and performance if it is well articulated and managed.

The need for a vision of perfect safety will always be set against competing forces such as expediency, greed, profit motive, poor ethics, power-seeking and shareholder returns, so trade-offs will occur. The research suggests that an organisation's long-term 'perfect' safety vision can only come into reality if vigilant safety systems support it.

Vigilant safety systems must be constructed by competent managers exercising ethical behaviour. The organisation needs to have a clear safety ethos deliberately constructed out of a concern for others, along with accountability, which is ensured by stringent compliance requirements.

Recognising both evidence and context in accidents.

The research for this book seeks to interpret, understand and reveal competencies at senior levels of corporate management that were not triggered, which led to failing to intervene in the chain of signals and precursors that resulted in each accident.

One of the principal reasons for examining actual cases is that Commissions of Enquiry reveal this chain of ignored signals by showing 'hard' evidence of failures at the level of the dominant coalitions of organisations – evidence that Senior Management adopted unsafe management priorities and agendas.

Some examples of the *contextual* questions Commissions of Enquiry demand answers to in actual cases include:

How did the accident occur?

Who was involved?

What technology was involved?

What were the decision antecedents to the incident?

Who made the decisions?

Was the person responsible a competent operator?

What competencies were absent?

Did any responsible person act unethically?

Were systems in place to ensure incidents did not occur?

What were the components of the systems that failed?

Why did the systems fail?

What priorities influenced the systems that failed?

Was there a review or checking process in place to update decision-making as new information became available or capacity was diminished?

Did the failed systems have vigilance indicators in place to respond to conditions leading up to the incident?

What conditions existed at the moment of the incident?

Senior management could have and should have asked these simple questions. Failure by the individuals even after fatal accidents to ask such systemic questions shows how incompetent these management coalitions were in the lead up to the accident. However, their focus tends to be on managing public relations.

Questions such as these suggest a thread of reasoning that might be available to help management to learn from its mistakes. Such questions may help to prevent accidents in the future.

The book is grounded in primary Coroners Inquests and Commissions of Enquiry and asks such questions. This form of conjecture is characteristic of the methodology known as 'grounded theory' and is relevant to examining the behaviours of individuals and groups, such as managers and dominant coalitions, in situations where it is impossible to apply quantitative methods.

These cases illustrate an important shift in approach to the way accidents are reported. Rather than blaming front line operators, they point to the failure of managerial responsibility. They also show that dominant coalitions can reign powerful forces against enquiries into accidents and that senior management often acts in its own interests with hubris and contempt for safety.

An integrating theory of safety system management would hold as its central principle that safety system management must be a *prime* investment function of the dominant coalition in high-reliability organisations, rather than the low priority given to safety (as an expense) by relegating it to the Human Resources department, demonstrated in these examples. A grounded theorist might ask if there could be relationships among organisational strategies, structures, and managers' personalities, as Marcus Aurelius seems to suggest?

Remember, it is the secret force hidden deep within us that manipulates our strings; there lies the voice of persuasion, there is the very life. There, we might even say, is the man himself. - Marcus Aurelius, Meditations

Kets de Vries (1984) makes the case that decision-making, leadership, strategy formation, structuring, and organisational change are influenced in both subtle and complex ways by 'invisible' long-standing psychological forces of which the individual is unaware. These covert forces can act to produce organisational outcomes that appear irrational and dysfunctional. These forces can also be both pernicious and destructive at the same time in high-reliability organisations.

The cases chosen for analysis show that these self-interested forces are at work in many accidents and near miss incidents. Based on the evidence, one can make a case that high-reliability organisations that isolate themselves from their social milieu (a phenomenon known as autopoiesis) are most likely to experience fatal accidents. This may be a fruitful line of further academic or postdoctoral research.

3. IMPERFECT SAFETY SYSTEM MANAGEMENT: HIGH-RELIABILITY ORGANISATIONS: A REVIEW

THIS CHAPTER PROVIDES A COMPREHENSIVE OVERVIEW OF EXISTING research on high-reliability organisations, examining their defining characteristics, operating principles, and successful practices. It explores various frameworks and theories relevant to understanding how HROs achieve and maintain high levels of safety and performance.

"The use of silly and meaningless safety language matters, it creates a distraction and delusion that safety and risk are being addressed. We may feel good about speaking such words but they dumb down culture and distract people from taking safety seriously."

Dr Rob Long

Imperfect Safety System Management

High-reliability organisations are seen as part of a larger social system. Like all social systems, they can be deconstructed and reconstructed in response to criticism, ethical issues, negative consequences, ineffectiveness or failure, as well as the results of research, new knowledge and insights from other disciplines. Hence, safety system management in such organisations can never be perfect or 'finished'. There seems little doubt that safety system management must be organisation and issue specific.

Each organisation must establish its own considered safety system management goals and not rely on 'off -the-shelf' or even 'tried-and-true' safety system management solutions that may have worked for other organisations or even for different sites in the same organisation (Hopkins, 1999).

While the literature shows that effective safety system management arises from specific safety system management goals appropriate to a particular environment or cultural context, stable and predictable safety system management may be an idealised goal not possible to achieve—but it is worth aspiring to and pursuing because a few core competencies can make a material difference. It is the difference between life and death.

The work should interest managers, organisation development consultants, and management training specialists. Academics teaching and studying policy, organisational behaviour, management and other social/behavioural sciences should also find it relevant. Its prime interest should be to members of the dominant coalition of HROs and their principal stakeholders.

Core Assumption:

Accidents occur because incompetent, responsible personnel governing organisations ignore available 'safety-critical' information even though the organisations concerned espouse compliance with current safety regulations and standards.

This book examines factors named as specific and distinctive issues of concern by commissions of Inquiry and coronial inquest reports on actual accidents that have not been treated or are only just emerging as matters of concern in the literature over the last thirty to forty years. These factors describe the dominant coalitions of directors and managers in organisations in relation to their Competencies for Safety-Conscious Practice.

These competencies are identified in accident and incident reports as direct contributors to the causes of accidents, confirming the core assumption. Two critical questions concerning competencies and the need for regulatory compliance in the absence of competencies arose from the research.

Principal Competency Question

What significant underpinning capacities, organisational factors, and performance capacities are revealed in accident reports, and what competencies flow from these to enable dominant coalitions in high-reliability organisations to engage in accident prevention effectively?

Subsidiary Compliance Question

What significant factors are revealed in accident reports and key literature as being required by dominant coalitions in high-reliability organisations to enable compliance with accident prevention regulations and intervention strategies in unfolding accident scenarios?

This book aims to identify and determine the role of these factors and the specific forms of each that contribute to enabling safety in high-reliability organisations and to present them as competencies that can be taught and mastered.

Conclusion

This chapter claims that the paradox of an organisation aspiring to an 'ideal of perfect safety' is not unrealistic, even if perfect safety itself is not achievable. It makes a case that accident prevention competencies can be identified by dominant coalitions and introduced into the culture of organisations. Then purporting high levels of safety in post-accident Public Relations releases might have a ring of truth to such claims.

We all know the wording of the standard PR release: "The company takes its safety responsibilities seriously." When these managers and directors later face formal inquiries, that is the first claim to be demolished because the assertion is fatuous and unsupported by evidence from the organisational culture.

The work also asserts that if preventable accidents occur, then punitive measures should be taken against the individuals most responsible - the senior management decision makers. Dominant coalitions should not be able to hide behind the 'corporate veil' masked by empty, unsupported PR releases.

This argument is developed in the next few chapters by examining the body of literature salient to the competency and compliance questions, followed by a brief examination of several accident cases which make it clear that competency and compliance failures were responsible for the each accident cascade .

4. RELEVANT TAXONOMIES & DATA ANALYSIS

THIS CHAPTER OUTLINES THE METHODOLOGY EMPLOYED IN THE research, specifically focusing on the application of grounded theory to analyse qualitative data from accident reports, inquiries, and relevant literature. It details the process of coding, categorizing, and interpreting data to develop a robust framework of managerial competencies.

'If I have seen far, it is because I have stood on the shoulders of giants.'

Sir Isaac Newton

Relevant Taxonomies

This chapter introduces relevant taxonomies or terms and ideas by identifying ten core managerial *competencies*, and it argues a role for a compliance regime so that in the event of a system failure, error is attributed where the error rests. Such compliance protocols can and must be done with almost scientific indifference and precision and without fear or favour. The research shows that inadequate or timid compliance compromises competencies and organisations learn nothing from what is often catastrophic failure.

Supporting theories such as 'memes', 'habitus', and 'psychopathic behaviour' are explained so that they make sense when used in the chapters that follow. The case evidence also claims that the dominant coalition handles safety, and the literature in this chapter supports that finding.

A brief description of the research method used to develop the ideas for this book points to the four critical areas of competence: underpinning capacities, organisational factors, the capacity to perform in high-reliability decisional roles, and regulatory and compliance capabilities and constraints.

Five important theoretical perspectives are examined to show how the literature views orthodox management theory, stakeholder theory, decision-making theory, organisational theory, and sociotechnical issues in relation to preventable high-reliability accidents. Several key sources, such as Perrow's (1999) Normal Accident theory and Hopkin's (1999) review of lessons learned from a preventable mining accident, are examined in some depth to further illuminate critical findings in the specific competency chapters that follow.

Critical theoretical perspectives are then identified to establish direct sources for the data. These sources tie management coalitions to prevention of accidents in high-reliability organisations. Prior knowledge and misinformation are now considered to be critical factors in the prevention of accidents, are examined in the text and linked to concepts such as 'habitus', 'autopoiesis', 'memes', 'psychological fitness' and 'reflective practice' are established as essential to govern high-reliability organisations.

High-reliability Organisations (HROs)

High-reliability Organisations (La Porte, 1996; La Porte and Consolini, 1991; Perrow, 1984, 1999; Rasmussen, 2000; (Roberts, 1990a, 1990b); Rochlin, 1987; (Weik, 1987, 1993; 1999)) are characterised as being reliable over time, while maintaining high levels of hazard accompanied by low risk.

The work makes it clear that effective management of such organisations results in low failure and accident rates. The effect is called the 'five-nines' principle: 99.999% accident free. This book examines cases in which these high-reliability capabilities were purported, or required under governing acts, to be maintained but were not. The organisations concerned could not keep a record of safety over a long period. Roberts (1999a:160) offers the clearest view of this core capability:

One can identify this subset by answering the question, 'how many times could this organisation have failed resulting in catastrophic consequences that it did not?' If the answer is in the order of tens of thousands of times, the Organisation is 'high' reliability.'

Key Sources

Several sources of information were used:

1. Commissions of Enquiry, Coronial Reports, and OH&S (Occupational Health and Safety) legal cases along with traditional 'orthodox' management sources.

2. Qualitative analysis using modified grounded theory techniques was employed to discover which core managerial competencies were necessary to enable greater safety in high-reliability organisations. HyperRESEARCH1 computer data collection and analysis identified 260 behaviours and phenomena at saturation of data from the items in item 1 (Commissions of Enquiry, Coronial Reports, and OH&S legal cases along with traditional 'orthodox' management sources).

These sources also informed the compression of this data to ten core behaviours or competencies.

3. Several non-orthodox theoretical sources informed and appear to be more relevant to safety in high-reliability organisations and to the concerns of the commissions of Enquiry than traditional orthodox management theory.

4. Safety in high-reliability organisations suggests that if managers and directors are not competent to run HROs2 (High-reliability Organisations) they must be held accountable. Relevant documents such as Acts regulating industry safety and theoretical legal texts related to regulating workplace safety were also examined.

Further, more detailed literature sources are provided in the appropriate sections of the data analysis.

Other sources:

Newspapers, coronial enquiries, commissions and boards of Enquiry and archival records were also consulted, such as:

Australian Transport Safety Bureau

Court of Marine Enquiry (ATSB - Australia

Civil Aviation Safety Authority - Australia

Marine Incident Investigation Unit - Australia

Transportation Safety Board - Canada

Marine Accident Investigation Branch - United Kingdom

HM Railway Inspectorate - United Kingdom

National Transportation Safety Board - United States

International Transportation Safety Association

Transport Accident Investigation Commission - NZ

The Safety Network (NSCA) - Australia

National Safety Council of Australia – NSCA

Relevant aviation-specific sources consulted.

Air Navigation Orders, as amended, Australian Commonwealth Department of Aviation, Canberra.

Air Navigation Act 1920-1960 as amended, Commonwealth of Australia, AGP.

Annual Report of the Department of Civil Aviation, Australia 1945/46, AGP.

Manual of Aircraft Accident Investigation, International Civil Aviation Organisation, Montreal, 4th Edition (1970).

Medical Officers Incident/Accident Check List, Royal Australian Air Force, Canberra (1981).

Air Accident Investigation Branch - United Kingdom

Bureau of Air Safety Investigation - Australia

Key Terms

1. HyperRESEARCH is a computer application that allows the researcher to identify tracts of text (and other data) and to code the selections.

2. HROs are high-reliability organisations that require reliable, safe systems to operate over time. They can be thought of as airlines,

mines, shipping, and other organisations such as hospitals, where failure can cause serious accidents or fatalities.

For those who pick over the bones of other people's disasters, it often seems incredible that (these) warnings and human failures, seemingly so obvious in retrospect, should have gone unnoticed at the time. Being blessed with both uninvolvement and hindsight, it is a great temptation for retrospective observers to slip into a censorious frame of mind and to wonder at how these people could have been so blind, stupid, arrogant, ignorant or reckless . . .

First, most of the people involved in serious accidents are neither stupid nor reckless, though they may well be blind to the consequences of their actions. Second, we must beware of falling prey to the fundamental attribution error (i.e. blaming people and ignoring the situational factors).

Reason J (1991) Human Error

This quote from James Reason reveals much of the task and direction of this book and establishes its essential framework. It alludes to failures of managerial competencies such as *vigilance, foresight and judgement* in the first sentence (…these warnings and human shortcomings, so obvious in retrospect, should not have gone unnoticed at the time), and then to failures of *compliance* and other competencies, such as *salience, and particular and multidisciplinary performance* (…people involved in serious accidents are neither stupid nor reckless… blind to the consequences of their actions… blaming people and ignoring the situational factors) inferring that the system itself is at fault and its responsible actors may have prevented such accidents if they had established the necessary systemic protocols or had intervened in the 'failure' process early enough. Insights such as these guide the analysis of the cases and framed the scope of the relevant literature.

5. CRITICAL PERSPECTIVES: COMPETENCIES

This chapter introduces the concept of "competency" and its significance in the context of high-reliability management. It examines different definitions and models of competency, exploring their relevance to understanding the skills, knowledge, and attributes necessary for effective leadership in hazardous environments.

"A good decision is based on knowledge and not on numbers."

Plato

Decision Making

Orthodox Management Perspective

'Relationships between individual managerial decision making and the relative effectiveness of organisations has been of particular interest, not only for executives and scientists, but for society itself.' (Streufert & Swezey, 1986). The author assumes that the reader does not require detailed explication of the literature in general management or postmodernist decision theory (Cooke & Slack, 1984; Cooper, 1989; De Michaelis, 1996; Heller, 1988; McCall & Kaplan,

1990, Mitroff & Emshoff, 1979; Parker, 1992; Burrell, 1988). These and others contain little to suggest that current theories of management and the decisions made by managers and boards of directors concern themselves with preventing accidents in organisations or accidents caused by organisations.

The broad sweep of organisational and management theories (Shafritz & Ott, 2001; Robbins & Barnwell, 1998; Hatch, 1997) focuses on how individuals, groups and entire organisational entities are structured (morphology), how they interact (dynamics), how they are lead and managed, and an interest in their spheres of influence (stakeholders) and their cultures along with the dynamics of power and politics observed within them. While these provide perspective to the issues raised, they are not central to this book and therefore can be taken as fundamental givens.

Stakeholder Perspective

Other investigators, however, point to concerns which are relevant and do not arise from traditional management preoccupations, such as the need to pay dividends to 'stockholders', but which go the heart of much wider organisational and 'stakeholder' concerns in high-reliability organisations. For example, Kirkeby (2000) posits six core virtues that convey an important perspective on the issues of 'ethical' responsibility and safety related managerial competencies. Kirkeby's notions informed the three core competencies, *ethics* (the first of the ten core competencies referred to above), *balance* and *judgement*.

1. Euboulia, "the ability to deliberate on practical matters, both relating to one's own private life and to public life. Placing public interests before one's own...a secular piety." (185–187).

. . .

2. Enthusiasm (or euphoria), "a commitment that reduces the significance of one's own person, of one's own personality" since the leader (e.g. Martin Luther King or Nelson Mandela) is absorbed into the cause itself. (187)

3. Hypomone, the leader's ability to be patient and exhibit courage, stamina, and endurance – the core of self-management. (190).

4. Prolepsis, "the ability to enrich common knowledge with the powers of personal experience" (192).

5. Epibole, acts of gestalt intuition rather than discursive insights in acquiring knowledge that goes beyond simple rule following (as in Peirce's abduction as opposed to simple deduction and induction). (193)

6. Maieutic, the art of the real leader, a form of midwifery, or the Socratic competence of stimulating another person to seek the truth and find his own moral character. (196).

Kirkeby observes the critical relationship between power and leadership (this book adopts the term 'dominant coalition' to include all organisational personnel who purport responsibility for an organisation's decisions). He points to critical theory critiques of economics such as surplus, exchange and use-value and management's long-standing war with labour. The 'leader', according to Kirkeby (2000:xi) is suspended between human, social, and capitalist rationalities, opposed stakeholders, and in the end 'between the realms of God and the emperor'. The implication of this view of leadership is seen, for example, in its consideration of the stakeholder model from the perspective of a radical-normative philosophy to show that in post-modern capitalism, dominant coalitions must deal not only with shareholders, vendors, employees, unions, and government but also a myriad of grass-roots groups concerned with ecology, labour rights, health effects of production and societies obsessed with consumption.

For example, it illustrates managerial blind spots when safety-critical organisations, such as hospitals, ask for FEEDBACK and send you a COMPLAINT form to fill in. This kind of 'feedback' is often presented to staff as a 'complaint', and it always lands like a lead brick on hospital staff, who gave their all to look after the patient. It does nothing to communicate to the patient that feedback is helpful to hospital administrations as 'user systems analysis', not a complaint – a paradox and the easiest of systemic processes to address rather than going blind to the problem and then repeating the whole thing over again.

As Kirkeby sees it, the leader is not only a negotiator among claimants but is often caught up amid corporate public relations campaigns that seem to 'spin' issues. Kirkeby challenged the 'Transaction-Cost-Model' of Williamson (1975) as 'idyllic ideology' and a 'naïve defence of the capitalist system' since it ignores both the Marxist consumption and the post-modern culture critique of subcontract networking. Kirkeby sees 'stakeholders' as a legitimate part of a political economy, networking in acts of distribution, production, and consumption, while narrating a phenomenology of commodities that conspires to cause ethical dilemmas. For example, he suggests that the dominant coalition should communicate to stakeholders how the firm deals with environmental catastrophes that threaten natural resources and threatened species (64-65).

The dominant coalition must prove to stakeholders that production and distribution are not adding to the problems of the third world, violating the spirit of applicable legislation, and meets the aesthetic image of their brand images. This view can also embrace responsibilities for the safety of people who can be affected by other hazards created by the organisation.

Kirkeby also asserts that Yukl (1994) is too cautious in refusing to set out the competencies of the 'good leader' (65).

These problems of ethical stakeholder relationships and managerial competencies have proven to be a core challenge to the research for this book, prompting its two primary research questions:

1. What significant underpinning capacities, organisational factors, and performance capacities are revealed in accident reports, and what competencies flow from these to enable dominant coalitions in high-reliability organisations to engage in accident prevention?

2. What significant factors are revealed in accident reports and key literature as being required by dominant coalitions in high-reliability organisations to enable compliance with accident prevention regulations and appropriate intervention strategies in unfolding accident scenarios?

Kirkeby's philosophical position is not far removed from Katz (1955) who also alludes to the role of competencies in managing organisations. He claimed that real skill in working with others must become a natural, continuous activity in decision making and day-to-day behaviour. He reasoned that this is because everything a leader (the dominant coalition) says and does (or leaves unsaid or undone) affects his associates, his true self, which will, in time, show through. This competence should be demonstrated in every action and every decision.

. . .

Decision Making Perspective

One may even consider these to be assumptions which construct an assumed orthodoxy of management when, in fact, management orthodoxy is failing to prevent preventable accidents. Decision-making theory offers views on how decisions are made and provides some insights of relevance to preventing accidents (Browne, 1993; Cooke and Slack, 1984; De Michaelis, 1996; Gilligan, 1983). For example, systems analysis was meant to address situations where urgent and large-scale problems were beyond the capability of individual decision-makers (DeMichaelis, 1996; Leavitt, 1973).

Critics argue that systems analysis is concerned more with technological information processing rather than with social structures and information processing amongst individuals (Rogers 1976).

In high-reliability organisations, it is clear that some critical problems may be beyond the capacity of individual decision-makers for a range of reasons - such as information complexity and response requirements of the situation or organisation - and in any case, even if decisions are bounded by the assumption that people know what they want and will choose the optimal course of action, individual and group decision makers tend to *satisfice*, to find the optimally best and easiest solution (often just a hunch!) Simon (1956, 1957, 1975, 1983) and Cyert & March (1963).

Simon (1983:13), describes the ideal formal machine of decision making as proposed by economists and mathematicians, such as Bayesian Theory, as 'a beautiful object deserving a place in Plato's 'heaven of ideas'. This 'Subject Utility Theory' he refers to makes four basic assumptions about decision makers – identical to assumptions that surface in media reports and critical analyses of accidents: (a) they have a clear picture of utility to the point that they can prioritise or assign a cardinal number to each decision alternative, (b) they have an exhaustive view of the strategies needed to implement each alternative decision pathway, (c) they can create a consistent joint probability distribution of scenarios of outcomes of each for each strategy, and (d) they will choose between the best alternatives in order to maximise their utility. However, cognitive reality departs from the formalised decision making ideal when people must choose between ambiguous alternatives at a time when they are under significant pressure.

Real-life decision-making falls far short of this ideal in that human beings do not work out all future scenarios, strategies and outcomes among alternative possibilities.

Fischoff, Slovic & Lichtenstein (1978) argue that important candidate alternatives are often neglected in decision making and those that are considered are poorly thought through. Simon (1983:18) says, 'particular decision domains will evoke particular values and great inconsistencies in choice may result from fluctuating attention.'

March (1978) and Simon (1975:198) earlier described this constrained keyhole view of a problem requiring a decision as *bounded rationality*. As society moves from the information age to the knowledge age, the complexity of business and contemporary sociotechnical systems of high-reliability organisations, exacerbates the problem of information overload and the related problem of "bounded rationality" (Hayek 1945:527).

Decision Making Models

Complicating the picture further is the evidence that other factors influence decision making. For example, decision models reveal several factors such as: *Systems Analysis* (Strauss, 1962; Jackson & Keys, 1987; Flood, 1990, 1993a, 1993b, 1995, 1996) – suggest that there should be an integration of human and technological processes for improved creative problem solving and decision making; the *Carnegie Model* (March & Simon, 1958) – introduces the concept that political coalitions form when problem identification is ambiguous and there is disagreement amongst decision makers; the *Garbage Can Model* (Cohen, March & Olsen, 1972) – shows that there are random interactions of problems, solutions, participants, and choice opportunities.

These elements exist within an organisation and only intersect at random. This means that problems may exist without being solved; solutions may exist without being identified; decision-makers may not identify problems; problems, though identified, may or may not be solved. Solutions often exist independently of problems.

'Choice' opportunities are occasions when decisions are made and are precipitated by urgent events or problems (such as crises or accidents).

While these models offer useful insights and suggest certain necessary managerial competencies, they are inadequate to make these competencies central to implementing them in high-reliability organisations. Rather they focus on other factors such as commercial and financial effectiveness and performance rather than 'safety'. This claim is confirmed by each of the various accident enquiries the author examined.

Decision Making and Contextual Cues

There can be little doubt that each organisational environment influences individual decision-making performance in situations related to high-reliability. Individual decision-makers do not operate in a void (Streufert, 1986), they make decisions within organisational environments that contain objective information and people who operate within a structure and set of established processes (Hogarth, 1981). However, 'influence' factors are always at play and can be explained by theories such as 'autopoiesis', (Varela, 1979), that suggest the organisation closes itself off from its environment when under stress, forcing managers to make decisions in a void. This claim was made concerning the behaviour over time of the Civil Aviation

Authority following a series of preventable fatalities in aviation in Australia by analysts such as Maurino, Reason, Johnston and Lee (1995:51), and Westrum (1992). There is no doubt that individual perception and decision style influence decision-making preferences.

Contextual cues that depend upon the specific context in which individual decision making occurs influence decisions (Kahneman & Tversky, 1979; Rowe, 1989; Hickson et al, 1986). This book considers such 'perceptual' factors under relevant theories such as 'meme theory' that suggest that dangerous unexamined assumptions persist in organisations to provide context for managerial perceptions and hence decisions (Blackmore, 1999; Brodie, 1996; Dawkins, 1976, 1982; Dennet, 1991, 1995, 1998; Zohar, 1997). Reason (1990) calls such factors *latent pathogens* and suggests they lie hidden in organisations having the power to become active, accident-causing factors under the right conditions.

Decision Making and Cognitive Style

Decision-making is also shaped by an individual manager's cognitive style and mental models. Analysing information to better understand a situation and estimate future outcomes is an essential component of decision-making in any field. The psychological experiments that are most relevant have been conducted with experts in such diverse fields as medical and psychological diagnosis (Oskamp, 1965; Goldberg, 1968) and horserace handicapping (Slovic, 1973).

The experiments reflect basic human processes that affect analysis of any subject. By controlling the information made available to a group of experts and then checking the accuracy of judgments based on this information, it is possible to investigate how people use information to arrive at analytical judgments. Stock market analysts, for example, work with information concerning price-earnings ratios, profit margins, earnings per share, market volume, and resistance and support levels, and it is easy to measure the accuracy of the resulting predictions.

When horse racing handicappers' predictions were compared with the actual outcomes of 40 races, it was clear that average accuracy of predictions remained the same regardless of how much information the handicappers had available. Three of the handicappers showed less accuracy as the amount of information increased, two improved their accuracy, and three were unchanged. All, however, expressed increasing confidence in their judgments as more information was received. With only five items of information, the handicappers' confidence was well calibrated with their accuracy, but they became overconfident as additional information was received (Slovic, 1973).

The same relationships among amount of information, accuracy, and analyst confidence have been confirmed by similar experiments in other fields such as psychological diagnosis (Goldberg, 1968).

A series of experiments to examine the mental processes of medical doctors diagnosing illness found little relationship between thoroughness of data collection and accuracy of diagnosis. As in other experiments, increasing information resulted in a strong rise in confidence but a negligible increase in accuracy (Oskamp, 1965).

Decision Making Sans Information

There is increasing evidence that failure of managerial foresight and judgement may be inherent in the role of managers. This is salient because the research considers man-made disasters. Turner and Pidgeon (1997:10) provide a classification of disasters in which two types of disasters are identified, (a) natural, and (b) man-made. The classification suggests that many natural disasters are not foreseeable but most man-made disasters are. This is despite advances in the understanding of work design methods for greater reliability from organisational psychologists and human factors experts (Muchinsky, 1993; Petersen, 1996).

Systemic and behavioural issues are in effect management issues, indicating blind spots that prevent managers learning from previous experience. Work by several organisational psychologists on vigilant information processing indicate that people can either share or not share a vigilant approach to information processing and this approach will affect decision-making tasks (Pugh and Morley, 1988).

Organisational Perspective

A cluster of faddish change management theories that suggest ways organisations might *change* (reengineering and sustainability) (Belbin, 1996; Dunphy & Griffiths, 1998; Stace & Dunphy 1994; Dunphy, 1981; Watson, 1994; Andrews & Stalik 1994), and *develop* (organisational learning and knowledge management) (Argyris and Schön, 1996), made no discernible contribution to anything, seeming more like theory than practical.

These theories provide insight into individual and organisational performance rather than accident prevention, and issues such as high-reliability requirements do not appear to be addressed by them. By 2004, change management was abandoned by most large international consulting firms. It is (in 2024) making its way into various university managerial and training curricula. One might observe that the show is well and truly over in the real world by the time universities start to teach something. However, these theories are relevant to the two identified competencies (*'particular performance'* and *'multidisciplinary performance'*).

Failure of organisational systems are a matter of concern for managers. Yet, the prescriptive (orthodox) texts on management and organisational behaviour pay little, if any, regard to mitigation or prevention of systemic failure. Notably, the seminal management literature falls short, considering the potentially catastrophic consequences of failure in high-reliability organisations. The literature in the management field that deals with strategy and rational approaches to planning and decision-making makes sparse mentions of failure, blunders, accidents, and disasters. The early classical literature in management provided some discussion of health and safety issues and the need to set up emergency plans, but these issues were treated as part of the responsibility of occupational health and safety departments, not from the point of view of managerial competencies.

Those classical texts that one would assume might deal with the subject, such as Simon (1957); March and Simon (1958); Cyert and March (1963); Woodward (1965, 1970); and Sayles (1989) to some extent deal with issues of constructing rational intent, but not the consequences of the failure of rational intent. Assuming it is possible to equate rational intent with *foresight* then the *failure* of 'managerial foresight' becomes a central focus of this book since more recent literature suggests understanding managers in possession of these competencies might contribute to the field of accident prevention as it pertains to the management of high-reliability organisations, in the areas of decision making, planning, strategy, policy, and management training.

The long tradition of examining management competencies, such as in the fields of 'management behaviour' and 'managerial work' (Hales 1986), which required managers to keep diaries, along with activity sampling, questionnaires, and having the researcher following managers around observing their actions of 'live' specimens. Managers are described in terms of their interactivity. Carlson (1951) studied nine managing directors, and Mintzberg (1973) put five chief executives under observation. Relevant to this book are Mintzberg's observations (1973 and 1989), which revealed that managers' activities are varied, of short duration – less than half an hour - and often interrupted. He also observed little time was spent reading, reflecting, or in solitary activity. These studies show that managers organise through 'live-action', moving around in networks of social relationships – often in relationships where they have no authority. This book establishes a case for the relationship between these poorly attended factors, the failure of foresight and other important competencies, and catastrophic failure.

Sociotechnical Perspective

Turner's (1978, 1997) 'disaster sequence model' based on his theory of 'man-made disasters' as postulated in his PhD thesis, *The Failure of Foresight* (1976), hypothesises that high-reliability organisations contain incubating accident-prone systems in which certain phenomena lead to disaster and crisis. In his later book (1978/97), Turner discusses disasters that exhibit these characteristics as 'sociotechnical', with social, organisational and technical processes interacting to produce failure.

Dunphy (1981) discusses sociotechnical systems theory in the context of organisational change as it relates to values, trends, and the characteristics of effective organisations. Dunphy suggests that planning must move from the technical to become sociotechnical, with multidisciplinary groups assessing the impact of technological innovations on personnel, work groups, and the social systems of organisations.

He also examines goals, structure, procedures, the work's meaningfulness, personnel competencies, politics and power, decision-making, availability of information, interpersonal atmosphere, performance expectations and reality checks, reward systems and environmental relationships. Dunphy's points may well be extended to support the argument of this book that individual managers may not be equipped to make some decisions. Dunphy's work is also relevant to Weick's (1987) observations from the Mann-Gulch study. He discusses roles and designing jobs to fit people and points out the differences between traditional job design and contemporary sociotechnical job design. It may be said that the collapse of roles and the inexperience of the firefighters who died, compounded by ambiguous leadership described by Weick, point to the nature of sociotechnical systems as a key aspect of understanding disasters.

A systems approach to building safety into socio-technical systems may enable a clearer understanding of accidents than is possible for complex, high-risk organisations. Such a system would emphasise the relationships between all parts of high-risk systems - how the parts interact and fit together (Ackoff, 1971). Thus, the systems approach concentrates on the analysis and design of the whole as distinct from the parts. A social and technical view of high-reliability systems must be taken (socio-technical). Complex system accidents are not linear. Analysis of accidents based on systems theory focus on the interactions among system components and do not specify single causal variables or factors (Leplat, 1987). Industrial (occupational health and safety perspective) analyses tend to focus on unsafe acts or conditions. A systems approach takes a broader view of what went wrong with the system's operation that allowed the accident to take place. The question then arises, 'Is complexity an adequate explanation for accidents?'

Perrow and Normal Accident Theory – Technological Complexity

A nomos (Gk: law - normative universe) acknowledges the complexity of the strands that weave through an amorphous concept such as 'safety'. One of the seminal works on the phenomena was written by Charles Perrow (1984, 1999) and is entitled *'Normal Accidents'*. It explores a nomos of acceptance of technological complexity as the acceptable cause of catastrophes (normal accidents). Perrow suggests that 'catastrophe' is made 'normal' and an 'inevitable' consequence of industrial activity. Such catastrophes are 'regretted' but considered 'normal' and therefore 'acceptable'.

A normal or system accident, as Perrow (1984) defines it, involves the unanticipated interaction of multiple failures of various of the system components. This is like the central idea Reason (1990) develops in his 'Swiss cheese' model. Where a system is complex, its components can interact in unexpected ways, and where it is coupled (where multiple failures can occur with little or no warning and there is not sufficient time to analyse and react to what is happening), then system accidents, he says, are almost inevitable. This was also true for the 'Longford', 'Seaview', and 'Westralia' cases.

Two Longford workers were killed in an explosion in the oldest of three gas processing plants near Sale, on September 25, 1998. The explosion also cut gas supplies to about one million homes and businesses in Victoria for almost two weeks.

On 25 July 1994, Seaview Air was licensed as a Regular Public Transport Operator. On 2nd of October 1994 the flagship of the Seaview Air fleet, VH-SVQ crashed while on a journey from Williamtown to Lord Howe Island. Nine lives were lost.

HMAS WESTRALIA disembarked Fleet Base West for the Western Australia Exercise Area. At about 10:30 a significant fuel leak was noticed near the port main engine, with fuel emerging under pressure like a garden hose. The ensuing fire killed four sailors.

The speed of the events surrounding the Columbia shuttle lift-off, in which a booster rocket insulation fragment hit the left wing of the shuttle, may be considered an example of this phenomenon. The window of opportunity to abort the mission was too small after the event occurred. The event was not anticipated, and the focus was on getting the shuttle into orbit (no matter what) rather than aborting the mission, and the systems were complex.

Lift-off was the system state, not re-entry. It requires high levels of vigilance and a certain way of thinking to carry such competing ideas at the same time.

Hopkins (1999) asserts that what became known as the 'Moura' mine explosion cannot be analysed in these terms. Moura coal mine in central Queensland was the site of an explosion in which eleven men died. The system was not complex in the above sense. On the contrary, there was nothing at all surprising or unexpected about the sequence of events; the process was quite foreseeable and had given rise to disaster on two occasions in Queensland in the past when spontaneous combustion and a methane gas build-up-were responsible for explosions. First, at Box Flat in southern Queensland in 1972, when seventeen miners were killed, then at Kianga, near Moura, in 1975, in which thirteen men died. Moreover, the system was not tightly coupled in Perrow's terms. Events unfolded slowly and resolute intervention at almost any point could have averted disaster and saved the mine. Perrow himself acknowledged that coal mine disasters could not be explained by his theory and Hopkin's analysis of the Moura accident confirms this conclusion.

Perrow (1999:244-255) states that mining is an inherently risky task. He points to frequent equipment failures, failures of the environment within mines such as collapses, and operator error. Perrow observes that mine disasters are avoidable and provide ample warnings of impending disaster. Mining is loosely coupled and is more complex than linear (Perrow, 1999:97), which suggests that when failures occur there is some room for recovery within the constraints of time-dependent processes. Perrow indicates that the dangers lie not so much in the processes but in the many invisible, unexpected, and unplanned interactions such as the emergence of explosive gases and complex pressures shaped by the shafts and passageways, along which gases and explosive forces can travel. In the light of Perrow's observations regarding the inherent dangers in mines and the propensity to blame the victims of mining accidents it is surprising that in cases such as Moura, where warnings were abundant and similar failures had occurred before that management let the lessons of these incidents and the critical hazard signals slip by. This insight contributed to the notion of the need for *regulatory compliance and intervention*.

Perrow (1984) and Mitroff & Pauchant (1990:122) point to a phenomena they characterise as 'naturalness' in that there is an incapacity to learn from crises because of a belief in technology. This concept is indicative of the need to ensure that this competency is in place as part of the capabilities of managers and organisations. Mitroff and Pauchant state that "there is an insistence on 'explaining the crisis away,' focusing on a narrow set of causes that seem to 'justify' the crisis, making it 'exceptional' or 'abnormal' or caused by 'human error', which is endemic to the belief in the 'naturalness of technology'. They suggest that this 'denial by exception' allows us to reinforce the basic assumption that a particular technology has emerged from nature itself and its use is thereby obligatory, 'natural', a 'fact of life', a 'given'. Therefore, a crisis can be explained as the result of human errors.

The media, at first, explained the Glenbrook rail disaster (December 2, 1999) as a 'signals failure', implying human error, then it was later attributed to speed, also implying human error. Yet the engine drivers both had contact by radio with the Glenbrook signals box – but not with each other because their radios were on different frequencies.

The Commission of Enquiry identified twenty-three matters that caused or contributed to the accident, demonstrating the complexity of factors and the role of *compliance interventions* in accident cascades (Venn Brown, 2001).

Turner & Pidgeon (1997:164) identify this phenomenon as 'limited information available to two parties,' each of whom would have been safe if the other had not been there. This is similar to that in Bangkok (BASI, 1999) between Qantas Flight 1 and 15, where the pilots could not talk to each other after QF 15 had aborted the landing. The question that jumps to mind is, who ordered the train radio frequencies to be different – considering the potential hazards reported to management over many years on the Glenbrook section of the line?

The Bhopal disaster (TED Case Studies, 2000) was first to 'explain away' the accident as an act of sabotage, Exxon Valdez (NMFS, 2004) as an alcohol problem of the captain, Chernobyl (Reason, 1987) as a failure of the power generating technology. This 'reasonable' process tends to prevent examination of basic assumptions about how 'natural' it is to produce dangerous chemical products in a densely populated area, or operating massive oil tankers in fragile environments, or operating nuclear facilities in populated areas.

Mitroff & Pauchant (1990) argue that as a technology is 'made natural' it becomes invisible to the executives who manage it and its dangers are not perceived by them, hence the need for high levels of *foresight* and *vigilance* and their relationship to *compliance* measures This was also applied in the Longford case where specific instructions regarding risk management routines were ignored by management. It may have also been a factor in the way that NASA's 'best minds' ignored the possible consequences of the damaged shuttle wing to the re-entry of Columbia. Mitroff and Pauchant claim that executives expect technology to always work. They point to an airline that is reported as saying: 'We do not have executive support for enhancing our technology; in many areas, we are walking right on the edge of a major disaster.'

This book suggests that *'foresight'* is critical to the relationship managers have with the causes of accidents. In each of the above cases management should have intervened, but they failed to exercise the necessary *vigilance* or managerial *judgement*. Gunningham and Johnstone (1999) consider this failure of *foresight* in relation to the need for the Law to punish such negligence. These issues are considered in depth in the reports on all of the accidents examined, except the earlier 'Lake Illawarra', which while steaming up the Derwent River to Risdon on 5 January 1975, collided with the Tasman Bridge at about 9.25 pm and sank. Several members of the ship's crew, as well as persons crossing the bridge, lost their lives as a result of the collision. This event was prior to these understandings entering the literature and court judgements. Intention (upon which many legal cases turn) is often confused with foresight, however, intention and foresight are not the same. One may have no intention to harm people but nevertheless do so as the result of erroneous judgements.

Multiple interacting influences introduced by people, organisations, and environments often lie behind an accident, and these often exist in the social and cultural fabric that connects individuals in an organisation. For example, an *organisation's cultural values* may prevent criticism of dangerous work practices reaching senior staff, and in some cultures senior managers do not tell each other the truth, which was also apparent in the reports of disasters such as the Challenger Shuttle explosion, Bhopal gas plant leak, Exxon Valdez oil tanker spillage, Chernobyl nuclear explosion (Mitroff & Pauchant, 1990; Reason, 1990). Such values may have a variety of manifestations including arrogance demonstrated by those in power, hasty propagation of unsound ideas, inhibition of individuals' capacity for judgement, an inward and defensive outlook, work systems that do not convey crucial information or allow accountability, masking of critical signals concerning potential hazards, and a tendency for decisions to be based on false consensus or group-think, and for management to blame operational staff (Mitroff & Pauchant, 1990; Mitroff & Linstone, 1993). Each of these problems is capable of causing a disaster.

Hopkins (lessons from Moura and Longford)

Hopkins (1999) identifies seven perspectives on disaster from his study of the Moura (1994) coal mine disaster. He suggests that each perspective illuminates different aspects of what went wrong. These perspectives point to failures of specific managerial competencies.

Hopkins comes to the following conclusions using the headings, normal accident theory, inevitability, the priority of production, misinformation, latent errors, the failure of organisational memory, and management system failure. His reasoning is important to understanding the managerial aspects of the disaster.

Inevitability

The disaster was far from inevitable. In the words of the Enquiry report, it was a result of `management neglect and non-decision that must never be repeated'. It was foreseeable and preventable. It could and should have been avoided.

. . .

The Priority of Production

Hopkins (1999) asserts that the view that the Moura explosion stems from the priority given to production has much more to recommend it. He observes that Moura was a mine whose economic viability was in doubt and there was pressure to maximise production. As Counsel for the miners put it in his final submission, `BHP ran a dangerous race against time to extract all of the coal from 512 [panel] in accordance with the plan'. There were numerous ways in which production was given a higher priority than safety at Moura. The routine practice of allowing men underground when a sealed panel was going through the explosive range involved a sacrifice of safety. Hopkins points out that shift-production reports were prepared at a higher level in the management structure than shift safety reports. Again, substantial financial incentives were paid for production but none for the conscientious management of catastrophic risk. He concludes (as did the Enquiry) that this led to a situation where safety did not pay for relevant decision makers. Moura was not unusual in this respect: Bhopal and the Herald of Free Enterprise were two other disasters where it seemed that safety did not 'pay' in the minds of relevant decision makers.

There is also a sense in which the government's very structure prioritises production. Hopkins refers to the location of mine inspectorates in government departments whose primary function is promoting the mining industry. This undermines the ability of inspectors to impose safety standards on mines. The regulator role is not congruent with the promotional role. This problem was also identified in the Piper Alpha report (1990) and led to a recommendation to relocate the offshore inspectorate within the general occupational health and safety organisation in Britain to ensure its independence from the industry it was supposed to regulate. This same structural problem is inherent in the regulatory regime for offshore petroleum production in Australia and, to some extent, in the aviation industry.

. . .

The Failure of Organisational Memory

Kletz's (1994) theory that disasters occur because of a failure of organisational memory has particular significance in the Moura context. It might be argued that its management should have learnt from the disasters in adjacent mines. Hopkins observes that the Enquiry found BHP, the mine operator, had experience of previous mine disasters, the most recent being the explosions at Moura No. 4 in 1986 and at Appin in NSW in 1979. It is BHP as an organisation whose memory was defective. Hopkins reasons because BHP had decentralised responsibility for disaster prevention to individual mine sites and had no central capacity or expertise concerning disaster prevention. BHP's corporate memory failed to retain the lessons of the various disasters it experienced. Disasters are often `carbon copies.' of earlier disasters (Braithwaite 1985:34-8). If BHP had attended to the lessons of earlier coal mine explosions, eleven men would not have lost their lives at Moura in 1994.

Management System Failure

Hopkins (1999), observes that the system for managing catastrophic risk at Moura was inadequate. Management had not applied itself systematically to managing the problem of spontaneous combustion. It had, of course, given some thought to the matter. Management had installed a gas monitoring system, and it was assumed that this would give warning of any spontaneous combustion that might be occurring. But no consideration had been given to just what would count as a warning and how the mine would respond to any such warning. No thought had been given to how the CO (carbon monoxide) results would be interpreted and what readings would trigger action. There was no action plan, that is, no set of procedures to be followed for dealing with a suspected spontaneous combustion. No procedures were specified for using the sophisticated detection equipment purchased after the previous explosion. This had echoes in the (Jan 2003) Waterfall rail disaster where the black box installed after the Granville rail disaster had not been turned on. The result was that this equipment lay idle throughout the critical period in both incidents. No thought had been given to who would be responsible for doing what.

Management system failure is perhaps the most practical of all the perspectives considered in that it highlights management competencies in planning for disaster prevention. No doubt, for this reason, it is the perspective emphasised by the Moura Enquiry and other recent disaster inquiries. It led to the recommendation that mines develop specific plans for the management of a small number of specified catastrophic hazards such as spontaneous combustion and it has led inspectorates in NSW, WA and Queensland to draw up very detailed guidelines as to what mine managers should include in these plans.

Management system failure incorporates several of the other perspectives considered above. Turner's misinformation, Reason's latent errors and Kletz's organisational memory failure are relevant. It does not supersede these, however, since it is these other perspectives that provide the insights into just how management systems fail.

Management Failures at Moura

Hopkins concludes that:

There was no adequate system for communication of decisions down the mine hierarchy.

There was no adequate system of communicating information about warning signs up the hierarchy. In particular, people at BHP headquarters had no access to such information.

There was no feedback mechanism to ensure that those reporting hazards or warnings were notified of what action, if any, was taken.

There was a hierarchy of knowledge that led to a misplaced reliance on personal experience and on oral communication and a tendency to ignore written reports.

The system for communicating production figures was more developed than the system for communicating safety information.

There was a norm at the mine that unless warning signs were verified and confirmed they could be ignored.

There was a series of beliefs at the mine, amounting to a culture of denial. One belief, in particular, `normalised' the evidence-that is, it reinterpreted the indications of abnormality as lying within the bounds of normality.

There were no specified actions that were mandatory when warning signs were detected.

No one was identified as responsible for critical, safety-relevant decisions.

The system of auditing by the company was inadequate.

The mine was using the wrong safety indicator-the lost time injury frequency rate. This provided no indication of how well catastrophic risk was being managed.

There were no incentives for mine managers to concern themselves with disaster prevention.

BHP had decentralised responsibility for the control of catastrophic risk, along with all other aspects of safety, to the mine level. It had no corporate expertise in disaster prevention, despite its history of mine explosions.

The law does not in practice hold the company or its senior management accountable for disaster prevention in the mine.

Coal mines inspectorates are hamstrung in their enforcement efforts by their position in mining departments.

. . .

Communication System

Hopkins argues that the system for communicating production figures was more developed than that for safety information. This suggests the desirability of computerising information and transmitting it via e-mail or some other system to a range of people with relevant expertise at company headquarters and elsewhere. Computerisation would also mean that databases on warning signs could be maintained, and patterns of warning signs identified and feedback to those who report information could be facilitated so that these reporters know how their reports have been received and have a chance to comment on whether the response is satisfactory.

Cultural Impediments

Hopkins identified the paradox that production could continue at top speed only on the understanding that the mine was safe, and this requirement generated an elaborate set of beliefs that provided this required reassurance. A hierarchy of knowledge developed at Moura and Longford that gave most weighting to information acquired by personal experience. Information acquired via oral communication was next in line while written communication was least effective. Hopkins argues that this involved an explicit belief that personal experience was the best guide and a belief that anything of importance in written reports would be transmitted orally. These beliefs undermined the value of the written safety reports.

Hopkins observed a second cultural phenomenon that he characterised as a culture of denial - a set of beliefs that discredited indicators that something might be wrong and nullified warnings of impending disaster. They included the following beliefs: that the mine was safe unless it was proven otherwise; that abnormal high rates of CO were to be expected because of the novel mining method in use;

that CO rates in any case had to show an exponential rise before there was cause for concern; that the mine was protected from spontaneous combustion by a six-month incubation period; and that no single indicator meant anything unless it was placed in context. This matrix of beliefs meant that the isolated and spasmodic indicators that something was wrong could be discounted. This very same phenomenon was evident in the Challenger disaster where a belief evolved that O-ring malfunction was normal and acceptable. This belief served to disguise the fact that safety was being sacrificed so that launch schedules could be met.

Getting Organisations to Attend to Risk

Hopkins suggests that the whole problem can be summed up as one of organisational inattention. The attention of the organisation was not focused on the control of catastrophic risk. The failures identified above and the principles of control to which they give rise are not specific to underground coal mining. They apply with perhaps some variations to the management of catastrophic risks. Similar failures occurring in organisations that do not have the potential for disaster nevertheless result in inefficiencies, irritations and suboptimal performance.

One could make a case in the light of all of the above examples that there should be a 'Devil's Advocate' who is employed in High-reliability Organisations to take an opposite mental view of events. For example, in the case of the Challenger disaster, someone charged to adopt an 'abort on incident' mental state while everyone else is taking a 'lift-off' perspective on the event. This person would have powerful 'abort' capabilities, depending on the area of a potential incident – mining, shipping, nuclear power, aviation, space, and so on.

6. COMPETENCIES: UNITS OF COMPETENCE

THIS CHAPTER DELVES DEEPER INTO THE SPECIFIC UNITS OF COMPETENCE identified through the research, breaking down the broader concept of "competency" into more manageable and measurable components. It organizes the identified competencies into a structured framework, offering practical guidance for developing and assessing leadership capabilities in these critical environments.

"It is easier to do a job right than to explain why you didn't."

— Martin Van Buren

Messick (1984) and Norris (1991) assert that 'competence' is a potential and performance is carrying out the task. Soucek (1993) makes the critical point that different circumstances require different competencies. These views taken together suggest that managers require both the potential and the capacity to perform their roles in different situations.

. . .

The following ten competencies plus compliance are elicited from the sources identified above and compressed from the 260 codes identified in the HyperRESEARCH analysis outlined in the following section. The codes fall into four categories: underpinning capacities, organisational factors, capacity to perform, and regulatory compliance and intervention.

Underpinning Capacities

1. **ethics** (organisational and individual manager's values and behaviour as they influence the determination of right from wrong in decisions concerning safety)

2. **foresight** (attitudinal 'stance' and 'intelligent looking ahead' as factors in decisions concerning safety)

3. **vigilance** (hazard perception and awareness and an alert 'way of seeing' are necessary to signal detection)

4. **judgement** (weighing up, trading off, and deciding - often in circumstances that make little sense or meaning, are factors in all competencies)

5. **balance** (psychological tenor, courage and persistence are essential in safety versus financial decisions)

Organisational Factors

6. **organisational ethos** (open or closed [autopoietic] organisational cultures shape hazard management capabilities)

7. **constructing a culture of safety** ('intention' to establish a culture of safety, 'ways of seeing', and persistent personal or organisational ideas - 'memes' influence the systemic capacities for managing safety)

Capacity to Perform

8. understanding the salience of the situation and its context (awareness of organisational and incident factors peculiar to particular hazardous environments)

9. performance in a particular setting (managerial capacity to deal with stress, conflict, and unfolding disaster in hazardous environments)

10. multidisciplinary performance (bringing together skills from different and complementary domains to manage a particular hazard)

Regulatory Compliance and Intervention

11. compliance (compliance and regulatory factors, legal and other punitive responses to managerial failure)

Key Competencies - Industry Competency Standards

The potential and actual capabilities that people bring to the job in the form of talents, abilities, and capacities are the focus of the Key Competencies (Mayer 1992). On the other hand, systemic attributes of the job itself in the form of task demands, role requirements, and what positions demand, permit and encourage are allied to Industry Competency Standards (NTB 1992). The data analysis examines the part played by managers (using their talents and capacities - Mayer Key Competencies) in several incidents that occurred in high-reliability organisations while they occupied dominant coalition roles of supervisor, manager or director (job or 'systemic' situational factors - NTB).

The essential elements of 'competency' portrayed by the Key Competencies and Industry Standards and relevant to this book are:

1. 'Competency' is being able to do something: This involves not only physical or mental manipulation or the practiced ability to perform managerial tasks with facility, but an ability to bring knowledge,

understanding and skill to bear on performance. For example, in situations where high reliability is either espoused or expected because of the higher risk involved, such as in mining or aviation or shipping or surgery. Further, 'competence' is about being able to do something well while being consistent, not just it so it is merely sufficient.

2. 'Competency' is multi-disciplinary: It draws on a variety of knowledge, understandings and skills. It challenges traditional boundaries of disciplines and knowledge areas. For instance, for an Air Traffic Controller, to display 'competency' might require the fusion of radar skills with knowledge of mathematics, interpersonal communication, spatial separation abilities and established practice. This principle also suggests that safety should be managed by people with 'complementary skills'.

3. 'Competency' is judged against contextualised criteria: The criteria by which, say, 'competency' in mathematics is judged are derived from settings in which the mathematics is used. The criteria by which aircraft are separated must be judged in the setting of aircraft separation required in air traffic control. The criteria for safety management in HROs should be judged against the setting pertaining to each high-reliability organisation. Off-the-shelf safety and training programs are very likely to miss the mark because of poor congruence with the context in which the competencies are performed.

Classification of Competencies

Competencies can be characterised in many ways. The National Training Board (NTB) specifies (a) Units of Competence) and (b) Performance Criteria). These are general specifications, but they are specific to managing safety systems in high-reliability organisations. An example, using the NTB guidelines, that shows how the principles and theory outlined in this book could be applied to advanced and cyclical refresher training programs for CEOs and senior managers of High-reliability Organisations, is included in Appendix 3.

(a) Units of competence are convenient collections or clusters of competencies. They provide a structure that enables many competencies to be managed, and to provide additional meaning to the competencies classified under them. Units may be formed to assist with definition and to describe tasks. For example, the 'salience of setting' in a particular high-reliability organisation may include communication, leadership skills, and ethical judgement sufficient to demand investment in safety in an organisational culture that prefers to invest in capital equipment or marketing.

Salience is a psychological way of seeing a 'particular' situation and the events that pertain to it. It is necessary, therefore, to be able to manage the 'salient' psychological space. This leads to a requirement for a capacity to manage the 'particular' background and the 'salient' physical factors. Managing the physical space is a different task for each operational site and depends on the capacity to manage the psychological space. These capacities are necessary to constructing the mental schemata needed to exercise the level of expertise characteristic of multidisciplinary performance.

(b) Performance Criteria enable us to describe a competency more concretely. The performance criteria tell us how we would know if the person had (or had not) achieved the competency. This is evidenced in the cases where performance by managers was found to be wanting or, in some cases, negligent.

(c) Further specifications, including Range Statements and Evidence Guides, are also employed. (c) Range Statements (range of variables) put boundaries on the scope of coverage of the competencies and their performance criteria. For example, they might indicate that the Unit of Competency might only apply to specific materials, equipment or size of an organisation. In general terms, these should not be needed because, as far as possible, NTB suggests, competencies should be generic (transferable to other safety systems-related areas). However, the literature [i.e. Souceck (1993)] points to management competencies being situation-specific. The cases support this view (ie, BHP's safety protocols used in one mine failed to prevent the accident at the Moura mine).

(d) Evidence Guides indicate what kinds of evidence would apply to measuring competencies within a specific Unit or Cluster. Gonzci (1993) provides guidance on competency-based assessment strategies for the professions.

The ten competencies and compliance (in section 2.4) [Eleven in all] are equivalent to units of competence - convenient collections or clusters of competencies. The 260 codes or descriptors are comparable to the competencies. They are a smaller grain size, and because they are behavioural, they can function as performance criteria to enable us to describe a competency in more concrete terms. In accident and risk management as revealed in this book they also proscribe the boundaries of the taxonomy of relevant competencies. The NTB model lends itself well to the design of training programs utilising these units of competence and competencies. Two types of useful training-related data became apparent in examining the sources: performance data relating to the job or role requirements expressed in terms of key result areas, key tasks or activities and performance indicators, and competency data relating to skills, knowledge and attitudes expressed in observable behaviour terms. Performance characteristics of each safety-related management role are important in the design of training curricula.

Sources of Accident and Risk Management Competencies

Key theorists use a range of equivalent and synonymous terms and approaches to describing the phenomena under study. There is significant agreement and triangulation from the literature, cases, commission reports and the Mayer/NTB insights on the ten core 'capabilities' (in section 2.4) as prerequisites for safety in high-reliability organisations. These capabilities and attributes required of the person in the managerial role along with analytical ability, decision making, problem solving, empathy, caring, establishment of relationships, interactions with colleagues and a range of other attributes that are difficult to measure but which can be inferred from a person's actions Heywood (1992) form the competencies revealed in this book.

The competencies observed in the *cases* are confirmed through the mainstream risk and accident-related *literature*, which includes the work of authors such as Perrow (1984), Reason (1990), Turner (1976), Mitroff (1990), Hopkins (1999), and Petersen (1996). It is further illuminated by emerging ideas found in orthodox organisational theory, psychology, and law, and in non-traditional management fields such as Darwinian ideas developed in meme theory (Dawkins, 1976), autopoiesis (Maturana, 1980), and also education and training (i.e. Mayer and NTB).

This book also shows that in each *case* where accidents occurred there was an amplified concern for 'the bottom line' and 'stakeholder returns' and a range of other 'production' related pressures, rather than safety. The accident reports make it clear that the ten core capabilities were lacking or not employed and tend to fail or are overwhelmed when financial or production pressures take precedence. This line of reasoning is suggestive of the need for a powerful compliance regime to ensure that such pressures do not prevail over the competencies needed to ensure safety. Gunningham (1999) suggests that where fatalities occur, significant sanctions against such managerial and organisational lapses are warranted.

These factors are at the core of this book's principal argument: If managers have the competencies listed above and use them to intervene in unfolding accident sequences, accidents will be less likely to occur. This claim also requires considering the corollary that the organisation must possess these competencies.

. . .

Competencies, Prior Knowledge, and Misinformation in Accident Scenarios

The relationship does not appear to have been well made before in the general orthodox management literature that prior knowledge of potential accidents is related to managerial competencies. The key literature pointing to prior knowledge as a factor in accidents (Turner, 1984, and Turner and Pidgeon, 1997) has been developed by others to indicate that individuals are less to blame for accidents than the systems that allow them to occur (Reason, 1990). Reason is reflecting on Turner's observation that disasters often occur because crucial information that is available at lower levels of the organisation is not systematically assembled in a coherent way and not passed up the hierarchy to a point where it can be acted upon. Turner claims that critical information: can be buried in other material, too widely distributed, limited to a few parties, wilfully withheld, or rendered useless by being ambiguous. For example, there were various reports of smells and of abnormally high CO (carbon monoxide) readings before the Moura mine disaster. But there was no system for capturing and collating this information or retrieving it for review, and so it was rapidly lost. Turner suggests that the central question to ask is: 'What stops people from acquiring and using appropriate information?' Hopkins (2002) and the Longford Royal Commission (1999) noted that in the Longford explosion, there were continuous alarms sounding that people habituated to and ignored. The capacity to utilise prior knowledge depends on the organisation's nature and the mental world or habitus it creates. The concept goes beyond that seen in the organisational theory of 'culture'.

Habitus

The roots of habitus are found in Aristotle's notion of 'hexis', elaborated in his doctrine of virtue, meaning an acquired yet entrenched state of moral character that orients our feelings and desires in a situation and, thence, our conduct. This book uses these senses of the term as it concerns ethics (competency one) and balance (competency five) and suggests an environment framed by ethical and balanced schemata. The term was translated into Latin as habitus (past participle of the verb *habere,* to have or hold) in the thirteenth century by Thomas Aquinas in his *Summa Theologiae,* in which 'virtue' acquired the added sense of competence or ability for growth through activity, or durable disposition (mental stance) suspended mid-way between potency and purposeful action - the competence of balance. The term was used by Emile Durkheim (in his course on Pedagogical Evolution in France, 1904-5), his nephew and close collaborator, Marcel Mauss (in the essay *Techniques of the Body,* 1934), as well as by Max Weber (in his discussion of religious asceticism in *Wirtschaft und Gesellschaft,* 1918) and also by Thornstein Veblen (who reflects on the "predatory mental habitus" of industrialists in *The Theory of the Leisure Class,* 1899). Turnbull (2000) later explored the influence of a predatory mental habitus on corporate governance in Australia.

The phenomenologist Husserl (1973) defined habitus as the mental conduit between past experiences and forthcoming actions and to that extent foreshadowed Turner's (1977, 1978, 1997) theory of 'prior knowledge'. Husserl also developed the connection between competency and judgement.

Of most importance to this book, however, is the way 'habitus' also figures in the work of Bourdieu (1997), that the way a social system (such as that in an organisation) - be it healthy or sick, consonant or dissonant - becomes deposited in persons in the form of lasting dispositions, or trained capacities and structured propensities to think, feel, and act in determinate ways, which then guide them in their responses to the their surroundings. This connects well with the work on 'meme theory' by Maturana and Varela (1980, 1981, 1987) on autopoiesis [used in this book to describe how organisations can cut themselves off from their surroundings (ie the CAA - see section 2.9 in this chapter]. Bourdieu proposes that practice is:

> ...the product of a dialectical relationship between a situation and a habitus, understood as a system of durable and transposable dispositions which, integrating all past experiences, functions at every moment as a matrix of perceptions, appreciations, and actions, and make it possible to accomplish infinitely differentiated tasks, thanks to the analogical transfer of schemata" acquired in prior practice (Bourdieu 1972/1977: 261).

Bordieu's idea is seminal to this book because of the way it interprets concepts such as 'competence', 'memes', and 'autopoiesis', in the sense that, as Bourdieu suggests, individual and group history is sedimented in the body or social stance becomes mental stance. As such, the managerial capacity to create an organisational habitus designates a practical competency, developed here as competencies six and seven, that connects underlying capacities of individuals to organisational capacities, because it (i) encapsulates not a natural but a social aptitude, which for this very reason is variable across time, place, and distributions of power; (ii) it is transferable to various domains of practice, which explains the coherence that obtains within and amongst individuals of the same class and it grounds their distinctive lifestyles (Bourdieu 1979/1984) and (iii) 'yet it is endowed with built-in inertia, insofar as habitus tends to produce practices patterned after the social structures that spawned them, and because each of its layers operates as a prism through which later experiences are filtered and subsequent strata of dispositions overlaid and so ensures that permanence within change that makes the individual agent a world within the world' (Bourdieu 1980/1990: 56).

Habitus informs this book as a principle of sociation and individuation: sociation because our categories of judgment and action, coming from society, are shared by all those who were subjected to similar social conditions and conditionings (thus one can speak of a high-reliability habitus); individuation because each person, by having a unique trajectory and location in the world, internalises a matchless combination of schemata.

This principle takes on particular resonance when considering that the organisations examined in this book are high-reliability organisations operating under specific socio-technical conditions. Therefore 'memes', running like viruses throughout organisations, amplified by the individual but 'sociated' schemata of individual managers and the polices they implement, can produce socio-technical consequences consonant with the organisation's mission or dissonant with it. Habitus operates as the unchosen principle of all choices, guiding actions that assume the systematic character of strategies even as they are not the result of strategic intention and are 'orchestrated without being the product of the organising activity of a conductor' (Bourdieu 1980/1990: 256).

Because the habitus in an organisation is both structured (by the past, ie, the old RAAF culture of the CAA) and structured (of present representations and actions, i.e., the need for safety in an era of high technology), the economic actor (manager) is not the isolated, egoistic individual of neoclassical theory, a computing machine that seeks to maximise utility in the pursuit of clear goals; but instead a carnal being inhabited by historical necessity who relates to the world through an opaque relationship of "ontological complicity" and who is tied to others through the "implicit collusion" fostered by shared categories of perception and appreciation (Bourdieu 1997/2000: 163, 2000/2004). This view illuminates the dangerous anomalies found in the autopoietic behaviour of organisations under significant stress, such as the CAA.

Habitus can "misfire" and produce 'critical moments of perplexity and discrepancy' (Bourdieu 1997/2000:191) if it does not generate practices that conform to expectations and can magnify hazardous situations. Boyer (2004) suggests that this idea is congruent with March's (1958) conceptions of bounded rationality, confirming the classical theoretical antecedents of Bordieu's insights.

High-Reliability Competencies

High-reliability theory suggests that over time, high levels of hazard accompanied by low risk, characterise high-reliability organisations (Roberts, 1990a 1990b). Framed by the theory of habitus outlined in 2.5.6, this book suggests that certain organisations develop a culture in which failure-tolerant managers create hazardous conditions in their pursuit of downward pressure on costs and increasing shareholder dividends. When it comes to managing what purport to be high-reliability organisations, the managers concerned are found to be unable to engineer organisational cultures that value high-reliability. The evidence suggests that managerial competencies revealed by the various boards of Enquiry and accident reports are deficient, if present at all, in the organisations studied.

A high-reliability 'competency' suggests considerable breadth and complexity and moves well beyond the realm of ability, simple skills and instrumental, mechanistic learning. For example, La Porte and Consolini (1991:19-47) claim that in high-reliability organisations, the leaders prioritise both performance and safety as Organisational goals, and consensus about these goals is unequivocal.

High-reliability competencies (section 2.4) are relevant to the cultures of organisations that are evolving from bureaucratic to more flexible forms (Bolwijn and Kumpe (1990) and Burns and Stalker (1961). Heywood (1992) states that 'competency' is a demonstration, through performance in the workplace, of an individual's underlying personal experience. This definition is illuminating in the context of the accidents examined where safety experience was lacking or available but not employed; for example, in the cases of Moura and Longford where it was available but not captured and transferred because of pathologies within the organisations (BHP in both cases) due to 'production pressures'.

High-reliability organisations socialise and train staff to provide uniform and appropriate responses to crisis situations (Weick, 1993).

The employment of empowered competent staff initiatives are supported in the HRO philosophy. This is called, a 'decentralised response'. 'Simultaneous centralisation,' refers to maintaining clear chains of command in crisis situations. For example, La Porte and Consolini (1991) argue that while the operation of aircraft carriers is subject to the Navy's chain of command (simultaneous centralisation), even the lowest-level seaman has the authority to abort landings (decentralised response).

High-reliability competencies therefore, differ from normal industrial competencies only in the clear hazard setting in which they occur. Managers should maintain simultaneous centralisation of control, while front line operators should have the authority and necessary competencies to make an appropriate decentralised response. This book is interested in the capacity for managers to allow decentralised responses by front-line operators. It requires an order of managerial competence far beyond the limited capacity to issue instructions.

Boyatzis (1982), the psychologist who pioneered much of the earlier work on competencies during the 1970's, defined competencies as: "underlying characteristics of a person that result in effective or superior performance in a job". Others have suggested dimensions such as 'roles', 'skills', and 'attitudes' (Hayton (1994). Evidence of distinguishing attributes of managers operating under various conditions was collected over the last two decades of the 1990's. For example, Scott (1990a, 1991) suggests that *'stance'*, *'way of seeing'*, and *'important performance skills and knowledge'* are salient. 'Stance' as used by Scott means the affective or emotional dimensions of appreciating a situation. Stance as used here is suggestive of 'ethics' since one's *ethical* appreciation of a situation constructs one's feelings of consonance or dissonance. Stance is also central to understanding *foresight* and the other underpinning capacities, *judgement, vigilance and balance.*

The cases studied in this book make it clear that these factors play a significant role in the outcome of a dangerous situation. For example, the CEO of Seaview falsified safety reports and removed safety equipment from aircraft. He experienced no cognitive or ethical dissonance at doing so. This is an example of a situation where, if ethics fail, then compliance with regulatory standards must be rigorous to prevent accidents, and if an accident is found to have been avoidable, then sanctions must be severe (Gunningham & Johnstone, 1999). This compliance argument, which sees 'ethics' as a critical managerial competency, is well supported both by the case evidence and the literature.

However, Soucek (1993) argues that competencies are situation specific and are therefore difficult to specify in advance of them being needed and once acquired may not guarantee competent performance if circumstances change. He argues that different situations require deep mechanisms of understanding if a person is to apply competencies acquired in one situation to perform in an unforseen situation. This book suggests that there is often a separation of understanding and performance, and both should underpin the performance of safety-related management competencies. This would suggest 'knowledge management' is needed to pass on learning from previous accidents, but this information cannot be depended on to prevent future accidents. BHP's safety protocols used in one mine failed to prevent the accident at the Moura mine (Hopkins, 1999). Soucek (1993:168) states, 'It's focus on performance rather than knowledge is unlikely to equip the future practitioner with the capacity to deal with unforeseen, situationally specific problems.' The selected cases make it clear that BHP did not understand this principle when previous accident knowledge did not transfer from other similar incidents to the Moura or the Longford sites. This book recognises that transferability of managerial competencies between situation specific settings and the relationship between a performed skill such as intervening in unfolding accident scenarios and the deeper understanding that underpins it is at best tenuous.

Wood and Power (1987) argue that competence and performance are not the same and define competence as resting on '... an integrated deep structure (understanding) and on the general ability to coordinate appropriate internal cognitive, affective and other resources necessary for successful application.' This paradox of knowledge transfer is relevant in situations where corporate and personal ethics may be the only determining factors capable of mitigating the pathological pressure to cut costs, produce more and meet deadlines, resulting in scenarios where accident signals and prior knowledge are ignored.

High-reliability Pathologies

High-reliability organisation theory suggests that organisations that are good at disaster avoidance systemically mobilise as many pairs of eyes as possible to scrutinise critical information. This maximises the likelihood that the organisation will respond to signs that things are going wrong. However, such signs were being discounted and dismissed at Moura and Longford so effective information transfer and feedback did not occur. This process is typical of a broad range of failures of competence, which form part of the pathological trajectory of accidents in many organisations and accident scenarios (Turner 1978, 1984; Turner and Pidgeon, 1997; Reason 1990, 2000; Hopkins 1999, 2000, 2002). Turner identified numerous reasons and phenomena to account for such failures. His line of reasoning suggests that when information is not captured and is then confounded by errors in communication then the system by which the information was processed has failed. While the people involved are not the system, they are nonetheless part of it. Reason argues that the 'system' means the risk management processes and the culture within which they are embedded. Hopkins observed that the Moura disaster occurred because vital information was rendered ineffective, both by an inadequate information processing system (technical) and by a culture (social) that neutralised it.

These social and technical (sociotechnical) dimensions of a high-reliability organisation together constitute its capacity to function as a 'high-reliability system'. The Longford Commission report and subsequent court case made it clear that 'management' constructs the 'system' and *systemic failure* is therefore 'management' failure. The literature (mainly Reason and Hopkins) suggests then that 'management' has failed, not the people involved at the accident interface. The questions pose themselves. Is there a pathology of some sort at work in organisations that could and should prevent otherwise preventable accidents but fails to do so? Is there a managerial personality type that ignores information even when this prior knowledge could prevent fatal accidents?

7. MANAGERIAL PERSONALITY: THE NEUROTIC ORGANIZATION AND PERSONALITY STYLES

THIS CHAPTER INTRODUCES KETS DE VRIES' THEORY, WHICH SUGGESTS that unconscious psychological forces can significantly influence organisational dynamics and decision-making, particularly in high-reliability settings. It explores the impact of neurotic tendencies on leadership behaviours and their implications for safety.

"You will never leave footprints in the sands of time if you spend your time sitting on your butt. Managers think and managers do. "

Management folklore.

Remember, it is the secret force hidden deep within us that manipulates our strings; there lies the voice of persuasion, there the very life, there, we might even say, is the man himself. - Marcus Aurelius, Meditations

Three Views of the Problem of Managerial Personality

The links between organisational and human pathology are well established. Central to Turner's (1997) thesis is the premise that the information needed to prevent an accident is already known within the organisation and is not heeded - as a result people die or are injured - this failure can therefore be considered pathological. Organisations and their safety systems seem to reflect the personalities of their top executives, a premise that also finds support in the literature.

The First School

Kets de Vries (1984) suggests that organisations have dealt with psychological matters in one of three ways. The first is epitomised by the human relations school, which points to the existence of crucial social needs and their impact on job performance. The human relations theorists showed that it is important to treat workers with consideration and to behave toward them in ways that imply that they are responsible, sensitive human beings. It was shown, for example, how by giving people more interesting work, more power or discretion, or more attention, their productivity and contentment might sometimes be enhanced. He warns that there are important limitations to this type of research, such as the focus that is on front-line workers rather than managers.

The Second School

The second school, the trait or attribute school, Kets de Vries (1984) says, examines various psychological traits among managers in order to discern their consequences and determine how functional they are. Individual personality or cognitive attributes influence risk-taking, decision-making, leadership, and so forth. For example, the need for power or achievement can influence leadership behaviour, locus of control can affect strategy formulation, and cognitive styles can influence decision-making. The trait or attribute school, however, tends to characterise individuals along one simple psychological dimension or trait. So other aspects of personality and context are ignored and only the most general tendencies are described.

Kets de Vries (1984) identifies five neurotic styles which relate to the five most common types of dysfunctional corporations. He suggests that top executives' neurotic styles of behaviour can have on overall organisational functioning. He calls these paranoid, compulsive, dramatic, depressive, and schizoid. He makes the strong claim that these organisational problem syndromes seem to be *influenced* by the neurotic styles of their top managers, and suggests that each of these styles can give rise to particular problems of strategy, structure, decision making, and managerial culture. He also asserts that organisational configurations seem to *mirror* the psychodynamic neurotic configuration of the top executives.

The simple list below compares the five types identified by Kets de Vries with those described by the Diagnostic and Statistical Manual of Mental Disorders (1995). These personality types lend significance to the underpinning competency to exercise managerial *judgement* and *balance.*

Kets de Vries (1984) personality types and DSM IV (1995) personality types.

Kets de Vries five neurotic styles

•Dramatic,

•Compulsive

•Paranoid,

•Schizoid

•Depressive

DSM IV Classification

•Paranoid Personality

•Schizoid Personality

•Schizotypal Personality

•Antisocial Personality

•Histrionic Personality

•Borderline Personality

•Narcissistic Personality

•Avoidant Personality

•Dependent Personality

•Obsessive-Compulsive Personality

•Masochistic Personality

Kets de Vreis points out that it is important to establish more encompassing, more elaborate, and more realistic descriptions of managerial psychological states and behaviour in order to relate them to key organisational problems. This task is taken up in a limited way in examination of the underpinning competencies (competencies 1-5) and capacities to perform (competencies 8-10).

The author decided to preserve the DSM IV categories to preserve the integrity of the original research. It is better to use the current version of the DSM if you are doing a similar body of research. (DSM V at the time of writing).

. . .

DSM IV Classification

DSM IV Classification

The American Psychiatric Association's Manual of Mental Disorders (DSM IV) provides the following classification and descriptions of personality disorders, several of which have been found apply to members of dominant coalitions of high-reliability organisations (Babiak and Hare (2000), and Cleckley (1941, 1976).

DSM IV (1995) claims that these personality types begin by early adulthood and are present in are reinforced by a variety of contexts.

The Paranoid Personality

A pervasive distrust and suspiciousness of others such that their motives are interpreted as malevolent.

The Schizoid Personality

A pervasive pattern of detachment from social relationships and a restricted range of expressions and emotions with regard to interpersonal settings.

Schizotypal Personality

A pattern of acute discomfort in close relationships, cognitive or perceptual distortions, and eccentricities of behaviour.

The Antisocial Personality

A pervasive pattern of disregard for and violation of the rights of others. Most significant is the substantial lack of remorse for the crimes that they commit. They also often exhibit an inability to control their violent impulses. They erupt without warning.

The Borderline Personality

A pervasive pattern of instability of interpersonal relationships, self-image, and affects, and marked impulse behaviour.

The Histrionic Personality

A pervasive and excessive emotionality, theatricality, self-dramatisation and attention-seeking behaviour.

The Narcissistic Personality

A pervasive self-centeredness, an all-encompassing grandiosity about themselves, their achievements, and their place in life. Along with this exalted self-centred behaviour, there is also a discernible lack of empathy and a sense of entitlement that blinds them to all needs except their own.

Avoidant Personality

A pattern of social inhibition, feelings of inadequacy, and hypersensitivity to negative evaluation.

Dependent Personality

A pattern of submissive and clinging behaviour related to an excessive need to be taken care of.

The Obsessive-Compulsive Personality

A pervasive pattern of preoccupation with orderliness, perfectionism, and mental and interpersonal control, at the expense of flexibility, openness and efficiency.

The Masochistic Personality

An individual whose personality exhibits the need for suffering, complaining, self-damage, and self-deprecation.

If managers and members of the dominant coalition shape their world view, organisational cultures, and approach to safety through these abnormal personality filters then competency issues such as compliance and ethical behaviour may also become compromised and cause abnormal behaviour - as is seen in the example of the Russian submarine, Kursk (described in chapter 6).

Further analysis presents as a worthwhile undertaking since the core material would derive from more rigorous and more directed psychological research such as the relationship between the managerial traits revealed and standardised coded psychological abnormalities such as DSM IV. For example, the diagnostic relationship between the DSM IV antisocial personality disorder (F60.2:664-668) and psychopathic management as described in Babiak and Hare (2000) and Cleckley (1941, 1976) appears to be synonymous and on a behavioural continuum. DSM-IV Criteria for Antisocial Personality Disorder demonstrate a pervasive pattern of disregard for and violation of the rights of others occurring since age 15 years, as indicated by three (or more) of the following:

failure to conform to social norms with respect to lawful behaviours as indicated by performing acts that are grounds for arrest

deceitfulness, as indicated by repeated lying, use of aliases, or conning others for personal profit or pleasure

impulsivity or failure to plan ahead

irritability and aggressiveness, as indicated by repeated physical fights or assaults

reckless disregard for safety of self or others

consistent irresponsibility, as indicated by repeated failure to sustain consistent work behaviour or honour financial obligations

lack of remorse, as indicated by being indifferent from or rationalising having hurt, mistreated, or stolen from another

The individual is at least age 18 years.

There is evidence of Conduct Disorder with onset before age 15 years.

The occurrence of antisocial behaviour is not only during the course of Schizophrenia or a Manic Episode.

Note that the age criteria reflect a recognition that many persons who engage in antisocial acts during adolescence grow out of that behaviour. One must engage in these behaviours into adulthood to receive this diagnosis.

The concept of Psychopathy was first described in the 1940s by Cleckley (1941, 1976). It refers to a personality type reflecting lack of conscience development and excessive focus on one's own desires. Building on the work of Cleckley, Hare (1993, 1998) developed a 20-item checklist characterising the essential features of psychopathy. Hare claims that Psychopathy is a syndrome or a cluster of related syndromes. For each characteristic that is listed, the subject is given a score: 0 for "no," 1 for "somewhat," and 2 for " does apply." The cut-off score for a psychopath is 30 points.

Hare's Psychopathy Checklist:

Glibness/Superficial charm

Grandiose sense of self-worth

Proneness to boredom/Need for stimulation

Pathological lying

Conning/Manipulative

Lack of remorse

Shallow affect

Lack of empathy

Parasitic life-style

Poor behavioural controls

Promiscuous sexual behaviour

Early behaviour problems

Lack of realistic long-term plans

Impulsivity

Irresponsibility

Failure to accept responsibility for actions

Many marital relationships

Juvenile delinquency

Poor risk for conditional release

Criminal versatility

The characterisations in this checklist are more focused on personality than are the diagnostic features of Antisocial Personality Disorder. These characteristics represent two major dimensions. The first involves the affective and interpersonal core of psychopathy, including lack of remorse and empathy, exploitation of others, and promotion of self at the expense of others.

The second dimension focuses on impulsivity, aggression, antisocial acting out, and deviant lifestyle, and is therefore congruent with the DSMIV classification F60.2: Antisocial Personality Disorder. Also, because Psychopathy focuses on personality, it allows for persons who have the basic personality structure but do not engage in unlawful behaviour. Indeed, some persons who act in malicious ways with selfish disregard for others may rise to positions of prominence due to their ruthless approach, having the outcomes of the socially accepted while relying on asocial methods.

The following section also addresses psychological issues (psychological limitations), and the problem of identifying people with psychopathic (antisocial personality) disorders who are in positions of organisational influence. The later sections point to the difficulty of training dominant coalitions if psychopathic disorders characterise them.

The Third School

The third school, the cognitive constraint theorists, looks at the general psychological limitations of individuals in an organisational context. Both Turner and Kets de Vries cite the seminal works of Simon (1956), March and Simon (1958), and Cyert and March (1963), which show how cognitive limitations result styles of decision-making that limit rationality. For example, people consider only a few alternatives in choosing solutions to problems and decisions seem to be triggered by pressing problems rather than opportunities. Organisations seem to focus on short-term goals in making any one decision, supplanting these with contradictory goals in making the next decision and, according to the constraint theorists, most decisions are incremental and remedial (after the event), rather than innovative or bold (they lack foresight, balance, vigilance, salience and judgement).

Individual differences are ignored in these theories and are critical to any understanding of organisational dysfunction. For example, consider the effect an individual manager suffering from depression may have on an organisation's safety decision processes. Edwards (1995:887-888), writing in the British Medical Journal, points out that people with depressive disorders could be more liable to accidents than others for several reasons. These include impaired attention and concentration (often due to preoccupation with morbid or worrying thoughts); anxiety, which often accompanies depression; irritability; agitation or retardation; fatigue after sleepless nights; and weakness due to insufficient food intake. In addition, depressed people may take risks with little regard for the consequences of their actions or decisions, make suicidal gestures or attempts that go wrong, and take alcohol or other substances that impair functioning to relieve distress. Supporting these considerations are the reductions in performance in tests of cognitive and psychomotor function in individuals who are depressed.

Individual differences among managers are critical to understanding how accidents might be avoided. Managers have the capacity to discover and utilise adequate information already known in the organisation's systems to prevent accidents from occurring. Top executives' neurotic styles of behaviour can affect overall organisational functioning.

A critical dimension of managerial style is the influence on risk that different senior executives impose on an organisation due to their varying capacities for managing the psychological space of the organisation. Psychological limitations in a high-reliability organisation's workforce can inhibit safety awareness. For example, if power relations are poorly managed by certain individuals, then a range of pathological anomalies can occur. 'Mobbing' illustrates one variation of neurotic behaviour that senior executives initiated, supported or allowed.

Davenport (1999:40) claims that 'workplace mobbing' is defined as 'a malicious attempt to force a person out of the workplace through unjustified accusations, humiliation, general harassment, emotional abuse, and/or terror'). The term 'mobbing' refers to abusive group behaviour, instead of, for example, the term 'bullying' that refers to the actions of an individual. The phenomenon of 'mobbing' behaviour in the workplace has been studied by a number of researchers. Different terms are used to describe the 'mobbing' phenomenon, such as 'emotional abuse', 'harassment', 'bullying', 'mistreatment' and 'victimisation'. Leymann (1994) described 'mobbing' as 'harassing', 'ganging up on someone', or 'terrorising' others at work. Another researcher describes it as a deliberate 'campaign' by co-workers to exclude, punish and humiliate a targeted worker in a 'desperate urge to crush and eliminate' them in the workplace (Westhues, 2002). The outcome of mobbing is the target's 'expulsion' from the workplace, causing psychological and physical injuries as well as financial distress (Davenport, 1999; Einarsen., 2003; Leymann & Gustaffson, 1996). Some targets have committed suicide, and the symptoms of those who have been 'expelled' are similar to those of post-traumatic stress disorder.

Shallcross (2003) suggests that poor human resource management practices often result in qualified and capable staff leaving or being 'expelled' from their positions because they display qualities such as enthusiasm, integrity, and commitment that challenge the status quo or dominant culture. They are easy targets for passive aggressive and abusive behaviours, including micromanagement, constant criticism, fault-finding, gossip and slander, and false accusations. This thesis argues that capable frontline staff experiencing 'mobbing' and other forms of preventable harassment are unlikely to prioritise the safety of others and the organisation ahead of their own survival. Therefore, managing the psychological space is a high-level competency and may require specific training.

Psychodynamic Neurotic Styles

Reason (2000) identifies two approaches to the problem of human pathologies and fallibility: the *person* and the *system* approaches. The person approach focuses on the errors of individuals, blaming them for forgetfulness, inattention, or moral weakness. It focuses on the unsafe acts, errors and procedural violations of people at the sharp end, the accident interface. It views these unsafe acts as arising from aberrant mental processes such as forgetfulness, inattention, poor motivation, carelessness, negligence, and recklessness. If this were the prime cause of accidents, then the measures to avoid accidents would be directed at reducing unwanted variability in human behaviour, such as poster campaigns that appeal to people's sense of fear, writing another procedure (or adding to existing ones), disciplinary measures, threat of litigation, retraining, naming, blaming, and shaming. Followers of this approach tend to treat errors as moral issues, if bad things happen to bad people, what psychologists have called the 'just world' hypothesis.

Reason (1990) suggests that related psychological precursors lead to unsafe acts by individuals. Still, he sheets home the cause of the pathology to managerial decision-making, because it undermines individual and systemic resilience. It limits the capacity to form moment-to-moment adjustments to changing events and is often the most powerful factor in preserving safety in situations of uncertainty (Uren, 2000). For example, Reason showed that there are about 100 million errors on the flight decks of passenger aircraft around the world each year, but only about 25 "hull losses". The key to safety is the ability of the flight deck to use their initiative to overcome those errors. Reason quotes the case of a Boeing 767 that, after a series of blunders, ran out of fuel on a domestic flight in Canada. Without power, the plane lost use of its flaps for a controlled descent. The captain, a skilled glider pilot, used a manoeuvre known as a sideslip. He lost height without going into a dive, then kicked the tail back into a normal position for landing. The plane landed, although it was never included in any Boeing procedure manual. Reason calls this phenomenon 'resilience'.

This capacity involves the performance competencies (in section 2.4 above), (8) *understanding the salience of the situation and its context* (organisation and incident factors), (9) *performance in a particular setting* (stress, conflict, unfolding disaster, capacity for action) and (10) *multidisciplinary performance* (using skills from different and complementary domains). As well as empowering staff to act with initiative it also encourages them to take responsibility for safety.

A resilient organisation encourages people to report their blunders, because near misses are one of the best source of information about organisational safety. However, these near misses are covered up by all levels of operation when organisations where the ethos does not support passing them into the information chain. Such organisations can be pathogenic.

Perhaps Reason's (1990) most important contribution to the field was to identify the phenomena of latent pathogens. Maurino, Reason, Johnston, and Lee (1995:28) state that '...decisions taken in the highest echelons of the system – seed *organisational pathogens* into the system at large'. For example, many chief executives of companies with an engineering base put up signs listing the number of days since the last lost-time injury and set zero accidents as a corporate goal. Reason suggests that this is steering safety based on negative outcomes. It is an approach that is counter-productive according to Reason. It suggests that safety may be equated with avoiding injuries. Also, it acts as a powerful deterrent to anyone reporting them (Uren, 2000) and undermines trust. The injury rate had been halved at BHP's Moura coal mine in the year prior to a collapse killing 11 miners in 1994. Lowering injury rates is not the same thing as operating a safe organisation.

According to Reason between 80 per cent and 90 per cent of accidents include human error, so it is not surprising that managers see their job as trying to reduce the scope for human error. They do that by trying to reduce variability to ensure consistency of action through the application of systems. The system approach concentrates on the conditions under which individuals work and tries to build defences to avert errors or mitigate their effects. It asserts that humans are fallible, and errors are to be expected, even in the best organisations. Errors are seen as consequences rather than causes, having their origins not so much in the perversity of human nature as in "upstream" systemic factors. These include failed error traps in the workplace and the organisational processes that give rise to them. According to Reason, countermeasures call for us to examine the assumption that although we cannot change the human condition, we can change the conditions under which humans work. A central idea is that of 'system defences'. All hazardous technologies possess barriers and safeguards. When an adverse event occurs, the important issue is not who blundered but how and why the defences failed.

Reason explains that defences, barriers, and safeguards occupy a key position in the system approach. High technology systems have many defensive layers: some are engineered (alarms, physical barriers, automatic shutdowns, etc), others rely on people (surgeons, anaesthetists, pilots, control room operators, etc), and yet others depend on procedures and administrative controls. Their function is to protect potential victims and assets from local hazards. But there are always weaknesses. Each defensive layer should be intact. However, they are more like slices of Swiss cheese, having many holes though, unlike in the cheese, these holes are continually opening, shutting, and shifting their location. The presence of holes in one "slice" does not cause a bad outcome. This can happen only when the holes in many layers momentarily line up to permit hazards into damaging contact with victims.

Reason's (1990) theory of latent and active errors states that major accidents occur when latent failures arising in the managerial and organisational spheres combine with local triggering events (weather, location, gravity, etc) and with the active failures of individuals at the operational interface (errors and procedural violations). These ideas suggested the organisational competencies, *organisational ethos* and *constructing a culture of safety*.

Many organisational problems at Moura hid latent deficiencies (Hopkins, 1999). The local triggering event was the heating, and the active failures were the failures of individual managers to apply their minds to the possibility that heating might be occurring on the night of the explosion. Moura, in other words, is a classic illustration of the mechanisms that Reason identifies.

The Columbia shuttle disaster (February 2003) that claimed seven astronauts appears to have occurred for the same reasons. NASA failed to understand the salience of the fallen insulation on the left wing of the shuttle and ignored a key memo identifying the problem several days before re-entry along with an actual photograph of the cracked wing. The mission should have been aborted at lift off if they had heeded Reason's theory. NASA officials reported that they may not have been 'conservative' enough while still espousing their safety priorities in PR releases.

Reason's analysis acknowledges that actions or inactions of individuals are a part of the chain of events that lead to a disaster but it concludes that focusing on these active failures of individuals is not as useful from the point of view of disaster prevention as focusing on the latent or organisational failings involved.

8. DECISION TO FAIL: THEORY OF THE NEUROTIC ORGANISATION

- This chapter suggests that unconscious psychological forces can significantly influence organisational dynamics and decision-making, particularly in high-reliability settings. It explores the impact of neurotic tendencies on leadership behaviours and their implications for safety.

"I have not failed. I've just found 10,000 ways that won't work."

Thomas Edison

Reason's major contribution is an easily understood but powerful conceptual tool. It specifies the organisational and situational factors involved in the causal pathways of accidents. By using this tool, it is possible to identify dangerous latent failures before they combine triggering active factors to cause an accident. The same framework can also be used in reverse to track back from some incident or accident, via the active and latent failure pathways (trajectory of opportunity) to their organisational roots. These ideas contributed to the competencies, *vigilance, foresight,* and *understanding the salience of the particular situation.*

Reason (2000) goes on to indicate that:

1. Although some unsafe acts in any sphere are egregious, the vast majority are not. In aviation maintenance, a hands-on activity, some 90% of quality lapses were judged as blameless.

2. Effective risk management depends on establishing a reporting culture. (requiring competencies such as foresight, salience, vigilance, shaping persistent ideas in constructing a culture of safety [meme management], and an ethos of safety)

3. Without a detailed analysis of mishaps, incidents, near misses, and "free lessons," we have no way of uncovering recurrent error traps or of knowing where the "edge" is until we fall over it. The complete absence of such a reporting culture within the Soviet Union contributed to the Chernobyl disaster (and the Kursk tragedy). (failure of such managerial competencies as salience, ethics, ethos, establishing a culture of safety, and particular and multidisciplinary performance)

4. Trust is a key element of a reporting culture and this, in turn, requires the existence of a just culture, one possessing a collective understanding of where the line should be drawn between blameless and blameworthy actions. (requiring competencies such as balance, constructing a culture of safety - persistent ways of seeing [memes])

5. Engineering a just culture is an essential early step in creating a safe culture. (A managerial skill requiring all ten identified competencies)

6. Another serious weakness of the person approach is that by focusing on the individual origins of error it isolates unsafe acts from their system context. As a result, two important features of human error tend to be overlooked. First, it is often the best people who make the worst mistakes. Second, far from being random, mishaps tend to fall into recurrent patterns. The same set of circumstances can

provoke similar errors, regardless of the people involved. The pursuit of greater safety is impeded by an approach that does not seek out and remove the error provoking properties within the system at large. (requiring competencies such as salience, balance and judgement)

Psychopathological (Antisocial Personality) Styles

Neurotic styles of managing safety in high-reliability organisations subvert psychological balance and become amplified, if those responsible for safety decisions can be diagnosed with Antisocial Personality Disorder according to DSMIV (F60.2), or as psychopaths according to the Hare Psychopathy Checklist-Revised (PCL-R): 2nd Edition (2004) and its screening version (PCL-SV), which can be applied to corporate leaders as well as those already in gaol for serious crimes such as murder1.

Hare suggests that 1% of the general population of North America are psychopaths and that corporations reflect the general population. Results suggest that Corporate Psychopaths function incognito in high-powered professions like the law, politics, entertainment, the church, the military, trade unions, the media and the arts, as well as large corporations.

According to Babiak and Hare (2000), psychopathic behaviour is seen in toxic managers, irrational CEOs, backstabbing co-workers, serial bullies and malignant narcissists who are insincere, arrogant, untrustworthy, manipulative, insensitive to the thoughts and feelings of others, remorseless, seeming not to have feelings, and incapable of experiencing or understanding the feelings of others. They tend to blame others for things that go wrong, have low frustration tolerance and are impatient. They are also erratic, unreliable, unfocused, selfish, parasitic, and take advantage of the goodwill of people they work with as well as the company itself.

While these are characteristics that a lot of us display at some time, according to Babiak, the psychopath exhibits these tendencies throughout every aspect of their lives. Hare (1998) states that individuals with this personality disorder are aware of the consequences of their actions and know the difference between right and wrong, yet they are terrifyingly self-cantered, remorseless, and unable to care about the feelings of others. Perhaps most frightening, they often seem completely normal to unsuspecting targets. Babiak and Hare (2000) argue that the corporate psychopath's cold-blooded ability to manipulate others without remorse, coupled with a veneer of charm and high energy, can make them successful in many walks of life.

Hare and Babiak and have developed a questionnaire they call the 'Business Scan' or 'B-Scan 360' (2004)2. It is based on the 'P-Scan' (1995), which is considered to be the standard test for detecting criminals with psychopathic leanings. It is filled out by others above and below the 'problem employee' to pinpoint personality traits and behaviours which may be destructive. It is designed to prevent organisations from promoting psychopaths through their ranks or hiring them in the first place. (The following sample is taken from the B-Scan's core items.)

Answer Yes or No to the following ten questions:

1. Does your boss or workmate come across as smooth, polished and charming?

2. Do they turn most conversations around to a discussion about them?

3. Do they discredit or put others down in order to build up their own image and reputation?

4. Can they lie with a straight face to their co-workers, customers, or business associates?

5. Do they consider people they've outsmarted or manipulated as dumb or stupid?

6. Are they opportunistic, ruthless, hating to lose and playing to win?

7. Do they come across as cold and calculating?

8. Do they sometimes act in an unethical or dishonest manner?

9. Have they created a power network in the organisation, then used it for personal gain?

10. Do they show no regret for making decisions affect the company, shareholders, or employees in a negative way?

A score of six out of ten, is indicative of an industrial or 'corporate psychopath'.

Dr Paul Babiak indicates the psychopath usually enters an organisation and takes over in five stages (Gettler, 2003). The following five stage movement of a psychopath through an organisation from entry to dominant coalition should serve as a screening indicator for Human Resource and other personnel.

First, comes the entry phase, in which the psychopath charms the hiring team into selecting him or her for the job.

Then comes the assessment phase. Here, the psychopathic employee identifies the potential support network of Patrons (those who will protect and defend the psychopath), Pawns (those who can be manipulated into using their power in service of the psychopath's aims), and Organisational Police (staff in such control functions as audit, security, human resources who might get in the way).

Stage three is manipulation: the psychopath works the patrons and pawns, building the influence network through close and intense one-on-one relationships and at the same time moving up the organisation.

The next stage is confrontation. Individuals no longer deemed useful discover they've been wiped, relegated from close friend to Patsy. Two factions start forming: influential supporters (Pawns and Patrons); and powerless detractors (Patsies and Police).

Then there's ascension. That's when all that planning and manipulation pays off - the patrons are betrayed, the boss is shoved aside, and the psychopath moves in.

(Gettler, L The Age Feb 21, 2003)

1. PCL-R Self is a self-report instrument designed to assess psychopathy in clinical and forensic settings. PCL-R Self is useful for studying traits and behaviors related to psychopathy. This instrument is able to distinguish between the four subscales of psychopathy: Antisocial, Interpersonal, Affective, and Behavioural.

Sample: Adults 18+ years old; clinical and forensic populations

Item count: 87

Estimated completion time: 15-20 minutes

Component: Self-Report Form

Type: paper-and-pencil, web

2. The B-SCAN 360 is a multi-rater evaluation that is beneficial for companies concerned with the integrity and competence of their management candidates and employees in key leadership positions. The B-SCAN 360 items identify specific dysfunctional behavioural patterns that, if left unchecked, could have a negative impact on the organisation and its members. Specific behaviour patterns that are "red-flagged" by the B-SCAN 360 for management discussion or coaching and developmental planning include Personal Style, Emotional Style, Organisational Maturity, and Antisocial Tendencies.

Sample: employees in a business environment

Item count: 111

Estimated completion time: 25-30 minutes

Components: Observer Form (Item Booklet and Response Sheet)

Type: paper-and-pencil, web

3. The Hare PCL:SV was not designed to replace the PCL-R, but to offer a tool to screen for the possible presence of psychopathy. The Hare PCL:SV is a 12-item scale based on a subset of PCL-R items that can be completed in civic and forensic settings in under one and a half hours. In civic settings, the PCL:SV can be used in personnel selection. Cutoff scores indicate when to follow up the screener with the complete Hare PCL-R, so it is easy to integrate the two instruments for ultimate accuracy.

9. REFLECTIVE PRACTICE: HABITUS, MEMES AND REFLECTIVE PRACTICE

THIS CHAPTER EXAMINES THE RELATIONSHIP BETWEEN 'REFLECTIVE practice', 'organisational learning', and 'cognitive consistency', 'habitus' and 'memes' – the cultural warp and weft of an organisation. It illuminates the problem of making meaning out of the worn fabric of an evolving organisation that espouses high reliability.

"Following effective action with quiet reflection. From the quiet reflection will come even more effective action."

Peter Drucker

The literature suggests that ordinary (non-high-reliability) organisations suffer from systems that do not:

• look beyond the rational (mechanical, linear causal thinking) capabilities of individual managers to the organisation's systems (March and Simon, 1958; Perrow 1973)

• manage social as well as technical systems (Taylor, 1987)

- encourage a culture that is outward looking (Maturana & Varela, 1980)
- encourage systems that escape groupthink through, for example, dialectical processes (Mitroff & Linstone, 1995)
- encourage surfacing and examination of hidden assumptions (Weick, 1979; Mitroff & Linstone 1995).
- maintain individual's psychological balance (Argyris, 1996)
- screen people with psychopathic disorders from positions of influence (Hare, 1993, 1998; Babiak, 1995, 1996, 2000; Babiak and Hare, 2000), as described in 2.7.5.

Amongst the remedies for failures of sense-making in the literature on non-HROs and one of the most relevant to this research is Donald Schön's (1983, 1987) notion of reflective practice, a process of paying specific attention to the interconnections in systems. It is also one of the oldest and best grounded (in studies of practitioners' decision making. The inference is that safety-based managerial competencies are critical to organisational safety. Habermas (1979) whose sociotechnical view identified two roles for education to develop social skills, cultural understanding, moral maturity, and practical and emancipatory knowledge.

Dewey (1933) writes about a five-phase process he called Reflective Thinking; (1) Suggestion, (2) Intellectualisation, (3) Hypothesising, (4) Reasoning and (5) Testing the Hypotheses by action. In Dewey's first step, from a safety systems management perspective, the manager is confronted with a problem that needs to be understood. Then, the manager assesses the scale and scope of the problem, conceptualising it until it is possible to formulate a hypothesis that describes both the causes and the resolution of the problem. This third step in Dewey's reflective thinking should involve the lessons learned from prior accidents and 'prior information' existing in the organisation. This capacity to think reflectively is enhanced if the information has been gathered as part of 'organisational learning' systems. In high-reliability organisations, these hypotheses are framed as conjectural statements that explicitly posit the cause-and-effect relationships the manager believes are at play in a risk scenario.

This clear relationship between 'reflective practice', 'organisational learning', and 'cognitive consistency' suggests a way managers might evaluate and be judged in high-reliability organisations. In Dewey's fourth step, the manager deduces possible interventions and the presumed consequences. The final step consists of consciously experimenting (action research) with selected interventions to see whether the causal relations contained in them are verified and confirmed or disconfirmed. These are the steps Lewin (1948) used when conducting his action research programs. Allied to this is the British tradition in particular that linked to education - which tends to view action research as research focused on enhancing direct practice. For example, Carr and Kemmis (1986) provide a classic definition:

Action research is simply a form of self-reflective enquiry undertaken by participants in social situations in order to improve the rationality and justice of their own practices, their understanding of these practices, and the situations in which the practices are carried out (p162).

This understanding is firmly located in the realm of the safety systems management practitioner in high-reliability organisations - it is tied to self-reflection. As a way of working it is very close to the notion of reflective practice coined by Donald Schön (1983) who brought 'reflection' into the centre of an understanding of what professionals do while on the job. These views anchor both '*judgement*' and '*balance*'.

The notions of reflection-in-action and reflection-on-action were central to Schön's theories. The former (reflection-in-action) is 'thinking on our feet' while the event we are dealing with occurs. It involves looking at past experiences, connecting with our values, and attending to our theories in use. It entails building new understandings to inform our actions in the unfolding situation. In an ideal situation, the manager recognises and permits surprise, puzzlement, or confusion in an uncertain or unique situation. Such a manager would reflect on the phenomenon unfolding and on prior knowledge.

Given time, the manager would carry out an experiment that serves to generate both a new understanding of the phenomenon and a change in the situation (Schön, 1983: 68). This is to test out 'theories' or, as John Dewey might have put it, 'leading ideas' and this allows us to develop further responses and moves. We must think things through since every case is unique. A manager in this reflection in action phase of reflective thinking should draw on prior knowledge. In many respects, Schön uses a distinction here that would have been familiar to Aristotle – between the technical (productive) and the practical.

This can be linked to the process of reflection-on-action. This is done later – after the encounter. Depending on the situation managers may write up or record their experiences, talk things through with a colleague and so on. This should enable a manager to develop sets of questions and ideas about activities and practice.

The notion of repertoire is a key aspect of this approach. Managers build up a collection of images, ideas, examples and actions that they can draw upon. Donald Schön, (1983), like John Dewey (1933: 123), saw this as central to reflective thought.

When a practitioner makes sense of a situation, he perceives to be unique, he sees it as something already present in his repertoire. To see this site as that one is not to subsume the first under a familiar category or rule. It is, rather, to see the unfamiliar, unique situation as both similar to and different from the familiar one, without at first being able to say similar or different with respect to what. The familiar situation functions as a precedent, or a metaphor, or... an exemplar for the unfamiliar one. (p138)

. . .

In this way managers and other people involved in incidents engage with a situation. It is not necessary to have a full understanding of things before acting, but it would be possible to avoid major problems while assessing the situation (carrying out crisis assessment and management). When looking at a situation where prior knowledge is involved, that information might become the repertoire and frame of reference. Managers should be able to draw upon certain routines to build theories and responses that fit the new situation.

Stringer (1999: 18; 43-44;160) developed a model of Action Research Process found in use in current Organisational Development practice that involved the following three steps:

Look - building a picture and gathering information. When evaluating we define and describe the problem to be investigated and the context in which it is set. We also describe what all the participants (educators, group members, managers etc.) have been doing.

Think – interpreting and explaining. When evaluating we analyse and interpret the situation. We reflect on what participants have been doing. We look at areas of success and any deficiencies, issues or problems.

Act – resolving issues and problems. In evaluation we judge the worth, effectiveness, appropriateness, and outcomes of those activities. We act to formulate solutions to any problems.

It becomes apparent that the paradox of asking managers to think in a reflective way so they may anticipate and avoid accidents by reflection-in-action and reflection-on-action, which requires significant psychological balance, while at the same time requiring them to create optimally productive organisations, which subverts psychological balance, will produce internal conflict (dissonance - see also chapter 5, s5.4.4). Aram (1976) pointed out that dilemmas such as this are about exclusive interests and disparate needs that, despite everything, are tied together. The case data that follows shows that these irreconcilable tensions in high-reliability organisations are often decided by untrained and unprepared people called 'managers'. The problem is further complicated by the relationship between culture and psychology, which has been shown to be an interaction of mental processes. This viewpoint dominates works in cultural psychology such as Harre (1986), Kleinman & Good (1985), Lutz (1988), Shweder (1990), Shweder & LeVine (1984), and Shweder & Sullivan (1993).

Closed 'Autopoietic' organisational cultures

Organisations can exhibit psychopathic cultures (habitus) and attract psychopaths (Hare, 2004). Professor Hare states that:

We estimate, on the basis of some decent data, that about 1% of the general population will meet our criteria for psychopathy. And in the business world, the prevalence debatably could be somewhat higher, dependent upon the organisation. The problem for the organisation is that only one or two of these people can do enormous damage if they get very high up in the organisation.

Interviewer - Ian Walker: "You said it depends on the corporation, so tell me what difference the corporate culture makes to fostering psychopathic behaviour?"

Robert Hare: "Well I suppose some people would argue that the very nature of the corporate culture almost compels psychopathic behaviour. There was this documentary that was just completed about seven or eight months ago, a Canadian one called The Corporation, and the premise of the whole thing is that corporations are, by their nature, psychopathic. Could they be impulsive? 'Yes.' And could it lack empathy? And I'd explain: 'Well, yes, under certain circumstances. If you look at the corporation as an entity, as a person.' And that was taken as evidence that the corporation is, by definition, psychopathic. And I would argue that corporations of that sort are prime targets for a psychopath, because he or she will function very well in a corporate culture that is designed to manipulate, con, lie, steal and cheat. But most corporations aren't like that."

(ABC Radio National - Background Briefing: 18 July 2004 - Psychopaths in Suits)

In the same interview, Manfred Kets de Vries said:

"I always make the joke the moment [someone becomes a] senior executive they're liars, and it's your task to keep the lying to the minimum, and hear what people are trying to tell you. But many people start to live in their own world and lose their touch with reality. And that's the reason companies go astray."

(ABC Radio National - Background Briefing: 18 July 2004 - Psychopaths in Suits)

Kets de Vries describes the phenomena of autopoiesis at the level of the dominant coalition. Organisations also 'live in their own world'. Autopoietic organisations, which by definition, are focused on themselves, can amplify psychopathic behaviour because they are isolated from their environment. Maturana (1980) suggests that autopoietic systems operate homeostatically and have their organisation as the critical fundamental variable that they maintain constant. The term was coined around 1972 by combining the Greek *auto* (self) and *poiesis* (creation; production). An autopoietic organisation engages in behavioural circularity and directs much of its resources and energies to maintain its own form. There is a sense of separation from its background rather than a proactive pursuit of its purpose.

In the case of safety-critical or high-reliability organisations, this can result in failure to observe set safety regulations and procedures. A relevant example is suggested by media reports of CASA. The Civil Aviation Safety Authority (CASA) is the Australian statutory authority responsible for oversight of the regulations and safety oversight of Australia's civil aviation. CASA was formed on 6 July 1995 under the Civil Aviation Act 1988 when the Civil Aviation Authority was split into two separate government bodies. The Aircraft Owners and Pilots Association President Bill Hamilton (West Australian (1993) Jan 23:16), is reported as saying that "...middle management at CASA (Civil Aviation Safety Authority) are contemptuous of legislation and frustrate government policy." There is a sense that the attention of CASA staff is not directed to safety but to protecting their own interests. An example of self-referencing culture was when the Chairman sent out a detailed video explaining the new Air Operators Certificate guidelines. One office returned the video unopened with a note saying that the entire staff had declined to view it. CASA's chief, Mr Michael Toller described its rules and practices as the 'Galapagos' approach to aviation (Weekend Australian, (1992) Aug 22-23:7). Toller's deliberate Darwinian characterisation is salient.

His point is that CASA is an organisation evolving apart from the rest of the world. James Reason asserts that CASA's culture "...has become a negative or dysfunctional culture that is characterised by what psychologists have termed, learned helplessness (Reason 1990). He suggests that its mission and culture play no positive part in the achievement of its organisational goals. It manifests circularity and directs its energies to maintain its form, and it operates in a state of cleavage from its background – it is, in this sense, autopoietic.

Mitroff & Pauchant (1990) suggest that accident and crisis prone organisations have structures that can be characterised as 'dinosaur', to suggest their inability to adapt to changing conditions of global pressures. Maturana and Varela's theory of autopoiesis deals with this dysfunctional behaviour because, as Maurino et al (1995) suggests, there is evidence that it is symptomatic of potential disasters.

Meme Management, Sense Making and Meaning

Systems that structure meaning

A considerable body of literature suggests that organisations suffer from systems that do not:

• look beyond the rational (mechanical, linear causal thinking) capabilities of individual managers to the organisation's systems (March and Simon 1958; Perrow 1973)

• manage social as well as technical systems (Taylor 1987)

• encourage a culture that is outward looking (Maturana & Varela, 1980)

• encourage systems that escape groupthink through, for example, dialectical processes (Mitroff & Linstone 1995)

• encourage surfacing and examination of hidden assumptions (Weick 1979; Mitroff & Linstone 1995).

While attributing the cause of an incident to human error and blaming the operator, such problems are often not the outcome of failure by individual operators but instead are systemic (Turner, (1978/97); Reason, (1990); Hopkins, (1999). Weick (1993) argues that systems that structure meaning can be viewed as unstable *processes* that can amplify any deviations from safe practices.

Managers have access to a range of antecedent sources for the 'meme' concept in organisations. One of the classical treatises that addresses the role of language in organisations, March and Simon (1958), states that organisations develop distinct vocabularies, and this means that certain kinds of information get highlighted and other kinds get filtered out. Meaning is conveyed through a system by its communications processes as ideas and messages. Many ideas and messages in organisations are not original but are copies of older unexamined ones (Blackmore, 1999; Dawkins, 1989). For example, most budgets are only copies of previous ones, but with minor modifications.

Since memes are ideas that replicate, understanding the nature of the organisational space in which they do so is salient because it can distort the construction of meaning and the nature of information. Again, the proviso of 'survival' of the meme and its space is the key factor. This book examines the nature and consequences of the means of transmission of organisational culture acting in its own best interests. Do managers have control over things they think they have? Is an organisational culture an autonomous phenomenon?

Events that structure meaning

Weick (1993) establishes, in the Mann-Gulch case (13 fire-fighters died), that meaning constructed during strange, unanticipated or catastrophic events is 'continually produced' and therefore prone to distortion. He describes it as 'the collapse of sense-making'. Based on this idea he makes a case that the shared interpretive schema component of a system collapses along with the system's rules, roles, procedures and authority relationships in a crisis. He cites a growing body of 'structuration theory' to support this notion of the collapse of sense making in systems, for example, the mutual constitution of frameworks and meanings, Riley (1983); relations, DiMaggio (1991); and reversals of structuration, Giddens (1984).

Burns and Stalker (1961) also point to the further complexities inherent in *multiple* systems in organisations (adding another level to the view of complex single systems). This capacity for failing to make sense of a crisis may explain why organisations that place a high premium on the actions of individuals to ensure safety by making sense of sudden events continue to experience the sorts of disasters where sense making collapses.

For example, the fire aboard the RAN vessel Westralia off Fremantle (four killed) in 1999, should not have happened because new fittings were installed just before departure. It did not make sense that new fittings would fail.

A similar set of circumstances preceded the explosion at Esso's Longford plant that resulted in two deaths and eight injuries and caused severe cuts to Victoria's electricity supply.

The Columbia disaster might have been avoided if the impact on the left wing at lift-off had made sense.

Making sense of prior events suggests that such systemic collapse might have been foreseen.

Memes and resident pathogens

The following unattributable, but illustrative, urban myth, is anchored in fact and reported in engineering texts, military specifications, NASA folklore and on the internet and points to the power of the 'meme'.

The US Standard railroad gauge (distance between the rails) is 4 feet, 8 and a half inches, because that's the way they built them in England, and the US railroads were built by English expatriates.

The first rail lines were built by the same people who built the pre-railroad tramways, and that's the gauge they used because they were using the same jigs and tools that they used for building wagons, which used that wheel spacing. The spacing of the wagon wheels was the same as the old wheel ruts found worn into roads in Europe that were built by Imperial Rome for the benefit of their legions. The initial ruts were first made by Roman war chariots. The United States standard railroad gauge of 4 feet, 8 and a half inches derives from the original specification for an Imperial Roman army war chariot.

The Space Shuttle uses two booster rockets attached to the sides of the main fuel tank. These solid rocket boosters, or SRBs are made by

Thiokol at a factory in Utah. The SRBs had to be shipped by train from the factory to the launch site to utilise the state rail freight system. The railroad line to the factory runs through a tunnel in the mountains. The SRBs had to fit through that tunnel. The tunnel is a little wider than a railroad track, and the railroad track is about as wide as two horses' behinds. So, a major design feature of what is the world's most advanced transportation system was determined by the width of a horse's rump.

The point of this urban myth is that 'copying' or 'imitation' from one system to another of critical factors occurs in an unconscious way. Such copying can be subject to mutation and result in serious error. Hence the contribution to high-reliability management theory by meme theory may prove to be valuable for its capacity to explain and illuminate a range of issues such as communications and assumption surfacing. Orthodox theories in management and organisational research, organisational culture, systemic management failure, organisational communications, and systems theory do not offer this perspective, and understanding of high-reliability processes is enriched by it and herein lies its *specific* contribution: that unexamined assumptions are memetic and pathogenic.

However, just as the herpes virus lying dormant in the human nervous system, expresses as a cold sore under the right circumstances, so latent pathogens may exist in organisational systems, hidden from the operational interface until they express themselves as front line incidents when circumstances are favourable. Simon (1957) coined the term *incubation*, and Reason (1990), prefers *resident pathogens*. They *promote* unsafe actions and also lower the system's defences against disastrous consequences. Pathogens show up as poor decisions arising from inattention or overconfidence, poor application of rules, deficient documentation, inadequate resources, and poor problem-solving skills and performance failures (Reason, 1990). Reason demonstrated that latent failures were present in the following accidents: Three Mile Island, Challenger, Bhopal, Chernobyl and Piper Alpha.

Latent failures are systemic, different from active failures (associated with train drivers, ships' crews, signalmen, pilots, air traffic controllers etc.) Latent failures are decisions or actions, the consequences of which lie dormant in an organisation's systems for a long time and only result in incidents when they combine with local triggering factors (active failures, technical faults, atypical system conditions) to breach a system's defences. The critical defining quality of latent failures is that they were present as pathogens in the system long before the onset of a recognisable accident sequence. The system most prone to pathogenic activity in an organisation is its culture. This is where the norms, ethos, and modes of decision making are most likely to nurture the growth of pathogenic ideas and habits.

Forensic contribution of meme theory

A more detailed, perhaps forensic, view is suggested in Richard Dawkins' (1976) concept of the "meme". A meme is a contagious idea that replicates like a virus, passed on from mind to mind. Memes function in an analogous way to genes and viruses, propagating through communication networks and face-to-face contact between people over time. Memes can be considered as units of information residing in the brain. Memes also have 'phenotypic', or visible, effects and consequences on the outside world. This second level of activity, in which memes influence their own survival by their effects on the carrier vehicle (people and organisations), is memetic theory's main contribution to the field of systemic management.

Memetic phenotypes

Hoskins (1991:216) points out that people, organisations, and environments each, to some extent, make the other (echoed in the 'phenotypic' argument of the meme theorists who suggest that ideas can affect and shape their environment and so enhance their 'fitness' for their own survival and replication, (Dawkins 1976:212, 1999:110) and Dennet (1991:206). He also says that individuals and groups tend to make their organisational environments either hostile or munificent. A powerful example of this phenomena is the 'faith/religion' meme, which discourages the exercise of critical judgement, resulting in a potent phenotypic effect of making its carriers intolerant of new and unfamiliar ideas. The 'race' meme operates in a similar way, as do many political memes.

Circumstances in which destructive forces come about because of lack of integration or coordination of people, organisations and environments is captured by Weick's (1979) use of the term, 'enactment', which suggests that following an incident people attribute it to any context rather than their own actions – 'acting' as if the organisation, for example, was to blame. However, 'enactment' arises from conflict with the pool of memes which the group have normalised. Meme theory lends a richer perspective to this 'blaming' process through its 'survival' explanation.

Because accidents are not 'normal', always unintended, unexpected and violent they do not make sense, so most people find something or someone else to blame for the surprise and violation of their expectations. A 'normal' environment has become hostile, and everything is unfamiliar. The meme for 'normal' is not served by such conditions. The phenotypic state of 'normal' needs to be re-established as soon as possible for the meme's preservation.

The 'normal' phenotypic effect for the human host is safety and the expectations of safety. It is in the self-interest of the meme (the idea of safety and well-being) to recreate its most favoured state for its host. Memes have a phenotypic effect that systematically disables the forces that threaten their survival.

The system most prone to pathogenic activity in an organisation is its culture. This is where the norms, ethos, and modes of decision-making are most likely to nurture the growth of latent pathogens. This book argues that an organisation must ensure it has a stake in managerial reflective practice. While managers benefit from reflective practice, the organisation must also benefit.

If a manager who made a decision or set up a particular policy framework is no longer responsible later, when the effects of those decisions are felt, then the organisation itself must be in a position to ensure its capacity to act as a responsible entity. It therefore must also engage in reflective practice at a systemic level.

Issues for consideration as pathogenic agents might include an organisation's values, ethos, ethics, management competencies, decision-making, and human relations.

Other more obvious and potent agents within cultures of organisations include bullying and machismo. Even positive exercises such as building alternative decision scenarios through intelligence gathering and other decision support systems and practices can act as precursors to pathogenesis. However, the organisation that builds reflective practice into its organisational systems by enabling managers to reflect on their own managerial practice is inoculating itself against the conditions for pathogens to express and against the virus itself.

Dennet's view of Culture

Organisational Culture as defined by Frost et al (1985) presents a rich nutrient medium for the transmission of ideas, shared assumptions, priorities, meanings, and values, and patterns of beliefs. Dennet (1991) and Dawkins (1999) use the term 'meme' to describe the content of the transmission of culture but go beyond the process of transmission to its very nature and state that memes incubate as (management) fads, and are transmitted between peers, and social contacts (cultural transmission) (of managers).

Dennet (1991:209) suggests that '...transformations of the brain by infestations of memes are a major alteration in the competence of that organ.' Dennet's ideas rarely surface in the mainstream management literature but may well prove to be of value in understanding dysfunctional intentional action (which the management literature describes as 'rationality' and as planning, decision making 'satisficing', and strategy).

Dennet's (1991:251) construction suggests that although we *can* perform elaborate practical reasoning leading to a conclusion, followed by a conscious decision to do that very thing, culminating in doing it, however, these are rare experiences because the memes that shape our intentions are more interested in enhancing each other's opportunities (Dennet, 1991:207) and acting in their own best interests.

If indeed memes are selfish and also propagate cultural content then the Dawkins-Dennet concept goes well beyond the view (Frost, 1985) that culture propagates ideas that reside in people's heads.

The 'selfish' aspect of the meme may be a powerful aid to forensic analysis of the transmission of culture.

Stochastic attention and infection by management memes

Managers have very large social networks (Kotter (1982:67) with peers (Landsberger 1962). Kotter suggested that the managing directors he studied developed relationships with all people on whom they felt dependent because of their jobs. Dependent social and business contacts over which the manager may have some influence, but no authority also act as breeding grounds for ideas 'caught' from credible peers and influential others, a phenomenon Dawkins (1976), Dennet (1991), and Blackmore (1999), attribute to organisation groups and individuals the capacity to replicate ideas. This aspect of a manager's high level of interaction is echoed in structuration theory as: 'meaning constructed during strange, unanticipated or catastrophic events is 'continually produced' and therefore prone to distortion' (Weick, 1993).

In summary, memes are cultural phenomena and are important theoretical constructs because they illuminate systems and events that have the power to structure meaning in organisations. They also provide a way of understanding the destructive capacity of unexamined assumptions and those things we take for granted, expressed in language such as, "That's how we do things here." They also explain the dangerous connection between latent and resident pathogens and autopoietic behaviour.

1. Kurt Lewin is also credited as the person who coined the term 'action research'.

The research needed for social practice can best be characterised as research for social management or social engineering. It is a type of action-research, comparative research on the conditions and effects of various forms of social action, and research leading to social action. Research that produces only books will not suffice (Lewin 1946, reproduced in Lewin 1948: 202-3) His approach involves a spiral of steps, 'each of which is composed of a circle of planning, action and fact-finding about the result of the action' (ibid.: 206).

2. Daniel C. Dennet is Distinguished Professor of Arts and Sciences and Director of the Center for Cognitive Studies at Tufts University Massachusetts. He is the author of Content and Consciousness (1969); Brainstorms (1978); Elbow Room (1984); The Intentional Stance (1987); Consciousness Explained (1992); Darwin's Dangerous Idea (1995); Kinds of Minds (1996); and Brainchildren (1999). Dennet is a credible author in both the fields of Philosophy and Cognition. His work related to replication of ideas is developed from a premise developed by Richard Dawkins (1976/89) in The Selfish Gene and other works. This notion of Dawkins that ideas can replicate is seminal to this book. Dawkins ideas are also developed, and referred

to in this book, by Professor Susan Blackmore in The Meme Machine (1999); and by Richard Brodie in Virus of the Mind (1996). The work is relevant for a range of reasons including its explanations of the persistence of beliefs, insights into the nature of assumptions, and the notion that certain decisions are made based on earlier copied decisions. It is salient because of its power to provide a perspective on organisational communications not found in mainstream management literature to date.

10. GOVERNANCE, REGULATION, COMPLIANCE, AND INTERVENTION

THIS CHAPTER EXAMINES THE ROLE THAT LEGAL REQUIREMENTS PLAY TO ensure safety in organisations, particularly when safety measures fail. It also demonstrates that competencies and compliance are inseparable in 'high-reliability' organisations.

"The biggest corporation, like the private citizen, must be held to strict compliance with the will of the people as expressed in common law."

Theodore Roosevelt

Competencies and compliance are inseparable in high-reliability organisations.

This section examines two cases from the literature (Esso - Australian, and Zeebrugge - European) to elicit the role that legal requirements play to ensure safety in organisations when safety measures fail.

It seeks to provide some insight into the nature of breaches and the resulting impositions on organisational management and governance. It assumes that while some accidents may result from inadvertence that inadvertence is not an excuse in law or an avenue by which an organisation or its dominant coalition might avoid responsibility. This section also assumes that failure of responsibility resulting in accidents may arise from more serious motives such as criminal behaviour and negligence. It will attempt to discover what factors might trigger such behaviour through an examination of the cases and their judgements at law.

An organisation preoccupied with safety must have strong measures against reckless behaviour. Reason (2000) does not believe efforts to measure the economic benefit of "the accidents you don't have" will produce the correct strategies. Economic and management theory tells us that the forces of production are managed with detailed measurement, procedures and rewards. They are intrinsically more powerful than the extrinsic forces of protection, which produce few direct measures. It is for this reason that companies have focused on the 'lost-time injury rate'. Reason contends that a better approach is to treat safety as an exercise in due diligence. It is about ensuring that the conditions for the survival of the business are preserved.

Reason (2000) points out that blaming individuals at the accident interface for accidents is emotional and more satisfying than targeting institutions. He suggests that if something goes wrong, it seems all too obvious that an individual (or group of individuals) must have been responsible because people are viewed as free agents capable of choosing between safe and unsafe modes of behaviour. Seeking as far as possible to uncouple a person's unsafe acts from any institutional responsibility is obvious. It is in the interests of managers. Its legality is also more convenient.

Safety in high-reliability organisations is not enhanced by blaming organisations for the oversight and actions of individual managers. If managers and directors are not competent to run HROs they must be held accountable through stringent compliance regulations and sanctions for breaches. The following two cases point to these concerns.

. . .

Esso Case

In his sentencing of Esso (DPP v Esso Australia Pty Ltd) for breaches of the Occupational Health and Safety Act 1985 – in relation to the catastrophic failure at the gas processing plant at Longford, Victoria, which led to death and personal injury in a workplace designated as a major hazard facility – Justice J. Cummins (2001) found against Esso in *all* of the charges brought. He also identified key legal and compliance issues such as risk to non-employed persons, unsafe workplaces and systems of work and lack of safety training and imposed a further penalty under s. 53(a)(i) of the Occupational Health and Safety Act 1985. His considerations in sentencing were the Occupational Health and Safety Act 1985, ss. 4, 6, 21, 22, 47 and 53.

The date of the sentence brought compliance with the Occupational Health and Safety Act 1985 up to date at the end of 2001. It sets out the responsibilities of the dominant coalition in such high-reliability organisations. There are serious governance implications set out in the judgement and sentence that require consideration of managerial competencies and ethical factors, in high-reliability organisations and industrial engineering operations. Breaches of the Act are designated as 'criminal' and that alone has further consequences for those who would act as managers and directors of companies.

In his judgement, Justice Cummins set out the reasoning for his sentence as follows:

His Honour, Justice Cummings' Reasoning:

1. The objects of the Occupational Health and Safety Act 1985 are set forth in s. 6 of that Act. They are -

"(a) to secure the health, safety and welfare of persons at work; (b) to protect persons at work against risks to health or safety; (c) to assist in securing safe and healthy work environments; (d) to eliminate, at the source, risks to the health, safety and welfare of persons at work; (e) to provide for the involvement of employees and employers and associations representing employees and employers in the formulation and implementation of health and safety standards."

2. These are serious matters. The provision by employers of a safe workplace and safe systems of work is a serious matter.

3. Under s. 21(1) of the Occupational Health and Safety Act 1985 it is provided that an employer "shall provide so far as is practicable for employees a working environment that is safe and without risks to health". That is the basal legislative requirement.

4. The section proceeds in sub-s. (2) that:"Without limiting the generality of sub-s. (1), an employer contravenes that sub-section if the employer fails - (a) to provide and maintain plant and systems of work that are so far as is practicable safe and without risks to health; (b) to make arrangements for ensuring so far as is practicable safety and absence of risks to health in connection with the use, handling, storage and transport of plant and substances; (c) to maintain so far as is practicable any workplace under the control and management of the employer in a condition that is safe and without risks to health.... (proceeding then so far as is relevant to (e)) (e) to provide such information, instruction, training and supervision to employees as are necessary to enable the employees to perform their work in a manner that is safe and without risks to health."

By sub-s. (4)(d), an employer is required - "so far as is practicable ... (to) monitor conditions at any workplace under the control and management of the employer."

Further, under s. 22 of the Act, an employer is required to - "ensure so far as is practicable that non-employed persons are not exposed to risks to their health or safety arising from the conduct of the undertaking of the employer".

5. The fundamental consideration is prevention. That is the purpose of the legislation. The standard of compliance and of knowledge is objective. In deciding what is practicable as provided in ss. 21 and 22, what is looked to is (s. 4):

"(a) the severity of the hazard or risk in question; (b) the state of knowledge which the employer had or ought to have had about the hazard or risk and any ways of mitigating or removing the hazard or risk; (c) the availability and suitability of ways to remove or mitigate that hazard or risk; and (d) the cost of removing or mitigating that hazard or risk."

6. "Hazard" means the potential to cause injury or illness. "Risk" means the likelihood of injury or illness arising from exposure to a hazard.

Item 6 (above) offers a legal definition of hazard and risk in relation to the Occupational Health and Safety Act 1985. "Hazard" means the potential to cause injury or illness. "Risk" means the likelihood of injury or illness arising from exposure to a hazard.

These findings support the earlier findings from the Zeebrugge case, described in the following section.

Zeebrugge

Crainer (1993) examines the capsize of the car ferry, *Herald of Free Enterprise*, off Zeebrugge in March 1987, in the light of failure of corporate responsibility and concludes that responsibility for safety must be taken by the board of directors. In the case of Townsend, managerial responsibility for safety was unstructured and vague. Since Zeebrugge, the company has accepted that safety demands commitment at a senior level and a board director has been assigned overall control of safety. Part of this managerial responsibility must be to ensure that the importance of safety, and everyone's involvement in maintaining high safety levels, must be regular and supported with clear communications. Safety policy needs to be understood and people's understanding of it monitored. Communication, and its impact on safety, was a crucial aspect of the Zeebrugge disaster. It revealed that human fallibility has to be accepted and systems developed that minimise the risk of human error.

The profit motive

Crainer (1993:3) observes that short-term thinking characterises the decision-making of British boardrooms and confronts the following issues:

1. Profit versus safety.

2. Need for expert input and the ability to listen to operational staff.

3. Safety is a board-level responsibility.

4. Micromanagement of employees is hazardous.

5. There are clear dangers in poor communication systems.

6. Managers cannot hide behind the corporate veil (they handle day to day operational responsibility.

7. Takeovers can be hazardous factors - look beyond the balance sheet.

8. Consider the links senior managers have with related government departments.

Crainer (1993:153) cites Kenneth Andrews (1998), who says that 'Management's total loyalty to the maximisation of profit is the principal obstacle to achieving higher standards of ethical practice.' Crainer suggests that while managers from all areas of the business world have espoused an increase in long-term thinking little happens to change the pressure on business people to produce annual dividends for shareholders. The emphasis on producing yearly and half-yearly figures means that managers need to produce impressive results. Crainer is concerned that the fundamental changes in attitude needed to support safety are compromised by management thinking that is inextricable from reporting and pursuing success yearly.

This thinking leads to a propensity for takeovers rather than the pursuit of organic long-term growth and where the profit motive overcomes more stringent examination of a company's activities. He observes that the case of P&O's acquisition of Townsend Thoresen provided a textbook example of a takeover that added up on paper but would have presented a somewhat different picture if a closer look had been taken at managerial systems and standards of operation.

The conclusion that presents itself is that regulatory and compliance pressures need to be brought to bear on companies with poor safety management profiles, rather than relying on market forces to bring about critical safety management changes. All systems fail at some point; therefore, senior management should anticipate such failures and prepare themselves and their organisations.

Communications

The Herald disaster demonstrated the need for employees to exercise their own responsibilities. Managers ignored the worries of employees. If employees think something is important enough, and if it affects something as fundamental as safety, they have a responsibility to express their views. It is strange that in a free society, there is little protection for employees who see something wrong or dangerous and then tell others. If this continues, companies will be allowed to become even more secretive, and employees will become even less powerful.

The communications issues raised by Zeebrugge was also subject to external dimensions. Communications in a crisis now form a substantial part of the skills expected by managers. A *Daily Telegraph* survey (6

April 1987) of the Times Top 1,000 companies showed that 63 per cent agreed a crisis is as inevitable as death or taxes. In another survey only 24 per cent of chief executives said they had training in crisis management. Over 91 per cent thought their firm was vulnerable to an external crisis. In one *Daily Telegraph* survey (9 April 1987), 42 per cent of chief executives said that the crises they faced were due to poor management.' Their inability to collect and communicate vital information was a telling reflection on their training, sensitivity and knowledge of the business they purported to manage.

Suppose the general causes of systems failure can be specified in a form suitable for use by managers and others in daily practice, for example, in a checklist. In that case, this should go some way towards inoculating organisations against the damaging effects of systemic pathogenesis.

This is important in high-reliability organisations if managers retire or change jobs. If a manager who made an earlier decision, or set up a particular policy framework, is no longer responsible at some later time when the effects of those decisions are felt, then the organisation itself should have developed the capacity to act as a responsible entity.

Design

Crainer (1993) claims that Zeebrugge proved that it is unacceptable, in any business, to wait for the product or machine to go wrong before acting. The instrumental or mechanical failure is contingent on a competency failure. The Zeebrugge accident reports show that addition of simple indicator lights would have told the captain whether the bow doors were shut. Bulkheads would have slowed the capsize. The evidence for the importance of these design modifications was well documented, though not insisted on in law. P&O's declared policy has been to comply with the standards laid down by current legislation. Ferry operators claim that they are 'dedicated to safety'. Crainer says all this means is that they have satisfied whatever regulations have been forced upon them by bodies whose track record is one of belated response rather than foresight. Crainer's observation points to the need for special consideration of the issue of compliance and regulation in accident prevention. Crainer claims that safety of employees and customers is both a moral and a commercial imperative.

Crainer leads an argument that designers of high-reliability products should take responsibility for safety. This raises the further issue of the design brief and its specifications. Viscount Caldecote and Alex Moulton of the RINA according to Crainer, said in 1987: If our profession of engineering is to be regarded, every engineer involved in design must be prepared to refuse to be associated with a design that is not fully fit for its specified task, regarding its reliability, its life and most of all its safety.'

Crainer claims that the design function has been historically under-valued and isolated and suggests that to be effective and responsive, it has to be integrated and linked to overall strategy. Those in charge of design should have a clear mandate for action. Their work should not be restricted to new products, but they should be continually improving and enhancing the design capabilities of existing ones.

At Townsend Thoresen, design input seemed to come to an end once new ships were in operation. The design function was isolated - inland - and did not carry the necessary power to effect change. Such isolation from the mainstream of a company's activities has clear repercussions. Operating procedures are likely to expose frailties in the design that are not communicated to the designers. The company is unlikely to be involved in the wider design debate, the innovative thinking that improves and enhances product performance and safety. The overall design lesson of the Zeebrugge disaster is that no product, however large, however costly, exists in a vacuum. Its efficiency has to be reassessed again and again in the light of changes in operational requirements and in the behaviour of those using it.

. . .

Duties and standards adopted by an organisation must always be viewed in the context of the expectations of the various groups (stakeholders) within society, who pay for, and rely upon, that profession's services. Gunningham and Johnstone (1999:142)) suggest that primary responsibility to provide and update a safety management system lies with the employer. They also note that there is then a need for that system and its implementation to be monitored, otherwise there would be a risk that, either deliberately or through ineptitude, the system could fail to achieve its stated goals. The emphasis under the traditional regulatory approach is on inspection, and on compliance with specification, performance and process standards. The main aim is to bring enterprises up to the minimum level of performance prescribed by law, and inspection, coupled with enforcement.

In contrast, Gunningham and Johnstone (1999 suggest, the future may see an emphasis on the performance of the system, and on the effectiveness of the company's internal monitoring of that system. That is, audit and oversight of the system itself will take priority over conventional inspection and enforcing the rules, because the former will be more effective than the latter in ensuring that the system is operating effectively.

There is a key role for utilising self-regulation by individual firms because the enterprise itself has the greatest capacity for making a systems approach work to optimal effect. Gunningham and Johnstone are aware that, given limited inspectoral resources, self-regulation is also the only way that the workplace can be realistically monitored on a continuous basis. However, experience suggests that pure self-regulation, without outside scrutiny or oversight, is rarely capable either of overcoming the gap between public and private interest, or of providing the credibility necessary for public acceptance. For these reasons, those regulatory analysts who nevertheless see virtue in self-regulation have commonly advocated its use in conjunction with some form of government or third-party oversight, or both.

. . .

Gunningham and Johnstone (1999:144) propose self-enforcing, self-referencing safety management systems based on the concept of 'reflexive law'. They point out that reflexive law recognises the limitations of command-and-control regulation, in terms of its limited impact, its rigidity, and its tendency to produce regulatory overload. Reflexive law 'focuses on enhancing the self-referential (autopoietic) capacities of social systems and institutions outside the legal system, rather than by direct intervention of the legal system itself through its agencies, detailed statutes, or delegation of great powers to the courts . . . [it] aims to establish self-reflective processes within businesses to encourage creative, critical, and continual thinking about how to minimise . . . harms and maximise . . . benefits' (Gunningham and Johnstone, 1999:144; Orts, 1995:1227, 1232; Teubner, 1983:239).

While this reinforces Schon's concept of reflective practice in that it seeks this is the aspiration of this book, which seeks to encourage internal self-critical reflection within enterprises about their managerial competencies, and to establish processes and procedures that encourage self-reflective learning and thinking about reducing injury, in organisations that espouse safety, nevertheless safety and where the fatalities ensue from failure.

Gunnigham and Johnstone (1999) are specific that this path should only be available to enterprises that can show an existing high level of safety performance. Governments, they suggest, should require participating firms to commit themselves to several 'bottom lines'. Each participating enterprise would be required to commit itself to implementing a safety management system with prescribed minimum components. These would be identified in the code of practice.

. . .

Minimum requirements under such a code might include:

periodic review;

education and training of personnel at all levels,

documenting and monitoring activities and results,

setting up procedures for investigation and corrective action in cases of system failure,

establishing internal and external communication procedures concerning OHS practices,

establishing operational procedures designed to maintain 'operational control',

keeping a register of legislative, regulatory, and other policy requirements,

keeping a register of OHS incidents deemed significant at a participating site

This book is focused on item 2 (education and training of personnel at all levels), but with an emphasis on management since it is essential that there is provision for internal auditing, monitoring, reporting, and tracking systems, including continuous on-site monitoring by trained personnel and independent checks on the status of the system. For example, the enterprise could be required to establish an independent inspectoral audit group, responsible for identifying problems, taking action, and reporting to a nominated member of senior management, who themselves would be required to 'sign off' on the system, undertaking to government that the system did indeed meet government criteria and that it was being implemented effectively. (Gunnigham and Johnstone:148). However, they suggest that a betrayal of the trust implicit in such a self-self-regulatory arrangement must not only lead to loss of accredited status but also to rapid escalation up the enforcement pyramid.

Conclusion and initial model deduced from the literature.

An attempt was made in this chapter to identify the key sources, references and related areas of knowledge, to establish the taxonomic framework for the book.

The Phenomena of Interest

Reason's exhortation at the beginning of this chapter points to both people and situational factors as central factors in accidents. The key literature makes it clear that accidents happen as the result of management failure (a people factor) that has become systemic (situational or job factors). Aviation, shipping, mining, power generation, engineering and even person to person services such as medicine are becoming more and complex - and progressively more difficult for organisations to deliver safely.

Most authors writing in the discipline argue that the tendency to 'blame and shame' the front-line operator ignores the causes of *most* failures that arise from levels of systemic complexity that human beings cannot cope with rather than irresponsibility or wickedness, even if these are shown to have been factors in some accidents.

Individuals and organisations cannot readily assimilate and apply the vast amounts of technical knowledge they may need, and regulatory, financial, performance, and stakeholder demands may just add to the burden and the lessening of the flexibility needed to allow people at the operational front line to deal effectively and creatively with evolving circumstances. Managers need to acquire many skills and competencies, in particular the following competencies:

Underpinning Capacities:

•ethics (organisational and individual manager's values and behaviour as they influence the determination of right from wrong in decisions concerning safety)

•foresight (attitudinal 'stance' and 'intelligent looking ahead' as factors in decisions concerning safety)

•vigilance (hazard perception and awareness and an alert 'way of seeing' are necessary to signal detection)

•judgement (weighing up, trading off, and deciding - often in circumstances that make little sense or meaning, are factors in all competencies)

•balance (psychological tenor, and psychological consonance or consistency, emotional intelligence and maturity, and courage and persistence are essential in safety versus financial decisions)

Organisational Factors

•organisational ethos (open or closed [autopoietic] organisational cultures shape hazard management capabilities)

•constructing a culture of safety ('intention' to establish a culture of safety, 'ways of seeing', and persistent personal or organisational ideas - 'memes' influence the systemic capacities for managing safety)

Capacity to Perform

•understanding the salience of the particular situation and its context (awareness of organisational and incident factors peculiar to particular hazardous environments)

•performance in a particular setting (managerial capacity to deal with stress, conflict, and unfolding disaster in particular hazardous environments)

•multidisciplinary performance (bringing together skills from different and complementary domains to manage a particular hazard)

Regulatory Compliance and Intervention

•compliance (compliance and regulatory factors, legal and other punitive responses to managerial failure)

Despite the concerns raised by the literature that some senior managers can be diagnosed as having serious personality disorders that make training extremely difficult, the literature suggests that this may be overcome by a stringent compliance regime, so that if These competencies emphasise the role of management in safety systems. They lead one to conclude that normal managerial practice would insist on internal auditing, monitoring, reporting, and tracking systems, including continuous on-site monitoring by trained personnel and independent checks on the status of the entire system, at nodal points where assumptions, if left unexamined, may lead to erroneous ways of thinking and responding to signals and warnings.

For example, the enterprise could be required to establish an independent inspector level audit group responsible for identifying problems, acting, and reporting to a nominated member of senior management, who themselves would be required to 'sign off' on the system, undertaking to government that the system did indeed meet government criteria and that it was being implemented effectively. If fatalities or serious breaches of compliance regimes and safety regulations can be established, then these should provide a basis for prosecution or other enforcement action against individual managers. Such a compliance regime should be characterised by a 'carrot and stick' approach so that appropriate regulatory authorities trigger training and cyclical retraining programs as a requirement for holding office in high-reliability organisations.

The literature also suggests that dominant coalitions in high-reliability organisations are responsible for accidents, since it is this group that creates the habitus or climate in which prior knowledge of impending accidents is not signified; therefore, the direction the book assumes that *if* these senior managers had the competencies necessary to initiate safety related interventions, then preventable accidents should not occur.

The literature was chosen because of its salience to the findings of the cases examined in the data analysis chapters and its illumination of the problem of preventing preventable accidents. The review examined the relevance of orthodox management literature to the problem. In general, it was found wanting, and a range of other theoretical perspectives such as decision making, organisational theory, sociotechnical factors and the 'normalisation of accidents', were examined and found to offer much of value to understanding the problem.

The issue of stakeholders versus stockholders suggested the drive to make profits for stockholders could be responsible for stakeholder neglect. A 'competency' perspective on the problem provided insights into managerial competency failings that could contribute to accidents that should otherwise be preventable. These critical competencies can be identified and acquired.

11.COMPETENCY 1: ETHICS

COMPETENCY 1: ETHICS: DETERMINING RIGHT FROM WRONG IN MANAGERIAL DECISIONS

THIS CHAPTER EXPLORES THE CONCEPT OF "HIGH-RELIABILITY ETHICS" AS a foundational competency for effective leadership in hazardous environments. It delves into the ethical considerations and principles that guide decision-making, highlighting the importance of integrity, responsibility, and a commitment to safety.

'The psychology of the mature human being is an unfolding, emergent, oscillating, spiralling process marked by progressive subordination of older, lower-order behaviour systems to newer, higher-order systems as man's existential problems change.'

Professor Clare W. Graves, Union College, New York

INTRODUCTION

This set of competencies are considered to be the essential 'building blocks' of an 'Ethical' organisation. It analyses ethics, foresight, vigilance, judgement, and balance. The chapter poses a set of generative questions and a review of the literature salient to the concept and complementary to the main supporting theories.

WHAT ARE HIGH-RELIABILITY ETHICS

'Ethics' is concerned with reasoning through, deciding and acting upon what is right and wrong.

Ethics, can be grouped into several ethical systems that test for ethical principles.

For example, WHEN -

The moral rightness of an action is determined by considering its consequences. We test for results.

The moral rightness of an action is determined by laws and standards. We test for policies and procedures.

The moral rightness of an action is determined by the customs and norms of a particular community. We test for organisational values.

The moral rightness of an action is determined by one's conscience. We test for personal conviction.

Ethics, as a philosophical concept, is broader than these definitions indicate. However, they are useful in the sense that they direct the mind to deontological moral 'rules' (deontological derives from *deon,* the Greek word for duty), such as specification and performance standards to ensure 'duty holders' exercise 'duty of care' and comply with organisational and professional codes of conduct and regulatory regimes.

Each of the cases examined reveals that commissions of Enquiry into fatal accidents place considerable emphasis on ethical values in their analysis of an accident, which lends weight to identifying ethics as a core competency. Ethics is perhaps the most overlooked managerial competency since it competes with the demands of 'the bottom line'. The organisational and managerial dimensions of ethics become important as organisational and individual values and behaviours influence unfolding accident scenarios by potentiating or mitigating accident dynamics.

HyperRESEARCH computer analysis of the case data revealed descriptors of ethical concern. Placing the salient examples of the descriptor (HyperRESEARCH code) being examined into a panel is followed in each of the competencies described in the following chapters.

A representative sample of these behaviours is examined in the analysis that follows. Managers who can, but fail to, exercise initiatives to protect life in hazardous situations, are behaving unethically and this behaviour can also have profound accident potentiating systemic consequences. For example, ignoring hazards to make profits is a deliberate decision. It is an abrogation of managerial ethics and is, therefore, criminal. It is not uncommon in recent cases in Coroner's courts to hear the phrase, "It was a case of 'systemic failure.' This implies that systemic failure was generated separately from the people who run the organisation.

ETHICS, ETHOS AND JUDGEMENT

Turnbull (2002) asks why should people trust corporations when chairmen act in an unethical manner? He comments that fish rot from the head. He also asserts that Company chairmen routinely provide evidence of rot being universal. However, in high-reliability organisations, it is critical that good ethical conduct becomes part of the ethos (a memetic force) of an organisation if the drive to profits is to be mitigated to ensure safety.

Within the problem of unethical behaviour lies the ethical solution. By understanding the pathogenic nature and the memetic robustness of persistent and dangerous communications senior managers can model integrity and ethics.

Ethical behaviour in organisations rests on ethical behaviour by each and every individual in that organisation. Ethics bears a close relationship with each of the competencies, and in particular, organisational ethos. This broader organisational influence of ethical conduct is also important when considering ethical reasoning (deontological reasoning) and its role in 'judgement' (competency four). Ethical reasoning is different from ordinary decision making, even though a decision may well follow the reasoning process.

IDEAS ABOUT ETHICS

The Philosophical underpinnings of ethics are substantive. A way of positioning any particular view of ethics is to place it within an ethical taxonomy in which the consequences of our behaviours and the duties we have to others are considered.

WD Ross (in Boatright, 1993) says we have duties of:

1. Fidelity - to keep promises and tell the truth.

2. Reparation - to compensate people for injury we have inflicted.

3. Gratitude - to return favours that other do for us.

4. Justice - to ensure that goods are distributed according to needs and merits.

5. Beneficence - to do whatever we can to improve the conditions of others.

6. Self-improvement - to improve our own virtue and intelligence.

7. Non-Maleficence - to avoid injury to others.

The deontological (duty) theories argue for the nature of 'relationships' (French and Granrose, 1995). The commissions of Enquiry attached considerable importance to the ethical obligations between employers and employees and between high-reliability organisations and their stakeholders. Deontological (duty) theories also account for motives. For example, when two people give money to charity and we know that one did it for genuine reasons of compassion and the other to impress. The *consequences* are the same, but our deontological view is that we value the motives differently.

Immanuel Kant1 (1724-1804) in *The Critique of Pure Reason* (1781) and the *Foundations of the Metaphysics of Morals* (1785) argued that the ordinary person knows perfectly well which actions are right and which are wrong. Kant argues that *intention* describes the moral worth of an act more than *consequences*. If a person is motivated by the intention to do the right thing, then that person is motivated by a sense of duty. His moral law requires that one should do an act only if one would want others in similar circumstances to do the same thing. This goes to the heart of the notion that senior managers should perhaps place themselves in the same hazardous situations in which they place their employees and other stakeholders. Immorality is when we make an exception to the moral law in our own case.

Kant draws the conclusion that we must always act as belonging to a community and treat others with respect, since we all have intrinsic worth. Kant said that achieving real outcomes required 'categoric' action. Kant said, "If you want to ......, then do ...." He saw it as imperative that if you wanted to, for example, improve your organisation's safety then you would intervene in hazard potentiating situations. Not to do so could be considered unethical and dysfunctional. Kant said that achieving real outcomes required categoric action. He saw it as imperative that if you wanted, for example in the modern world, to improve your driving skills then it was imperative you would take proper lessons from a professional instructor. Kant then, took the premise further and said that one should, "act only according to that maxim by which you can at the same time will that it should become a universal law." Therefore, Kant would call the statement, *"Tell the Truth"* a 'categorical imperative'.

Ethically dysfunctional managers were identified by each commission of Enquiry as being central to the accidents they studied. This notion of dysfunctional management extends to a broader base than ethics alone and is central to this book. Dysfunctional management behaviour is congruent with high-reliability organisational theory in the sense that incompetence in the form of inattention or inadvertence, greed or neurotic behaviour, or worse, is not acceptable as an excuse for a fatal accident.

A manager's ethical constructs seem to be an indicator of a propensity for functional and dysfunctional behaviour and point to primary managerial perceptions held by any manager. Hitt (1990), for example, suggests we can identify organisational leaders in terms of how they might 'ethically' view their primary management function. He suggests that end-result ethics leads to manipulation; rule ethics bring about bureaucratic administration; social contract ethics promote professional management; and personal ethics can result in transforming leadership:

Manipulator. The primary function of leadership is to use deception and cunning to further one's own ends. (The end justifies the means.)

Bureaucratic administrator. The primary function of leadership is to communicate and enforce rules (structure is preserved through rules.)

Professional manager. The primary function of leadership is to get things done through people for the purpose of achieving organisational objectives. (Management is grounded in the responsibility for achieving results through the effective and efficient use of human and material resources.)

Transforming leader. The primary function of leadership is to lift followers to their better selves. (The most effective way to motivate is to bring out the best in others.)

This theoretical perspective and philosophical insight is helpful in understanding the ethical concerns of this book. For example, consider managerial concern for the financial bottom line in decisions that require a trade-off between investing in safety or profit.

The economic dimension encompasses good and bad decisions in a business sense, whereas the ethical dimension encompasses right and wrong decisions in a moral sense. Safety centred decisions in high-reliability organisations must be both good from an economic standpoint and right from an ethical standpoint.

In *'The Neurotic '* (1984) Kets de Vries and Miller examine how top executives' personal neurotic styles of behaviour effect overall organisational functioning. They identify five neurotic styles - more developed in the *Diagnostic and Statistical Manual of Mental Disorders,* DSM-IV (1995). These help shape and influence at least five types of dysfunctional corporations and suggest that organisational problems seem to reflect the neurotic styles of their top managers. They suggest that each of these styles is shown to give rise to issues of strategy, structure, decision-making, and managerial culture. They claim that the organisational configuration seems to mirror the psychodynamic neurotic configuration of the top executives.

Because of the relationships between the decision-making outcomes of individual managers, and their cognitive and decision-making styles, in novel and complex environments, it is unethical to allow personal neurotic dysfunctional aberrations to subvert or preclude proper safety management, in organisations that require high levels of reliability to function safely, such as in mining, oil and gas exploration and refining, shipping, aviation and military operations.

Simple common sense suggests that perhaps states such as lack of knowledge may not constitute dysfunctional behaviour. However, in high-reliability organisations managers who should have particular knowledge but do not and insist their decisions on hazardous situations, may bring about loss of life and property. In this sense their lack of knowledge is lethal and therefore the consequence of ignorance is dysfunctional.

. . .

The following list of examples of unethical behaviours offered by Nash (1990) resonates with the findings of the various Commissions of Enquiry that follow (Case data in section 5.2.5). She identified 30 ethical concerns that result in dysfunctional behaviour or are examples of dysfunctional behaviour. This is suggestive of a strong equivalence between dysfunctional and unethical behaviours when the deontological equation is applied to high-reliability organisations.

1. Greed

2. Cover-ups and misrepresentation in reporting and control procedures

3. Misleading product or service claims

4. Reneging or cheating on negotiated terms

5. Establishing policy that is likely to cause others to lie to get the job done

6. Overconfidence in one's own judgment to the risk of the corporate entity

7. Disloyalty to the company as soon as times get rough

8. Poor quality

9. Humiliating people at work or by stereotypes in advertising

10. Lockstep obedience to authority, however unethical and unfair it may be

11. Self-aggrandisement over corporate obligations (conflict of interest)

12. Favouritism

13. Price-fixing

14. Sacrificing the innocent and helpless in order to get things done

15. Suppression of basic rights: freedom of speech, choice, and personal relationships

16. Failing to speak up when unethical practices occur

17. Neglect of one's family, or neglect of one's personal needs

18. Making a product decision that perpetrates a questionable safety issue

19. Not putting back what you take out of the environment, employees, and/or corporate assets

20.Knowingly exaggerating the advantages of a plan in order to get needed support

21. Failing to address probable areas of bigotry, sexism, or racism

22. Courting the business hierarchy versus doing the job well

23. Climbing the corporate ladder by stepping on others

24. Promoting the destructive go-getter who outruns his or her mistakes

25. Failing to cooperate with other areas of the company - the enemy mentality

26. Lying by omission to employees for the sake of the business

27. Making an alliance with a questionable partner, albeit for a good cause

28. Not taking responsibility for injurious practices - intentional or not

29. Abusing or just going along with corporate perks that waste money and time

30. Corrupting the public political process through legal means

. . .

David Godsell (1993) suggests that the legitimacy of the duties and standards adopted by any profession can never be isolated from the expectations of the various groups within society, who pay for, and rely upon, that profession's services. Godsell was pointing to a general propensity to ethical malaise in the auditing profession. His remarks also apply to those who purport to manage high-reliability organisations.

Gunningham and Johnstone (1999) develop a legal socio-technical argument that both specification standards (that tell duty holders how to meet a goal by requiring compliance with detailed technical requirements) and performance standards (that define the duty in terms of problems to be solved or goals to be achieved) are needed to ensure 'duty holders' comply with regulatory regimes. They observe a trend towards replacing specification standards with both performance standards [duty] and principle-based standards [ethical values] (for example, very general 'duty of care' provisions) while complementing these latter with greater reliance on codes of practice rather than regulations. This shift to reliance on ethical values in compliance regimes lends emphasis to the critical importance of the weight given to ethics as a core competency in this book.

One of the more relevant elucidations of ethical judgement is found in the deliberation process posited by Hosmer (1996), who identifies five major ethical systems each providing clear benchmarks for reasoning. Hosmer argues that the major implication for managers is that there is no single system of belief, with rationally derived standards of moral behaviour or methods of moral reasoning, that can guide executives fully in making 'proper' judgements when confronting difficult moral problems, such as reasoning through the consequences of whether to invest in safety or not.

For example, in the Pinto case, Ford valued a human life at $11.

Hosmer argued that immoral acts can be rationalised by persons who are prone to self-deception or self-importance (evidenced in the CAA case findings), and there is no scale to judge between 'wills'. Because of these implications, it is the contention of this book that if day-to-day managerial (ethical) judgement fails, then legal compliance imposts must be sufficient to save lives and ensure adequate vigilance in high-reliability organisations.

CASES OF FAILURES OF HIGH-RELIABILITY ETHICS

The case data makes it clear that senior management is required to exercise competent responsibility for the welfare of others (the deontological ethic). For example, Windridge (1996) observes in examination of the Moura evidence:

Mineworkers place their trust in management and have the right to expect management to take responsible decisions in respect to their safety. They also have the right to expect management to keep them informed on any matter likely to affect their safety and welfare (p 412).

Windridge is suggesting that managerial decision making should prioritise safety before other considerations, such as the priority of production. He is also suggesting that management has a responsibility to proactively communicate safety concerns to those who might be affected by them. To deliberately withhold critical safety information from those who might die as a result of not having that information is also unethical.

All of the case reports point to a cluster of ethical failures characterised by dysfunctional or ambiguous behaviour modelling by 'duty holders' [the legal term for those with responsibility - derived from 'deontology'] such as managers and directors. These ethical descriptors are grouped together.

HyperRESEARCH Ethical Descriptors

ambiguous behaviour modelling, blaming, CEO lying, corruption, duplicitous conduct, espoused values, failure of responsibility, false representation, pressure to break rules, relationship between regulator and regulated

This pattern is followed in each chapter of the following analysis. For example, the descriptors above include: managers shifting blame to front line workers for accidents that arise from managerial greed or incompetence, CEO and other members of the dominant coalition lying, individual and systemic corruption, duplicitous conduct, espoused values that bear no resemblance to actual practice, failure of responsibility through inadvertence or incompetence, false representation, managers applying pressure on workers to break rules, and cultivating a dubious and opportunistic relationship between the regulator and regulated. The direct relationship between managerial competencies and ethical behaviour is established in the literature section above (Windridge/Moura) and demonstrated in the case example (Westralia) below where one example showing 'failure of responsibility' is selected from the text of the five cases:

<u>WESTRALIA case</u>: [CODE: failure of responsibility] Diesel engines with jerk pumps are known to be prone to pressure pulses in the fuel system.... The presence of these pulses is well known by the engine manufacturer and the International Maritime Organisation. There was no consultation with relevant experts by the contractor, subcontractor or ship's staff. Lloyd's Register of Shipping approval of the intended arrangements was not obtained as required in order to maintain the ship's certification, and as requested by the ship. (Item 60: Report of the Board of Enquiry into the fire in HMAS WESTRALIA on 5 May 1998 EXECUTIVE SUMMARY)

This model of naming the text data source from now on will be done by naming the case source in bold with underline at the beginning of the paragraph ie, **WESTRALIA.** [The HyperRESEARCH code is *italicised* in the square brackets in each example that follows]

In the Westralia case the fuel hoses did not comply with specifications. In effect, the ship sailed without certification. The Navy Enquiry tended not to engage in the kind of higher order analysis suggested by this book and furthermore, it leaned toward exoneration of its own personnel by suggesting that 'systemic failure' had caused the accident. However, such 'systemic failure' can and will happen again unless a forensic examination reveals the competencies, motivations and thinking of the individuals involved and that is factored into future practices. A forensic analysis would require asking uncomfortable questions such as, 'Who benefited from the contract?' The active exercise of such candour needs to be in place in all high-reliability organisations.

In the following extract from the Longford Commission of Enquiry text data, several sections dealing with ethical concerns are identified. Sections 13.1, 13.2 and 13.3 point to lessons from prior accidents that were identified and detailed in operational manuals but largely ignored in practice, resulting in the loss of critical hazard related competencies. The Eleven guidelines included the organisation's statement of its responsibility for managerial accountability, risk assessment, facilities design, training, management of change, incident analysis, community preparedness for accidents, and the integrity of the plant's operations.

LONGFORD: 13.1[espoused values] Following an oil spill from the oil tanker Exxon Valdez in 1989 and against the background of a number of other disasters arising from the hazardous activities of companies other than the Exxon Corporation and its affiliates, Exxon developed a framework for the safe and environmentally sound operation of its various undertakings. The framework was called Operations Integrity Management Framework (OIMF). Within this framework, Exxon Company International (ECI) developed a series of expectations and guidelines (the ECI Guidelines) that included the ECT Upstream OIMS Guidelines (the ECI Upstream Guidelines). The ECI Upstream Guidelines contained eleven primary elements with associated expectations, and a series of guidelines for the achievement of these expectations. ...

13.2 The eleven elements referred to In the Guidelines were:

Element 1 - Management leadership, commitment and accountability;

Element 2 - Risk assessment and management;

Element 3 - Facilities design and construction;

Element 4 - Information/documentation;

Element 5 - Personnel and training;

Element 6 - Operations and maintenance;

Element 7 - Management of change;

Element 8 - Third party services;

Element 9 - Incident investigation and analysis;

Element 10 - Community awareness and emergency preparedness;

Element 11 - Operations integrity assessment and improvement.

13.3[systems manual that espoused safety accountability procedures] Utilising OIMF and the ECI Guidelines, Esso developed its Operations Integrity Management System (OIMS). This management system was outlined within a manual known as the OIMS Systems Manual and was detailed in a series of supplementary manuals, charts and other "controlled" documents. A controlled document was one subject to regulation by document management guidelines. The OIMS Systems Manual was the centrepiece of OIMS. It set out the scope and objectives of each of the 11 elements and identified each system owner, as well as the manuals and other documents falling within each system or sub-system. The owner of a system was the person responsible and accountable to ensure that the overall system was working and achieving its objectives in an efficient manner. (The Esso Gas Plant Accident, Report of the Longford Royal Commission. 1999)

This failure to implement these espoused guidelines is tantamount to unethical behaviour by management. The Royal Commission makes the point in paragraph 13.5 of the Report.

13.5 [espoused procedures were not implemented] However, in many respects, there were shortcomings in the way in which Esso implemented its OIMS system at Longford and thus, in the way in which it implemented the ECI Upstream Guidelines.

It stated that the failure to implement the espoused "process that measures the degree to which expectations are met" and regarded that managerial requirement as essential "to improve operations integrity and maintain accountability". The Longford findings were also suggestive that these deontological ethical factors need to be addressed and identified so that organisational learning can occur. For example, the Commission emphasises management's responsibility for competency based training and organisational learning possibilities that flow from identification of unethical behaviours in paragraphs 13.6 and 13.7 below.

13.6 [espoused values emphasised training] The ECI Upstream Guidelines called for the careful selection, placement, ongoing assessment and proper training of employees. They also required Esso to maintain a management system that ensured that the necessary levels of individual and collective experience and knowledge were maintained. Further, they required Esso to provide for ongoing refresher training and also to understand and apply the proper protective measures to deal with safety, health and environmental hazards.

13.7 [failure of training resulted in failure of safety] The system of training at Longford changed in 1993 from a "supervisor based" format to a "competency based" format. The evidence was that a competency based training programme required trainees to demonstrate a knowledge of plant operations, to apply acquired skills and to have an appropriate attitude to safety issues in respect of fellow employees, equipment and the environment. It was unnecessary for the Commission to undertake a detailed investigation of Esso's training programme or its particular training techniques. This was because the accident on 25 September itself demonstrated the primary deficiency in Esso's training. That deficiency lay in the failure of its training programmes, however implemented, to impart or refresh the knowledge required to operate GP1 safely in the conditions that existed on the day. (The Esso Gas Plant Accident, Report of the Longford Royal Commission. 1999)

This direct connection between ethics and competencies is salient since it occurs in all of the cases in one form or another and illustrates the gap between espoused values (often in the form of 'mission statements') and actual practice. For example, an analysis of the Seaview case from an 'ethics' perspective should be set against the espoused corporate mission statement of the CAA (now the Civil Aviation Safety Authority) as a high-reliability organisation and as the regulator responsible for the administration of the Act governing the conduct of Seaview Airlines. The Seaview case was as much an examination of the CAA, as regulator, as it was an examination of Seaview Airlines. Both failed to act ethically. Both were instrumental in the accident. The Commission of Enquiry and various other reports pointed to the

CAA as a bureaucracy out of touch with its prime responsibility as the 'regulator'. It had a 'duty' to ensure aviation safety and it failed repeatedly to enforce 'compliance' with aviation safety regulations. This failure was characterised as systemic and proved critical to its inability to prevent the Seaview accident, which cost nine lives. It failed to act in accordance with its own espoused guidelines. The following espoused undertaking by the CAA is taken from the Civil Aviation Authority Industry Development Plan (1994) Q 354.79094 AUS:

CAA: [espoused values] Serving Australia and international aviation, by pursuing high standards of aviation safety, through effective and efficient safety regulation and provision of world class aviation traffic services.

With this regulatory 'duty' spelled out, Mr. Paull, the CAA's regulatory officer responsible for policing the Seaview operation, failed in his ethical duty in the following significant ways, which resulted in compromising the critical relationship between regulator and regulated. The Commission makes the following findings: (Staunton, J.H. (1996) Report of the Commissioner / Commission of Enquiry into the Relations Between the CAA and Seaview Air, Executive Summary: 40-41) {from now on referred to as Seaview Report, Executive Summary}

[diligence and vigilance were compromised by the unethical relationship between the regulator and the regulated] First, the Commission uncovered no evidence of the corrupt receipt of benefits by Mr Paull as an inducement to act in a particular way. (Researcher's note: However, the particular technical definition of 'corruption' applied here does not entirely exonerate Mr Paull's lack of integrity and his resultant failure to ensure safety. There can be no doubt his judgement and impartiality were compromised by accepting benefits.)

[individual manager's values and behaviour] Secondly, Mr Paull allowed himself to be compromised by the receipt of significant benefits from CareFlight, and, in the case of the fax machine and the CB Radio, requested those benefits. He must have appreciated that this was wrong. He knew of no other CAA officer who had received such benefits. He did not disclose these matters to his superiors. He was aware of the Code of Conduct. There was no evidence that he behaved differently toward CareFlight than he otherwise might have done, or that his conduct towards CareFlight was inappropriate. However, no detailed investigation was undertaken into his supervision of that organisation.

[relationship between regulator and regulated] Thirdly, Mr Paull appeared not to have appreciated the need for some distance between the regulator and the regulated. His dealings with Heliscene and Solitary Island Helicopter Service demonstrated an insensitivity to the possibility of a conflict of interest. The closeness of his relationship with each operator inevitably compromised his ability to act as a regulator.

[duplicitous conduct] Fourthly, Mr Paull's use of training allowances to have the CAA pay for what were unquestionably private excursions reflected no credit upon him. He exploited his position. The evidence demonstrated a lack of integrity.

[failure of responsibility] Fifthly, the same lack of integrity was apparent in the evidence relating to outside employment. Mr Paull knew that permission was required. He knew he would not be given permission if it were a paid position. He surely knew he was compromising himself by accepting a paid position with an operator he supervised. Yet he went ahead with such employment, and did so repeatedly.

[false representation] Finally, in the midst of all of this, Mr Paull, on a significant number of occasions, lied to the Commission to cover up or explain his actions.

[relationship between regulator and regulated] Mr Paull presented as an opportunist who enjoyed, too much, the company of operators, and saw matters too readily from their viewpoint, rather than the viewpoint of public safety.

[corruption] The crash came at a bad time for the CAA. Its competence and integrity were already being questioned as a result of a crash some fifteen months earlier, on 11 June 1993. On that day an aircraft operated by Monarch Airlines, another small airline, crashed near Young, with the loss of seven lives. (Seaview Report, Executive Summary)

The Seaview crash gave fresh focus to the media scrutiny of the CAA. A number of criticisms were made. The response of management was quickly contradicted by documents leaked to the Press. The documents appeared to demonstrate, first, a poor safety record on the part of Seaview, and secondly, prior knowledge of that record in the CAA. There was speculation that there may be corruption. The CAA had ample opportunity to deal with the issues at Seaview that eventually resulted in the fatal accident, but consistently failed to do so.

The Seaview case indicates the critical relationship that exists between managerial ethics and managerial success or failure in high-reliability organisations. It could become an exemplar case study for management training in defining and dealing with most of the issues revealed by this book. The most relevant outcomes of the Seaview accident were those that focused on managerial 'competencies' and 'values' at the most senior levels.

The Commission of Enquiry (Staunton, J.H. (1996) examined Seaview's activities over a period of approximately three years. In that time Seaview Air had three chief pilots: before August 1993, Mr John Green, the CEO and operator; between August 1993 and March 1994, Mr Gregory Matthews; and between March 1994 and October 1994, Mr Clive McIver.

The task Mr McIver inherited as chief pilot required pilots to change bad habits that had been formed over many years. Such a task was formidable. The Commission stated that Mr McIver's only hope of succeeding was if he were to demonstrate implacable opposition to overloading, and to demand integrity in the completion of documents. Regrettably, he seems to have done neither. The Commission observed that he did not set a good example of ethical conduct to his pilots:

[ambiguous behaviour] it seems that on occasions he flew overloaded and tolerated a degree of misstatement ("fudging") in documents recording the weight of passengers and freight; and though he urged pilots to record defects in maintenance releases (in accordance with CAR 50), he appears not to have done so himself.

[duplicitous conduct] On 2 October 1994, the day of the Seaview Air crash, Mr McIver recorded Mr Green's weight on the manifest of VH-IBF as 77kg (the standard weight), when it was obvious that Mr Green was considerably more (92kg).

[pressure to break rules] After the crash, the CAA suspended Mr McIver, referring, among other things, to the following:

"As a result the company would appear to have a culture wherein the regard for rules, regulations and general best practice is not appropriate to the class of operation proposed to be conducted - i.e. RPT."

Mr John Green, was the CEO and airline operator and its chief pilot prior to 1993. Mr Green denied that Mr Paull had ever disclosed to him the fact that Mr Matthews (chief pilot between August 1993 and March 1994) had complained. That denial was furnished to the Commission before Mr Green became aware of Mr Paull's position. Mr Green was lying. The disclosures were certainly made. The Commission found that:

[CEO lying] Mr Green denied having knowingly flown an overloaded aircraft. He also denied having put pressure on his pilots to fly overloaded. The Commission has found that Mr Green is lying in both respects. The evidence that he flew overloaded, and that he put pressure on pilots, was overwhelming.

Mr Green gave evidence that he had not destroyed or concealed any document, having simply discarded correspondence with Fastbook Travel because it was unimportant. This evidence was rejected. The Commission found that the agreements and correspondence with Fastbook Travel were deliberately concealed from the Enquiry.

[instance of collusion by dominant coalition in lying to the Commission] According to Mr Green it was not until VH-SVQ had failed to arrive at Lord Howe Island (after the elapse of another hour) that he recognised the possibility that the aircraft might have crashed. Mr McIver gave similar evidence.

The Commission found that Mr Green and Mr McIver were both lying. It stated that, 'It is impossible to believe that two experienced pilots, both mature men, would not have appreciated at once that VH-SVQ was in grave and imminent danger.'

The Seaview crash was one of many serious events that resulted in the Civil Aviation Authority (CAA) being abolished and replaced by two separate organisations: the Civil Aviation Safety Authority (the Authority) and Airservices Australia. New compliance and enforcement procedures were introduced by the Authority in January 1996 after the Seaview crash and other disasters.

DIAGNOSTIC TOOLS TO IMPROVE HIGH-RELIABILITY ETHICS

Deontological ethics is a primary competency needed by managers and organisations in which responsibility for the lives and welfare of others is essential. Seeding of unethical values into organisations occurs where managers are themselves prepared to act unethically.

This is supported by the evidence from the Seaview case in which the CEO was found to be lying. His influence reached deep into the into the organisation itself and into the regulatory authority, the CAA. These unethical propensities take on memetic (message survival) force so they become part of every communication. This was evidenced in the Longford observations of ignoring critical espoused values. This is perfectly congruent with Maurino's (1995) theory that, 'organisational pathogens ... are transported along two principal pathways to the various workplaces, where they act upon the defences, barriers and safeguards to create latent failures and upon local working conditions to promote active failures (errors, violations and component failures). Subsequently these active and latent failures may act to create an event' (Maurino, 1995:28). Unethical behaviour by managers both models and gives permission for unethical behaviour in other employees such as the evidence shows in the case of the chief pilots involved in the Seaview incident. The evidence suggests that univariate dysfunctional ethics in managers can lead to multivariate dysfunctional ethics in employees.

THINKING ABOUT ETHICS

This view of univariate dysfunctional ethics leading to multivariate dysfunctional ethics in employees is seen in the Seaview case where the CEOs dysfunctional behaviour entered the organisation and infected his senior pilots. The ethical failure of corporate responsibility can be very high. For instance, Ford could have installed an $11 shield for the petrol tank of the PINTO, but senior management did a cost benefit analysis and decided not to. Hundreds of people were incinerated in Pinto crashes. Employees knew of this aberration but did nothing to stop the deaths.

In another example of the failure of corporate responsibility, safety queries about Concorde's engines surfaced in 1998. New Scientist magazine, 12 August 2000 reported that, British Airways commissioned a risk analysis of Concorde's Olympus 593 engines because it wanted to keep the 30-year-old supersonic plane flying until 2012. The study...divided the consequences into five classes--ranging from trivial to "catastrophic". The latter included "non-containment of high-energy debris, engine separation, uncontrolled fire [and] multiple engine failures". The analysis identified 152 separate risks, but it showed that Concorde's engines did not fall short of the safety standards required by the Civil Aviation Authority in Britain and its counterparts in France and the US.

Nevertheless, a blazing Air France Concorde smashed into a hotel two minutes after taking off from Charles de Gaulle airport, killing 113 people. It seems prior knowledge of 'significant risk' was not significant enough to cancel flights. British Airways was quick to emphasise that in spite of the CAA knowing of the potential dangers the regulator in its role of safety policeman had not 'required it to improve the plane's engines'. This is another example of costs driving risk rather than safety. The Pinto and Concorde crashes were preventable accidents. There was a corporate ethical responsibility to act on clear hazard information. Furthermore, it seems that not only were the organisations failing in their due diligence, so were the industry regulators.

Evidence from each of the Commissions of Enquiry found that behaviour such as ambiguous behaviour modelling, corruption, lying, and duplicitous conduct could have prevented each of the accidents studied.

As demonstrated in the case analyses the various Commissions of Enquiry all came to somewhat similar conclusions concerning poor ethical conduct at senior level. But Australian corporate laws and practices are based on the opposite assumption, that when directors gather, they will always be good fiduciary agents putting the interest of others above their own.

However, this espousal of 'corporate responsibility' often rings ethically hollow. This is no surprise. Adam Smith in 1776 stated that business people "seldom gather together except to conspire against the public interest". Coincidentally, Australian directors have a number of powers that create conflicts of interest and the opportunity to serve their own interest ahead of the company, its shareholders and stakeholders and to entrench their position, status and influence to serve their own interests (Turnbull, 2002). Corporations governed by a single (unitary) board have absolute power to manage their own conflicts of interest (Turnbull, 2000). High-profile corporate failures and the preventable accidents revealed by this book confirm the adage that absolute power leads to absolute corruption.

It is reasonable to assert, hypothetically, that competencies that systemically ensure the seeding of responsible managerial modelling of ethical behaviour throughout high-reliability organisations are essential to safety. Practical methods are available to managers that they can use to instill ethical behaviour in organisations (Ross, 1993; Kets de Vries, 19940; Nash, 1990) and include: ethics committees, an internal ombudsman's office, judicial boards, ethics-training programs, and social audits.

HIGH-RELIABILITY DIAGNOSTIC QUESTIONS

Generative questions attempt to generate issues of relevance related to, or which might be construed from the concepts (Becker, 1993). For example, the following two questions: 'Are personal and organisational ethics emergent cultural phenomena that arise over time, or can they be acquired and sustained through training and development?' and 'Can organisational cultures be provided with conceptual tools to detect and limit the effects of unethical behaviours?' point to the issue of training managers in ethics.

. . .

Solomon (1994) raises several behavioural questions in his social-responsibility audit.

Given any planned activity:

Who is affected? How?

Who might be affected?

What criticism might be expected? By whom? Is it justified? How can it be avoided?

Who could be helped by the plan? Who could be helped by a slight change in the plan?

How much would that cost?

Is the planned activity one which you would be willing (even happy) to publicise and make known to the community? Are there social aspects of the plan that would be well worth your publicising?

If not, why not?

Does the activity involve (or encourage) any immoral activity?

If so, how could this be avoided?

Are the net effects of the activity just and fair? Will anyone be cheated out of something rightfully his or hers (land or its value, royalties, credit, dignity, health)?

Are there any laws likely to be violated in carrying out the plan?

Are anyone's fights likely to be violated?

Are there valuable social institutions that could be served by the action?

Are other people's customs or ways of living likely to be violated?

. . .

Such questions are directed to actual day to day ethical concerns of managers. The difference between each type of question is apparent in the sense that the ethical audit style of question asked by Solomon is different from the HIGH-RELIABILITY DIAGNOSTIC QUESTIONS about ethical behaviour. This pattern of formulating HIGH-RELIABILITY DIAGNOSTIC QUESTIONS about the competency is followed in this section in each of the following chapters.

1.Immanuel Kant (1724-1804). His two most important works are The Critique of Pure Reason and the Foundations of the Metaphysics of Morals. Kant believed that the ordinary person knows perfectly well which actions are right and which are wrong. Kant argues that intention describes the moral worth of an act more than consequences. If a person is motivated by the intention to do the right thing then that person is motivated by a sense of duty. His moral law requires that one should do an act only if one would will that anyone in similar circumstances would do the same thing. Immorality is when we make an exception to the moral law in our own case.

12. COMPETENCY 2: FORESIGHT: ATTITUDINAL 'STANCE' AND 'INTELLIGENT LOOKING AHEAD'

THIS CHAPTER EXAMINES THE COMPETENCY OF "FORESIGHT," emphasizing the importance of proactive thinking, anticipating potential risks, and developing strategies to mitigate them. It explores various tools and techniques for enhancing foresight, such as scenario planning and risk assessment.

"Hindsight is a wonderful thing, but foresight is better, especially when it comes to saving life, or some pain!"

William Blake

WHAT IS HIGH-RELIABILITY FORESIGHT?

No one can predict the future. However, we can adopt a stance congruent with our interests and look ahead and think about what might happen so that we can begin to prepare for it. This looking ahead is termed 'foresight'. Managerial foresight ('managerial stance' and 'looking ahead'), as it is used in this book, means an ability senior executives need to have to see ahead based on their awareness of how organisational systems in hazardous operations can be safely developed and deployed. (Scott, 1991), suggests that *'stance'* means the affective or emotional dimensions of appreciating a situation. The competency demands considerable insight into systemic breadth and complexity and moves well beyond the realm of individual ability, and simple skills of instrumental, mechanistic learning. At the same time, foresight demands an attitudinal stance informed by detailed knowledge of past events. Therefore, systemic mechanisms to retain corporate memory are critical.

The exercise of foresight requires that specific records are kept, such as Safety Systems Management [SSM] (Petersen, 1996) or prospective and retrospective HAZOP (hazard and operability) studies (performed in hazardous operations - often used with equivalence to SSM). Such records include information about alerts and hazard signals, identification of critical indicators and operational manual updating as well as ensuring necessary inspections and forensic investigations of previous incidents. It also requires shaping a culture in which these factors are meaningful and can be applied. Further, these tasks should be reinforced in a high-reliability SSM or enabling HAZOP organisation by cyclical refresher training and incentives to ensure the competency is not extinguished. A proactive 'attitude' or mental stance by senior management is essential to lead the practice of foresight into an organisation end ensure it operates properly.

The need for foresight is an enduring requirement in high-reliability organisations both in macro and micro focus. For example, if the organisation is in a period of change (macro) or its systems and processes are dynamically changing in vivo (micro) then systems need to be in place to ensure there are no surprises. Nevertheless, it makes no sense to claim to know already the facts you will learn in the future. Yet, paradoxically, information overload has become a well-known problem in high-reliability and technology-based organisations: pieces of knowledge pile up too fast for people to sort and make sense of them (Spezia, 1979). The need for intelligent prospective and retrospective HAZOP or Safety Systems Management (SSM) analysis to deal with this information, taking account of the known and making room for the unknown, is put into relief when we consider that the most rational of ideas may *appear* to be true, but in fact may not actually *be* true. Commonsense, which mostly relies on memetic filters and frameworks, can be a dangerous ally in managing risk. Stars do not sit on a dome above the earth. The sun does not revolve around the earth. Big objects do not fall faster than small objects. Leaving safety control systems to individuals to manage by exercising even the most rational of memetic hunches, assumptions or intuitions is about as effective as relying on the evil-spirit theory of disease and is not an adequate managerial response to hazard.

After ethics, the managerial capacity to exercise foresight is the next most important core competency. Good record keeping and prospective and retrospective HAZOP or SSM studies should be informed by reliable corporate memory and incentives to ensure prior knowledge is captured and utilised. High-reliability organisations undergoing change, which in today's changing corporate and business world probably includes all organisations, most of the time, must be required by the regulator to initiate forensic prospective and retrospective HAZOP or SSM studies to enable the foresight necessary to create useful and usable prior knowledge. The regulator should ensure that the dominant coalition should not be allowed to compromise safety in the pursuit of 'production', since Australian Corporate law allows directors to manage their own conflicts of interest. The CAA and the Longford cases, which reveal the dangerous play of uncertain contingencies in hazardous conditions, illustrate the tight relationship between managerial competencies and the need for a strong compliance regime in HROs.

The critical indicators and descriptors of 'foresight' revealed in the HyperRESEARCH analysis of case reports were:

HyperRESEARCH Foresight Descriptors

change related risk, corporate memory, critical safety indicators, failing to keep or supply records, failure to perform prospective and retrospective HAZOP study, incentives, prior knowledge, role of government, role of regulator.

FORESIGHT, CULTURE, JUDGEMENT

There is a striking overlap of core competencies throughout the book, as is to be expected in Grounded Theory analysis (Bennett and George, 1997; Richards, 1995). For example, the relationship between foresight and competency, 'constructing a culture of safety', is anchored by competency subsets in competency such as 'failure to utilise information' and 'failure of corporate memory', which are strong echoes of the need for 'foresight'. Foresight and the other competencies, such as judgement are also connected because of the memetic principle that ideas that have evolved to seem true (at least to uncritical minds) can, in fact, be quite false (Drexler, 1986). Facts and real skills are essential to the exercise of foresight and the other competencies rather than the simple aleatory exercise of alert intuition or hunches.

IDEAS ABOUT FORESIGHT

HG Wells (1932), put a strong case for what he called 'professors of foresight'. The theoretical base concerning 'foresight' is adequate for the task but may not warrant a university chair. There are several systems available to organisations who might wish to apply the skills of foresight. Schultz (1983) suggests the Manoa approach to scenario building as a technique for exercising practical foresight capabilities. She states that scenario building begins with the recognition of change occurring in the environment (environmental scanning), and an identification of specific changes critical to the specific activities and goals (issues identification). The benefits of scenario building, according to Schultz, rest not in the completed scenarios but in the process of development itself, and in the subsequent common language participants in the process share. They can use this common language as a tool to explore the benefits, costs, and trade-offs of any potential decision, initiative, or plan. She says, they can consider the short-term trade-offs in comparison to long-term trade-offs as the scenario-building process creates a language to facilitate that comparison.

Scenario building also clarifies priorities in considering trade-offs under very different possible future conditions. Schultz's approach is amenable to the foresight technique called 'incasting' - thinking up the specific details of a possible future based on a more general scenario description. Incasting begins with an array of possible futures: several different scenarios, all based on observed trends and emerging issues. The presumption essential to incasting the future is that you have awakened to find yourself living in it.

Schwartz (1996) focuses on eight steps in a formulaic foresight method by 'focusing' on future events and constructing possible scenarios: identify focal issue or decision; identify the key factors in the local environment that influence the success or failure of the key issue or decision; identify macro environment driving forces; rank these forces by most important and most uncertain; select possible scenario logics by location of crucial uncertainties on an axes of importance v uncertainty; flesh out the possible scenarios in term of connections and implications; select leading indicators and signposts needed for the scenarios.

Kets de Vries (2001) promotes a 'sociovision' approach to foresight construction. 'Scenario', according to both de Vries and Schultz is best characterised by Royal Dutch Shell, whose scenario building meant "thinking the unthinkable" - harnessing and mobilising ideas that are not obvious to all. Shell uses only two - at the most, three - scenarios at a time. This is because people must be able to keep all the scenarios in mind as a context for discussion and decision-making. The de Vries process is an organic, evolutionary scenario building process, built on a dialogue focussed by eight basic questions.

1) What is the significant issue, program, product, or event for which we wish to explore alternative outcomes and their implications? Write down the focal issue.

2) Map the present: what structures, feelings, reactions, values are on participants' mental maps right now with regard to the issue?

3) Ask, "what next?" What could be potential outcomes of this issue, program, product, or event? State the possible outcomes in a few words: a short, vivid phrase. Let participants spend some time exploring alternative possible outcomes, bearing in mind that those alternatives will in many cases contradict or exclude others on the list. This is the space in which to consider not only likely outcomes, but also unthinkable ones.

4) Let participants sit back and consider the list for a few moments. Identify those outcomes that indicate opposite possibilities, or a branching point in the evolution of impacts and outcomes. Focus on the strategic branching points of particular interest or that the group feels represents a critical pattern worth exploring.

5) Cluster elements on the list of potential outcomes that are consistent with the main "branches" you have identified.

6) For each "branch," look for a phrase that sums up or identifies the

deepest, most pervasive structure defining that branch of outcomes; that phrase is your scenario title.

7) Ask, with regard to each of your "branches" or scenarios, "what does this mean for the main players involved in this story?"

8) what your organisation or company, and the people in it, would do in the environment described by each scenario: how would your company deal with the conditions in that possible future? (Kets de Vries, 2001)

Harman (1976) discusses the necessity for thinking through the multiple causalities that produce an infinite array of alternative possible futures, and his work is relevant to the task of exercising foresight in high-reliability organisations. He describes how to mimic that pattern of development in scenario building. In its simplest form, this technique is based on group brainstorming but could also be expanded to include phases of background research such as SSM or prospective and retrospective HAZOP studies. Participants brainstorm evocative titles for twenty-two "snapshots" of alternative futures: not described scenarios, just quick images of possibilities. Post-it note jottings are arrayed so that they are visible to everyone. The group then discusses which of the "snapshots" seems closer to present conditions, and which seem to require longer-term, transformational changes. The post-its are rearranged to form rough groups of "near-future," "medium-term future," "long-term future," and "far future." Actual dates, or as in this example, sooner or later, are options. On a mural-sized sheet of paper, the group has prepared a fan diagram.

Participants then discuss where in the chronology represented by the fan template different "snapshot" images of the future fall, and whether neighbouring "snapshots" rely upon related trends and emerging issues of change. As the group discusses timelines and related lines of causality, the post-its are mapped onto the twenty-two different triangles on the fan. When the fan is complete, it may be used to tell different stories of how changes and situations emerge, blend, and bounce off each other when intersecting. The different triangles are like stepping stones into the future, and different paths create scenarios that unfold in different patterns.

Harman's approach is close in concept to standard crisis management techniques (Myers, 1986), which identify a critical envelope of executive concern in which time available to act, options available, dimension of the crisis and the extent of control over the factors are all considered in matrix form. SSM or prospective and retrospective HAZOP studies use a somewhat similar array of techniques borrowed from the 'quality' school of management theory, such as fishbone diagrams and fault trees, designed to capture critical information and identify issues.

In considering potential accident scenarios Heinrich (1950) indicates that there is a Chain of Multiple Events Model or Domino Theory of accident causation. His theory suggests a chain of events or factors that lead up to an accident, with each factor acting on the next over a period of time, implying that if any factor is removed from the chain, then the accident is unlikely to occur. This book suggests that management has prime responsibility to foresee and remove such factors, which might be achieved through immersion in the areas of concern by applying some of the foresight scenario techniques set out in this section. Such techniques require engagement at the highest levels of an organisation. Because there are many techniques and tools that can be used there can be no valid excuse for not applying them.

Most MBA programs in universities introduce future managers to the principles of strategic thinking through acquaintance with techniques such as SWOT analysis (analysing strengths, weaknesses, opportunities and threats). However, these are useful but often inadequate models to apply to SSM in high-reliability organisations. Their focus is on markets, profits and production rather than hazard prevention. So, no matter how competent a senior manager may be in their own estimation, foresight can be an area where one's earlier training in management may not be up to the task. Predictions based on competent managerial skill can be quite inaccurate. Even the steady advance of technology often eludes prediction by the most competent. For example, though the space shuttle was possible, predictions of its cost and initial launch date were wrong by several years and billions of dollars.

Development always involves uncertainties. Drexler (1986) argues that possibilities are quite distinct from predictions.

We look ahead with minds and cultures rooted in the ideas of more sluggish times, when both science and technological competition lacked their present strength and speed. We have only recently begun to evolve a tradition of technological foresight. (Drexler, 1986:54)

This mix of uncertainty and technological development is a potent combination in hazardous situations and makes mastery of managerial foresight critical in periods of change (both organisational and socio-technical). Foresight is enabled by the knowledge base of SSM and prospective and retrospective HAZOP studies during periods of change. In principle, if these were applied, they should go some way to mitigating preventable accidents.

For example, during a change from one air traffic control system to another system the likelihood of accidents is increased, therefore suggesting that heightened, rather than routine, foresight and vigilance are needed. Such a scenario is amenable to elucidation and development using any of the techniques listed above.

CASES OF FAILURES OF HIGH-RELIABILITY FORESIGHT

If proper organisational learning does not take place after an accident and foresight capabilities have not been deployed, then the conditions are still in place for the occurrence of similar accidents (as is demonstrated in the Mauro case examined in this book).

The Commissions of Enquiry data suggested that prospective and retrospective HAZOP studies would have revealed over time that systems, not individuals, were the main locus of most accidents in HROs and also where information to head off future accidents could be examined. The 'human element' approach creates a climate where blame is levelled at the front-line operators rather than managers (as in the Longford, Seaview, and Lake Illawarra cases).

To his credit, Viner (1982) points out that consideration of management's role has been a notable omission from the factors considered in accidents where rapid and dynamic change and uncertainty occur. He argues there has been a strong emphasis on a 'human factors' interpretation of accidents where an operator experiences 'overload'. The operator must continue to perform his usual tasks while correcting for the unusual additional system condition.

This issue of operator overload is thrown into relief in the Longford case where Esso - BHP had a philosophy about managing the change process and recognised the hazards that went with change but still pushed the safety envelope for the sake of production. It failed to carry out its own recommended risk assessment analysis and failed to foresee the impact of the proposed changes on the safe operation of the facility. Had it done so the problem of operator overload would have become obvious. The Longford Report states:

LONGFORD: 13.65 [risk resulting from change - prior knowledge - prediction of the consequence of change] Attached to and forming part of Element 7 was Esso's Management of Change Philosophy dated August 1993 (the philosophy). In the philosophy, Esso recognised that change was "necessary and desirable" as part of the operation of a facility but also recognised that "changes potentially invalidate prior risk assessments and can create new risks, if not managed diligently".

13.66 [HAZOP requirements specified prior to accident] The philosophy contained management of change procedures to be followed in undertaking, amongst other things, any modification or addition to an existing facility. These procedures required any permanent change to an existing facility to be accompanied by a risk assessment of the change, consistent with the procedures in OIMS Element 2, "Risk assessment and management". The primary purpose of such an assessment was to determine the impact of the proposed change on the safe operation of the facility.

Esso was in a process of organisational change at the time of the Longford accident. Taken together, paragraphs 13.65-68 illustrate that the organisation identified the need for risk assessments as part of the responsibilities it has to manage change related risk. At the same time, it occludes the actual tasks required by items 2 and 7 of its own 'Integrity' management system (OIMS) in managerial gibberish such as, "Production Technology operate(s) within a management of change procedure that is consistent with the EAL management of change philosophy" (quoted in 13.67). Clarke (1999) describes this as, 'the moral risks of risky systems are trumped by the bureaucratic standards demanded of fantasy documents and the administrative rationality they signal.' In spite of its awareness of the risk such change would bring, it failed to pay attention to information already in the system, hence it failed to connect prior knowledge to the potential accident conditions and the change process in train at the Longford plant. It overlooked or ignored the need to exercise straightforward foresight techniques.

13.67 [prior knowledge and change-related HAZOP requirements not converted into operational procedures and also masked by 'management speak'] However, OIMS Element 2 did not identify any procedures for risk assessment associated with management of change. The only reference to this topic was in the following terms: "Production Technology operates within a management of change procedure that is consistent with the EAL management of change philosophy."

13.68 [change related risk and failure to perform HAZOP study combine to subvert corporate memory and compliance requirements]. Moreover, neither OIMS Element 7 (Management of change) nor OIMS Element 2 (Risk assessment and management) made any attempt to define the breadth or scope of any risk assessment study to be undertaken to comply with management of change procedures.

There is ample evidence that prior knowledge of the consequences of change existed at senior corporate levels. Failure to perform the necessary prospective and retrospective HAZOP studies indicate a failure of corporate memory since this requirement arose from the organisation's prior experience of change related accidents and should have enabled adequate foresight. The following excepts from the Commission Report indicates that if the overload (job enrichment) margin becomes too large, or occurs at a critical time, a person may begin to make errors in his usual task performance or in the handling of the unusual additional system condition.

13.84 [change-related complexity associated with job enrichment masked critical safety indicators] In mid-1993, changes were made to the respective roles and responsibilities of operators and supervisors at Longford. Further changes were made in 1996 and 1997, with the consequence that operators assumed a greater responsibility for the day-to-day operation of the plant, including troubleshooting to overcome process irregularities. There was also a reduction in the number of plant supervisors and a reduction in the number of plant operating areas.

13.85 [risk assessments were required but these were not carried out] These structural changes were intended to alter operating and supervisory practices at the plant and thus required management of change risk assessment and evaluation pursuant to Esso's management of change philosophy. Again, no such assessment was carried out. (The Esso Gas Plant Accident, Report of the Longford Royal Commission. 1999)

Paragraphs 13.84-85 observe that risk assessments resulting from

management initiated efficiency changes were not carried out in spite of managerial policy alerts such as, 'changes potentially invalidate prior risk assessments and can create new risks, if not managed diligently'. This combined with the overload problem, masked critical safety indicators - such as audible alerts.

Central to the exercise of foresight is the attention given to the capture and application of 'prior knowledge' by Turner (1977, 1978, 1997). He suggests that prior knowledge of potential accidents already exists in organisations, however, this knowledge base of serious risk has often been ignored. For example, in the past, aircraft accident investigations were considered complete if 'human error' could be established as the cause. Aviation companies such as Boeing, for example, found that 73.9% of aviation accidents involving commercial jet aircraft could be attributed to failure of the 'human element' (survey from 1959 - 1985). Analyses such as these failed to garner knowledge of failing systems and little or no effort was then made to determine what other factors had resulted in accidents. This notion of winding up an investigation prematurely has some dubious support in the literature. For example, Viner's (1982:101) human factors approach suggests that human error results from man's psychological and physiological limitations and the demanding role he has been given in the aviation system.

The idea has memetic force as an assumption that appears to be true but which may not actually be true. For example, if an investigation finds that 'human error' is the principal cause of an accident, it has no reason to look further for 'cause' and will overlook all or most other factors necessary to feed into HAZOP studies or scenario building exercises. Hence the need for analysing accidents in terms of systemic factors (social and technical).

The literature points unequivocally to the need to engage in techniques of looking ahead by keeping critical prospective and retrospective HAZOP records and applying them to the task of scenario building. The problem of collecting and using prior information to feed into accident prevention often flows from an attitudinal stance by senior management and was strikingly observed in the following extract from the Seaview case. It shows the failure of both the company to keep records and the regulator to insist on such records being kept, as is required under the Act. If records had been kept they might have enabled the collection of already existing information sufficient to foresee the accident under study. The case also demonstrates the connection between such failures and how the attitudinal readiness to behave unethically and to breach compliance requirements limits the capacity for foresight. In this CAA-Seaview case the regulator failed to stop the airline, Seaview, from conducting unauthorised regular passenger flights.

CAA [failure to keep or supply records as unethical behaviour, duplicitous conduct and breach of compliance requirements showing contempt for the regulator] Seaview Air was obliged (as was the CAA) to produce to the Commission documents relevant to the Terms of Reference. It failed to produce agreements and correspondence with Fastbook Travel (a travel agency that arranged most nights). That material was made available to the Commission by the travel agency itself. It revealed the truth of Seaview Air's relationship with the agency, namely, the purchase of seats, not the charter of aircraft.

Mr Green gave evidence that he had not destroyed or concealed any document, having simply discarded correspondence with Fastbook Travel because it was unimportant. This evidence is rejected. The agreements and correspondence with Fastbook Travel were deliberately concealed from the Commission. (p15, Executive Summary)

. . .

Seaview was registered only to conduct charter operations, but it was running a six-day a week passenger operation in direct breach of its license. The core issue of ethics emerges as seminal to a competency such as foresight. Seaview's management, who failed to exercise foresight, simply broke the law in plain sight of the regulator, who also failed to exercise foresight, and against the specific advice of its chief pilot, who appeared to have exercised adequate foresight (and who was sacked), and consequently a fatal accident occurred. The Commission Report makes it clear that the Chief Pilot provided the regulator and the company management with sufficient prior knowledge of a potential accident. This prior knowledge should have enabled all who were involved to foresee the accident. Ethics, compliance and foresight are inextricably linked in the following extract.

[prior knowledge and the role of the regulator] On 7 March 1994 the chief pilot of Seaview Air, Mr Matthews, was dismissed by Mr Green. He was replaced by Mr Mclver, with the approval of the CAA. On 10 March 1994, Mr Matthews wrote to Mr Paull. His letter began with these words:

"SEAVIEW AVIATION operated by John Green is a disaster waiting to happen. (John's) attitude is extremely negative and dangerous. He does not know enough about Safety, Regulations, Orders, Aircraft limitations, and Pilot Management to run a safe and efficient operation. (His) opinion of the CAA is that "if they could get a decent job they would (not) be bothering him"; he also says, "that if pushed he would sell all his aircraft and retire to the (beach), drinking beer". It may be better for the travelling public that he does this?"

The accuracy of that statement has been demonstrated to the Commission. Seaview Air, while under the effective control of Mr Green (that included the period during which Mr Matthews was Chief Pilot), remained a poorly managed, and often wilfully non-compliant, organisation. Mr Green's attitude to many aspects of the operation was dangerous, for example, overloading, cheating on maintenance releases, failing to document defects, failing to restrain loads. Moreover, he manifested an attitude towards the CAA of contempt, which was not altogether unjustified.

Mr Matthews's letter catalogued the problems of Seaview Air. It is now known that Seaview Air was afflicted by each one of the problems he identified. He described an operation with which no sensible person would wish to fly. He identified the following:

- the failure of Mr Green to allow the chief pilot to control the operation;
- cheating on maintenance releases;
- overloading and the absence of a system of loading;
- the absence of documentation for each flight;
- failure to restrain loads;
- failure to maintain flight and duty times in accordance with CAO 48.0;
- failure to maintain adequate safety equipment (life jackets and life rafts); and
- the fact that the operations were, in truth, an unauthorised RPT operation.

This illustration of the dominance of the CEO and his capacity to treat safety with contempt emphasises the critical theoretical insight offered by Turner (1997) that prior knowledge of an impending accident is available within the organisation before the accident occurs, and in high-reliability organisations such accidents should be foreseen. However, in this case, the information that identified the serious risk contained in Mr. Matthews letter was ignored.

Instead of being the trigger for an investigation, Mr Matthews letter met with inertia. It was enough for the CAA that Seaview Air had appointed a new chief pilot, Mr Mclver. It was left to Mr Mclver to address the problems raised by Mr Matthews. With a new chief pilot, Seaview Air was to be regarded as having a "clean slate". The CAA did not even take the trouble to interview Mr Matthews to determine what evidence he could provide.

The alleged deficiencies of Seaview Air were so many, so serious, and reported so often (many being corroborated by information already available), that an investigation by the CAA, rather than by Mr Mclver, ought to have been undertaken at once. It was absurdly benign, and dangerous, to regard Seaview Air as having "a clean slate" simply because there was a new chief pilot. (Staunton, J.H. (1996) Report of the Commissioner / Commission of Enquiry into the Relations Between the CAA and Seaview Air:18, Executive Summary)

Coincidentally, Mr Matthews letter pointed to concerns later raised by the Commission and the CAA's failure to examine his evidence amounted to an extraordinary failure of foresight on the part of the regulator.

DIAGNOSTIC TOOLS TO IMPROVE HIGH-RELIABILITY FORESIGHT

Job enrichment (a managerial euphemism for job overload) can be dangerous in high-reliability settings if appropriate training and cyclical retraining is not a change-related requirement. High-reliability organisations that demonstrate increasing complexity should automatically become candidates for regulatory and board level scrutiny, if operational processes and systems are being managed by untrained personnel. Scrutiny of this type is predicated on observations that job enrichment or job overload can reduce a system's capacity to utilise or even capture accident relevant information.

The high probability of accidents under such conditions (almost always involving ongoing change) should be foreseen both by the senior organisational managers and by government regulators. These predisposing factors can be predicted whenever organisational or process change is put in place. If previous experience has been ignored prior to an accident, then such conduct goes beyond loss of corporate memory to individual negligence and culpable, if not criminal, behaviour.

It is relevant to observe that most system and process change is ordered by the dominant coalition to effect cost reductions, increase production, and so increase profits. Consequently, the dominant coalition is entirely responsible for change related accidents since it is their responsibility to foresee such accidents, because the information they need to identify accident potentiating factors is always present somewhere in the organisation (Turner, 1977).

THINKING ABOUT FORESIGHT

Grimaldi (1989:114115) observes that, "The qualifications for a safety practitioner should include (1) knowledge of hazards, safety principles and techniques; (2) knowledge of engineering; and (3) knowledge of business administration". It is salient that while chief executive officers and managers may have some knowledge of item three, business administration, it is rare that they have skills in items one and two. If this is the case it might be argued that priorities set by management interests may take precedence over those where knowledge of hazards, safety principles and techniques or even knowledge of engineering dynamics at play in the particular safety milieu are non-existent or poorly understood. Grimaldi's observation then, amplifies the need for these skills to be required of managers in high-reliability organisations or for the regulator to ensure that, if they are not then safety will not be compromised through the inability to foresee a potential accident.

Managers lacking these skills would find it difficult to convince an Enquiry that they had the competencies necessary to exercise foresight. For example, the Seaview Air case discussed in this book reveals core failures of foresight amplified by serious duplicitous behaviour. The CEO of Seaview could perhaps claim he had adequate knowledge of hazards, safety principles and techniques, knowledge of engineering, and knowledge of business administration, and yet these competencies still did not prevent a foreseeable and therefore preventable accident. Both the CEO and the regulator failed to exercise core competencies, foresight. Many indicators and behavioural descriptors relating to lack of foresight on the part of Seaview Air, and its regulator, were identified in the book.

Problems within Seaview Air included:

The company was not licensed to operate Regular Public Transport (RPT) services on the route in question

There was little evidence of compliance with the recording and processing of defects

Evasion of regulations was common-as admitted by several previous Chief Pilots.

Deficiencies on the part of the Civil Aviation Authority included:

Lack of effective procedures to review the issue of Air Operator Certificates

Poor operator surveillance

Inadequate follow-up of safety hazards identified in Seaview Air's operation.

Bureau of Air Safety Investigation. (1996) 9402804

. . .

A crash in the previous year on 11 June 1993 (ATSB Occ# 199301743, and the BASI (1994) Report, 9301743) should have rendered the Seaview crash foreseeable. VH-NDU, a Piper PA31-350 Navajo Chieftain operated by Monarch Airlines, was on a landing approach to Young Aerodrome, NSW, in conditions of low cloud and darkness. It struck trees, crashed, and was destroyed by impact forces and post-crash fire. All seven occupants were fatally injured. A combination of local and organisational failures led to the accident.

Local factors included:

The weather conditions were poor, and there were inadequate visual cues available to the handling pilot.

The pilot had a high workload, made worse by aircraft equipment deficiencies and inadequate procedures.

Deficiencies were identified within the regulator and the operator.

Organisational failures on the part of the operator included:

Poor training of flight crew

Poor control of the safety of flight operations

Inadequate supervision of maintenance

Inadequate resources allocated to safety.

(ATSB (1993), 199301743)

All of the above factors in both cases were foreseeable. These failures were made worse because operational staff in both companies felt unable to discuss their safety concerns with management. Management refused to see what the front-line operators could see.

. . .

The Australian Transport Safety Bureau web site1 details 486 aviation accidents between 22 December 1990 and 13 January 2003. Most of the fatal and serious category accidents reveal dangerous failures of foresight. Many of the accidents reported on the ATSB site contain data similar to the Monarch accident at Young and the Seaview accident, enroute to Lord Howe Island, cited above. There is also a disheartening similarity of event data in the marine accident investigation section of the ATSB site. It would be possible to list the details of several hundred accidents using the format of the accident of the Seaview Air Aero Commander and the Navajo Chieftain crash outlined above. All of them demonstrate deficiency indicators and organisational failures that point to break downs of the critical managerial competencies, such as foresight, discussed in this book.

Evidence from each of the cases examined in this book revealed that adequate prior knowledge was at hand to render each accident foreseeable. This capacity to intelligently look ahead for strange artefacts and possible anomalies to head off accidents should doubtless be a major concern for CEOs and the dominant coalition. It is clear from the warnings and signals received and ignored in the examples above, that routine managerial competencies, such as assessing critical safety indicators and carrying out HAZOP studies, are essential in managing safety in the change process. The examples also illustrate that corporate memory cannot be counted on and the Corporate regulator must play a significant role, when high-reliability organisations are going through change. Regulators should place themselves in a position to insist on the necessary capabilities required to the dominant coalition. Adequate responses to the knowledge that already existed or to the records that should have been kept and to the HAZOP procedures that should have been performed could have provided sufficient foresight to prevent each of the accidents studied. The various Commissions of Enquiry all came to somewhat similar conclusions.

Foresight is a trainable competency as demonstrated in the techniques and tools revealed in the work of De Vries (2001), Schwartz (1996),

Harman (1976), Schultz (1983), and Heinrich (1950), and in straightforward works that deal with the effectiveness of managing safety systems, such as Petersen (1996). The competency can be acquired with moderate effort by most managers and ought to be required of managers of HROs. It grows out of understanding the sorts of hazardous exigencies that can arise in high-reliability organisations during normal operations and during organisational or operational change. Both positive and punitive consequences for compliance and non-compliance with safety requirements are needed to ensure that the instruments and competencies essential to ensure foresight are in place and operating properly. Both organisational and regulatory interventions may be necessary.

HIGH-RELIABILITY DIAGNOSTIC QUESTIONS

Prospective and retrospective HAZOP studies both inform and are informed by reliable systems of capturing corporate information. This observation would suggest that management should put such systems in place at the outset to ensure critical systems and safety knowledge is captured and applied when needed. Romans were at the time raises such basic questions as:

•Should high-reliability organisations initiate forensic prospective and retrospective HAZOP studies to enable the foresight necessary to create decision usable prior knowledge?

•Then, because Australian Corporate law allows directors to manage their own conflicts of interest, one should ask if regulatory bodies ought to anticipate high level disinterest in safety, where safety is mostly seen as a cost.

•It is unrealistic in the present corporate climate to expect boards of directors to possess well developed safety-based competencies such as foresight without regulatory pressure to do so. Therefore, is there a need for a strong compliance regime in HROs if preventable accidents are to be avoided?

•This concern for a strengthened regulatory role raises the question, where willfully non-compliant organisations that fail to utilise prior information regarding potential accidents are allowed to operate high-reliability services, or are known to be otherwise at risk, to what extent is the regulator ultimately responsible for fatal accidents?

•This perspective on foresight as a regulatory failing also raises the further question, what systems or techniques could a regulator insist on to ensure critical safety information is captured and utilised in HROs?

These questions direct the booker to the scenario building foresight theories of De Vries (2001), Schwartz (1996), Harman (1976), Schultz (1983), Heinrich (1950) and the Turner's (1977) theory that underpins all of these, that prior knowledge of an accident exists somewhere in an organisation before the accident occurs.

13. COMPETENCY 3: VIGILANCE: HAZARD PERCEPTION AND SIGNAL DETECTION

THIS CHAPTER FOCUSES ON THE COMPETENCY OF "VIGILANCE," DEFINING it as the ability to actively monitor the environment for potential hazards and respond promptly to warning signals. It discusses the importance of maintaining a low threshold for detecting risks and the challenges of sustaining vigilance over time.

"Through vigilance, restraint, and control, the wise will construct an island that no flood will overcome."

Unknown

WHAT IS HIGH-RELIABILITY VIGILANCE?

Williamson (1975:21) observed that humans have limitations and that these 'physical limits take the form of rate and storage limits on the powers of individuals to receive, store, retrieve and process information without error'. Subsequently Spezia (1979), developed the 'task overload' concept to examine how system components and the pilot's limitations combine in the causation of the human error accident. Downs (1967:116–8) showed how information is typically subjected to increasing biases, errors and missing content as the number of levels in a hierarchy increases. Individuals and the systems they engage with need to constantly attend to risk. Vigilance is conceptualised as the capacity to attend to events that carry information significant to safety, and because they have different thresholds of significance they all must be above the vigilance threshold.

The psychobiological concept of 'threshold' is useful in distinguishing vigilance from other competencies. For example, we all have a pain threshold that can be mitigated through drugs or habituation resulting in an altered perception of pain. The vigilance threshold must be held very low through attitudinal and systemic foresight initiatives such as involving and valuing 'people', signal detection, and reporting skills. In consideration of Down's findings, this is critical in bureaucracies where supporting foresight systems may not be adequate.

Therefore, the competency also requires practical organisational systems to be in place to continually monitor and detect danger signals that move above the vigilance threshold, such as signal discriminating methods, feedback systems, attendance to records, monitoring of processes and flows, and attention to warnings and methods of calling attention to hazard signals that continually repeat and to which human operators can become habituated. Vigilance is necessary for the effective practice of 'foresight', competency 2, but should not be confused with it. The following 'vigilance' descriptors, which are significantly different from those for foresight, were identified in the HyperRESEARCH analysis of the text data.

HyperRESEARCH Vigilance Descriptors

attention to risk, auditing system, debriefing, discrepancies in reporting, equipment defects, error detection, failure of materiels, failure of safety systems, failure to discriminate signals, failure to monitor operating conditions, failure to utilise records, habituation to warning signals, failure to engage in or provide feedback, hazard identification, high-reliability - many eyes, ignored warnings, inattention.

VIGILANCE, FORESIGHT, ETHOS, AND CULTURE

This competency requires the information gathering and deployment capacities identified in competency two, foresight, and it is also closely linked to competency six, organisational ethos, and seven, constructing a culture of safety. If the culture is supportive and healthy, vigilance concerns will be expressed in healthy ways. Equally, if the culture is repressive these capabilities will be subverted and thresholds will be raised to protect the individual, where the culture supports individuals with agendas of their own. Senior management should encourage and reward expressions of human vigilance capabilities and be aware of their strong cultural connections.

Understanding the issues surrounding vigilance also informs organisational development and training concerns, which goes to the heart of issues raised in both competencies eight and nine that are concerned with performance in particular settings. Training may need to be site specific. This psychological perspective addresses the skills someone must acquire to operate a system safely and efficiently and how to select and train those operators whose abilities will match the competencies required by the job.

IDEAS ABOUT VIGILANCE

This competency is well covered in the literature, in fields such as human performance psychology, experimental psychology and engineering psychology. These fields of psychology are concerned with how the brain perceives and decides what to do with the sensory messages that are relayed from the environment by the eyes, ears, and other senses (perception) in the sensory register; then how the operator decides what to do with this information (decision) in the working memory and executive control centres of the brain; and then how the actions that are decided on are carried out (action) by the response generator (Wickens, 1992).

The *human performance perspective* also requires us to consider the rich interplay of variables among training, individual differences, and system design. This approach is very important because it accounts for several human-centred performance factors such as operator work load and performance, training, and selection (Spezia, 1979). This is congruent with the observations in the case data. However, while it is important to be aware of the role of these human performance factors it is vital not to be seduced by plausible psychological explanations of them to the point they capture a whole incident.

Reason's (1987:463-470) observation is of particular relevance to this study that 'human fallibility in one form or another is the major contributor to catastrophic failures in complex and hazardous process environments.' Heinrich (1959:13-16) asserts that only 10% of accidents are caused by unsafe mechanical and physical conditions, whereas unsafe acts of persons cause 88% of accidents. (The other 2%, he suggests, are classed as unpreventable, or acts of God).

The psychobiological approach to vigilance in HROs is very useful. For example, Reason (1987) shows us how an incident is planted as a virus very deep within the body of an organisation. The expression of that virus (the actual accident or incident) is often far removed in time and responsibility from the site of infection. Reason calls these causative factors *resident pathogens*. These viruses have memetic (survival and dispersion) force. They promote unsafe actions and also lower the system's defences against disastrous consequences. They reside at the human and systemic communication nodes of an organisation's communication channels. These nodes are easily located. They occur at the interfaces between one part of the process and the next.

Vigilance needs to occur at low signal detection thresholds with high sensitivity to ensure it is detecting the early event phenomena required to offset the cumulative effects of simple human induced error influenced by fatigue, uncertainty, background phenomena, and salience of signals (Wickens, 1992). Examples of poor vigilance can be seen in the simple errors in ordinary experience, such as turning on a car's headlights instead of the windscreen wipers because the controls are placed side by side. Other simple errors that are made because the process exceeds human capabilities (Spezia's 'task overload' concept) are making a mistake in using a set of controls because of ambiguous or poorly worded instructions or having to remember a ten-digit number and not remembering it long enough to complete entering it.

Because vigilance is a competency requiring the capacity to signify and attend to events that carry information significant to safety it is characterised by *perception, stimulus detection, recognition, identification* or *categorisation, absolute judgment* and *pattern recognition* (Wickens, 1992). It is a competency to be valued by management in front line operators in high-reliability organisations. Each of these factors is complex and can lead to competent performance or impediments to performance. For example, training for '*perception*' in Air Traffic Controllers requires that we distinguish between several levels of complexity in categorising a task brought about by the nature of the stimulus and the task confronting the operator. At a basic level, the competency may call for the simple human performance judgment of whether a *stimulus* is present or not, such as determining the presence of a blip on a radar screen. Only two perceptual categories are used, 'yes', and 'no', and the human performance operation is one of *detection* but still involves sensory processing, perception, attention resources and response execution. At levels of greater complexity, the competency may call for not just detection but also *recognition, identification* or *categorisation* of the stimulus into one of several possible groups, such as 'light aircraft converging with military or civilian jet traffic'. This level of complexity requires the use of the memory capabilities acquired through experience or training or both. The competency is learned and embedded in memory through repetition and use.

. . .

The process is made more or less complex depending on whether one physical dimension alone is to be used in perceptual categorisation of the stimulus, or whether instead several dimensions are to be considered in concert. As one example of the simpler, first case–the *absolute judgment task*--an operator may be asked to judge the velocity of several converging 'blips', the separation between them, and the aircraft characteristics they represent, and assign the stimulus to a particular categorical level. In more complex tasks, several dimensions need to be considered to match a stimulus category. Such multi-dimensional vigilance factors are typical of *pattern recognition*. Each pattern is specified by a combination of levels (called features) along the several dimensions. For instance, recognition of a particular malfunction of a complex system will occur when an operator can associate a unique combination (pattern) of dial readings (features) on several different instruments (dimensions) to the perceptual category associated with a particular malfunctioning state. For example, a particular collection of thermometer and barometer readings, satellite cloud cover photographs, and wind speeds may signal "storm coming" to a trained meteorologist.

Some aspects of perception do not involve *any* categorisation into discrete states but rather judgment of continuous events in which we do not consciously assign error into either 'large' or 'small' categories. This analogue perception, (in contrast to categorical perception), describes much of our perceptual experience with space and its perception in three dimensions - critical to both pilots and Air Traffic Controllers, ships captains and navigators, and the spatial mental modelling required in visualising complex plant processes while watching control room displays. This last item proved to be very important in the Longford explosion when critical stimuli were habituated to and the vigilance threshold was raised to the point where alarms were ignored.

CASES OF FAILURES OF HIGH-RELIABILITY VIGILANCE

Whereas the competency 'foresight' is mostly located in an organisation's systems, the problem of vigilance is largely located in an organisation's human component (giving rise to the term, 'human factors' and the fields of study identified above, such as 'human performance psychology'). The allocation of HyperRESEARCH-defined behavioural descriptors in the cases was based on this discrimination between predicting systems and psychobiological signal phenomena which, as in foresight, also includes relevant auditing and record keeping since these both enable signification of factors such as signal awareness and discrimination and most of the behaviours identified in the cases as vigilance related. The behaviours identified were:

•attention to risk,

•debriefing,

•discrepancies in reporting,

•equipment defects,

•error detection,

•failure of materiels (not 'material),

•failure of safety systems,

•failure to discriminate signals,

•failure to monitor operating conditions,

•failure to utilise records,

•habituation to warning signals,

•failure to engage in or provide feedback,

•hazard identification,

•high-reliability - many eyes,

•ignored warnings,

•inattention.

The following cases provide salient examples of failure in these capabilities and, in some cases, paradoxical findings. For example, it is stated in the *Court of Marine Enquiry (1975), Report Number 57: ss Lake Illawarra, (ON 178472)*, that the Minister required several questions to be answered during the Enquiry into the case.

The Commission revealed in answer to question 11, 'What caused the ss Lake Illawarra to collide with the Tasman Bridge and subsequently founder?' and to the related questions, 12 and 13, that 'The loss of the s.s. Lake Illawarra, the resulting damage to the Tasman Bridge and the subsequent loss of life...was due to the failure of Master, Captain Boleslaw Pelc to navigate with seamanlike care, skill and vigilance.' The Commission found that he failed to maintain a low threshold for discriminating signals, attention to risk, hazard identification, ignored warnings, and displayed inattention in the lead-up to the accident, and he failed to monitor ongoing operating conditions.

His failings met several of the performance criteria for failure of the competence, 'vigilance'. The Commission's findings went on to confirm a direct relationship between the concept 'vigilance', as described in these terms, and the claim that it is a competency.

The Commission cited several legal sources for its interpretation. However, it was found that Captain Pelc's conduct amounted to misconduct rather than incompetence within s.6C of the Navigation Act (1912-1973). This section of the Act relates to careless navigation.

For the purposes of Section 372 of the Navigation Act, "incompetence" is defined in the following manner by Section 6C(a): "An officer is incompetent if he is inefficient in the performance of any of his duties as an officer".

That view is supported by the definition of a shipmaster's duty of care given by Isaacs and Rich JJ. in *Spain v. Union Steamship Co. of New Zealand Ltd. (1923) 33 C.L.R. 555,* at p. 569: "... the legal standard of the Captain's duty was that he should take whatever precautions a hypothetical prudent and skilled navigator would reasonably be expected to take in the actual circumstances." (Australian Department of Transport (1975), *Court of Marine Enquiry:ss Lake Illawarra)*

The Illawarra case illustrates an interesting phenomenon; there is no single precipitating behaviour. The failure of vigilance is the collection of separate behaviours by individuals, which themselves are failed by poor systemic 'foresight' tools. The Longford case identifies in somewhat more detail how several critical behaviours which must occur together to maintain a low threshold of vigilance.

The threshold for discriminating stimuli from the environment on the night of the accident had eventuated over a period, all the while becoming more and more elevated. This elevated threshold means that stimuli, necessary to sense hazard information, does not activate a safety system management response.

In Paragraph 13.87, the Commission1 identified a problem in which necessary information did not get the attention of the operators, although there was a formal handover procedure. The foresight capability failed and consequently the vigilance capability also failed.

Longford: 13.87 The safe and efficient operation of a processing facility depends to a significant extent upon the dissemination of information and knowledge amongst those involved in the plant's operation. OIMS*, as applied at Longford, required certain channels of communication in order to facilitate the exchange of information. For example, it was a requirement that operators use the handover at the end of each shift for this purpose. Apart from OIMS, there were other protective systems, such as alarms, to ensure that essential information about the process came to the attention of plant operators. (Longford Royal Commission, 1999).

*Operations Integrity Management System (OIMS)

"... a quality management process that is aimed specifically at lowering the risk of incidents, and provides a means by which continuous improvement can be achieved."

Longfords's OIMS was made up of eleven elements

••Management Leadership

••Risk Assessment

••Design & Construction

••Information & Documentation

••Personnel & Training

••Operations & Maintenance

••Management of Change

••Third Party Services

••Incident Investigation

••Communication Awareness & Emergency Response

••Operations Integrity Assessment & Improvement

The following paragraphs from the Longford report are summarised to identify significant failures of vigilance. Taken together, they illustrate how several poor vigilance behaviours are collectively amplified by poor 'foresight' tools and, together, can precipitate a hazardous situation. Inadequate log books amplify shift handover problems.

The Longford Royal Commission (1999), in paragraphs 13.87, 13.88, 13.104 and 13.107, made a pointed accusation about the responsibility that management has to ensure these 'foresight' tools (log books and shift handover procedures) are effectively deployed.

13.88 There was no evidence that any system existed at Longford to eliminate unsafe or inefficient operations for the regular monitoring of operating conditions or operator practices.

13.104 Correct GP1 Control Room Log and Shift Handovers would certainly have referred to abnormal conditions in Absorber B and to the fact that the level of condensate in that absorber was still out of control.

13.107 Shift handovers and log-book entries were used ineffectively In the lead up to the accident on 25 September 1998. Moreover, laxity in the implementation of the handover requirements seems to have escaped scrutiny by management (Longford Royal Commission, 1999).

The core factor in this book, that prior knowledge of an impending accident exists in an organisation and if utilised, could prevent the accident from occurring, was forcefully made by the Longford Royal Commission in paragraphs 13.05, 13.08, and 13.09 (again, these are summarised).

13.105 The process difficulties experienced during the night shift were also known to the night shift supervisor, Wijgers. However, at the change of shift, Wijgers made no mention of the abnormal conditions of Absorber B to the relieving supervisor, Visser.

13.108 Log book entries were not subjected to any examination either by Longford plant management or by management in Melbourne. They do not appear to have been used by management as a means of monitoring process conditions at the plant nor were they passed on to any person or group in Melbourne for plant surveillance purposes.

13.109 The shift supervisors' log was available to management personnel both at Longford and in Melbourne. However, process upsets were construed narrowly both by Esso management and by operations personnel unless they were accompanied by injury to persons or damage to property and were not included. This meant that the shift supervisors' log was not a substitute for a maintained control room log, (Longford Royal Commission, 1999).

This prior information concerned key vigilance factors, such as warnings, which were ignored; error detection noted but not passed on; the need to attend to the increased risk not signified; and the operator habituation to hazard warning signals was not detected. There appeared to be a failure to engage in or provide appropriate 'foresight' feedback on these critical pieces of 'vigilance' information. The key rule applying to high-reliability organisations to use 'many eyes' in hazardous conditions was ignored.

There is significant resonance here (paragraph 13.145) between 'foresight' tools, 'vigilance' factors and 'organisational ethos', Competency 6, because they inform the lead-up to the Longford accident by telling us about the state of mind of the organisation and its management. Paragraph 13.146 of the Longford Royal Commission Report shows the connection between this failure of capability and 'prior knowledge'; information lost to the 'foresight' system and then lost as a necessary factor in the vigilance of the operators to signify the defective equipment, inappropriate operating conditions and the unsafe operating practices leading up to the accident.

13.145 The consequence of this practice was that process upsets that may well have signified defective equipment, inappropriate operating conditions, or unsafe operating practices to qualified and experienced personnel were not brought to their attention. Thus, valuable opportunities to learn from process upsets were lost.

13.146 A pertinent example of such a lost opportunity was the failure of operations personnel to report the cold temperature incident that occurred on 28 August 1998, (Longford Royal Commission, 1999).

Competency 7: *Constructing a culture of safety* is also implicated because it demonstrates a failure to actualise any real 'intention' to establish a culture of safety and demonstrates how 'ways of seeing' about critical vigilance factors such as allowing defective equipment, inappropriate operating conditions and unsafe operating practices to become persistent personal or organisational ideas. Over time this 'way of seeing' develops the characteristic of a virus of the organisational mind, or meme, that can then influence the systemic capacities for managing safety. (A parenthetical note regarding the many failures of opportunity BHP has demonstrated to master this facet of their management of safety is salient here, because even more recent catastrophic fatal accidents involving almost similar 'memes' have occurred since the Longford explosion.)

Like each of the organisations studied in this book, BHP set itself up for catastrophic failure (not for the first or last time) by not understanding the powerful memes at work. The Longford Royal Commission (1999), made this clear in relation to the 'state of mind' regarding reporting of the previous incident on the 28 of August ('prior knowledge') in paragraph 13.148 of its report.

If the incident on 28 August 1998 had been reported as it should have been, the danger of equipment becoming subject to dangerously low temperatures caused by the loss of lean oil flow for any length of time would have become known, as would the steps to avert the danger.

Failing to report this incident stands as another example of a failure in Esso's implementation of its management systems. In the case of the incident on 28 August, such failure deprived operations personnel of process information vital to the prevention of the incident on 25 September 1998, (Longford Royal Commission, 1999).

The real causes of the accident are identified in the paragraphs under 15.6 of the Longford Royal Commission Report (1999) are essentially all centred on the failure of the main strength, 'vigilance' and its role as a safety system management competency.

15.6 [debriefing, attention to risk, failure of materiels, failure of safety systems, error detection, failure to discriminate signals, failure to monitor operating conditions, failure to utilise records, habituation to warning signals, failure to engage in or provide feedback]

Notwithstanding the matters mentioned above, the conclusion is inevitable that the accident that occurred on 25 September 1998 would not have occurred had appropriate steps been taken following the tripping of the GP1201 pumps. [attention to risk, debriefing, failure of materiels, failure of safety systems, error detection]

When efforts to restart those pumps proved unsuccessful, it should have been realised immediately that cold temperatures would ensue downstream from the absorbers and render vessels not designed to operate at low temperatures dangerous. Had this been realised, steps could and should have been taken to isolate the outlets of both rich oil and condensate from the absorbers in order to prevent those cold temperatures from developing in the ROD/ROF area. [habituation to warning signals, failure to engage in or provide feedback]

Those who were operating GP1 on 25 September 1998 did not have knowledge of the dangers associated with loss of lean oil flow and did not take the steps necessary to avert those dangers. Nor did those charged with the supervision of the operations have the necessary knowledge and the steps taken by them were inappropriate. [failure of safety systems, error detection, failure to discriminate signals, failure to monitor operating conditions, failure to utilise records]

The lack of knowledge on the part of both operators and supervisors was attributable to a deficiency in their initial or subsequent training. [overall competency failure]

Not only was their training inadequate, but there were no current operating procedures to guide them in dealing with the problem that they encountered on 25 September 1998] [failure of safety systems], (Longford Royal Commission, 1999).

Examples reinforcing the 'prior knowledge' message from the Longford case appear in each of the other cases. For example, in the mining case, the Moura2 Enquiry (1966), revealed failures of vigilance when peculiar smells and high Carbon Monoxide readings were lost because there was no 'foresight' system in place to record them and deploy them to the people involved even though these were 'signified' locally. The hazard detection threshold shifted upward and these critical factors failed to register as stimuli and failed to produce a vigilance response.

Moura [ignored warnings, habituation to signals, hazard identification] At Moura, there were various reports of smells and of abnormally high CO readings. But there was no system for collating this information, or retrieving it for review, and so these isolated reports were rapidly lost (Queensland Warden's Court, c1996)

CAA

In the Seaview-CAA example, an engineering report of a suspected cracked cylinder (equipment defect) was detected, reported and then there was a culpable 'duty of care' breach made by the CEO of Seaview and this passed unnoticed because the engineer did not report the matter to the regulator. This meant that the pilot could not exercise the levels of critical vigilance because he did not know he needed to do so.

There was an additional aspect. It significantly aggravated the transgression by Mr Green. After he had taken delivery of the aircraft, he spoke to the previous owner. Because of that discussion, the aircraft was taken to the Monarch maintenance facility at Bankstown. The engineer at Monarch began an inspection. He noticed oil leaking from a cylinder and therefore suspected a cracked cylinder. Mr Green was informed. He elected to end the inspection in order to make his own arrangements for the repair of the cylinder. The engineer who had released the aircraft to Mr Green said this:

"My understanding is that the aircraft flew from Bankstown to Coffs Harbour. However, if I had believed that the plane would be used to carry passengers I would have taken steps to stop it flying." p8 Executive Summary (Staunton, J. H., 1996).

Westralia

In the Westralia case, the debriefing process after the accident was characterised by the Coroner as a 'contamination' of evidence that can occur through witnesses discussing matters among themselves. This process not only presents the compliance problem of possible contamination of evidence but also shows how an in house post-hoc forensic review can introduce an element of pseudo-psychology and a self-congratulatory discourse in which the possibility of gathering useful prior knowledge about safety system management to feed into future potential accidents is mitigated. The Westralia Enquiry (1999) did not miss this fact in paragraphs 51 and 52. An accident debriefing should be directed by senior management to gaining useful information to prevent other accidents. It should not be used to rationalise failure and exonerate senior managers.

[debriefing] 51. An informal 'de-fusing' was undertaken through the CO addressing the ship's company on return to Fleet Base West on the evening of the incident. An information session was conducted for the entire ship's company at STIRLING on 6 May, and group 'de-briefing' was conducted at STIRLING on 7 and 8 May. This de-briefing focused on each individual's recounting of their activities and was done in groups of about 30 personnel who had shared similar experiences on the day. The feedback from ship's company was mostly favourable, although some felt it was of little use and others attended against their will.

52. There was some suggestion that de-briefing conducted before personnel had had the opportunity to record their recollection of events, may have exacerbated the process of 'contamination' of

evidence that can occur through witnesses discussing matters among themselves (Department of Defence, 1999).

The Westralia incident was another example of how several factors can work together to subvert vigilance. What should have been a vigilance - foresight building opportunity was contaminated by Navy ethos issues. The process of group debriefing is prone to the effects of 'groupthink' where there is a strong tendency to conformity to group values and ethics. The Navy ethos ensured that the 'group' would overtly value loyalty and keeping issues 'in-house' above the forensic detailing of events. To that extent, inevitably, the 'group' would colour and shade the facts, if not distort them. Certain individuals could easily go on to hide the truth from the Commission and ignore their ethical responsibilities to reveal everything of relevance in some ill-conceived notion of loyalty to senior personnel and the Navy (organisation) itself. This ethos of loyalty is further reinforced by the broader Australian cultural ethos of not 'dobbing' on one's mates. Issues of duty of care, compliance, ethics, organisational ethos and organisational culture become overlaid on the core issues of foresight and vigilance and subvert their delineation.

The Westralia (1999) case also illustrates more concrete examples of failure of vigilance in paragraphs 56, 57 of the Commission report.

Paragraph 56 identifies fire-fighting safety equipment deficiencies and error detection, while paragraph 57 identifies error detection and shortcomings in the material state of the ship. Paragraph 18 identifies critical failure of fire extinguisher. These all speak to failing to engage vigilantly with hazards in the lead up to the fire.

56. [safety equipment deficiencies, error detection, equipment defects] Although the firefighting effort was successful, the report details equipment problems with breathing apparatus, protective clothing and safety equipment. The Board has made several observations and detailed recommendations of a fleet wide nature on these issues.

57. [error detection, materiel conditions, diagnostic failure] When WESTRALIA sailed, there were several deficiencies in the materiel state of the ship. The two serious deficiencies, the flexible supply and return fuel hoses and the CO2 system, were not clear. The flexible fuel lines gave no sign of any inherent flaw. The condition of the CO2 system, and the tension of the operating wires, would only have been apparent to an expert on close inspection.

18. [failure of safety systems] The drench was remotely initiated but some of the CO2 bottles failed to discharge and were discharged manually seven minutes later.

DIAGNOSTIC TOOLS TO IMPROVE HIGH-RELIABILITY VIGILANCE

There appears to be an attitudinal component modifying vigilance that determines how high or low an individual's vigilance threshold is. Each Commission of Enquiry found that 'alertness' and 'signal detection' were either weak or compromised by a poor organisational ethos and by a focus on priorities other than safety (such as concern with the bottom line). In such an environment it proved impossible to incorporate the experiences and insights available to people at the interface of an impending accident. In the cases examined in detail and in the other cases cited, staff who raised safety concerns were often seen by management as annoyances or 'out of order'. Such staff often paid a price in terms of career advancement. These people are often classed as 'whistleblowers'. However, both human performance and systems factors are characterised by strengths and weaknesses. Both require low vigilance thresholds to provide early detection of phenomena that may be predictive of an accident. The information from both sources must be valued by management and must also be incorporated into organisational learning.

THINKING ABOUT VIGILANCE

Turner's (1997) theory that disasters result from energy plus misinformation is relevant here. The Moura disaster occurred because vital prior information was rendered ineffective, both by an inadequate information processing system and by a culture that neutralised it. According to Turner (1997), disasters often occur because crucial information available at lower levels of the organisation is not assembled in a coherent way and is not passed on up the hierarchy to a point where it can be responsibly acted upon.

The insights of high-reliability organisation theory are also relevant here. Organisations that are good at disaster avoidance mobilise as many pairs of eyes as possible to scrutinise critical information. This maximises the likelihood that the organisation will respond effectively to signs that things are going wrong.

Evidence from each of the cases examined in this book revealed that adequate vigilance, the capacity to maintain low event thresholds and intelligently use many inputs, 'many eyes', to examine processes and practices for breakdowns and possible anomalies should be a major concern for CEOs and the dominant coalition. This requires both a human and systems approach to vigilance.

The data makes it clear that vigilance is a matter of maintaining low phenomena and event thresholds in a culture that values both human and systemic feedback. The case data is persuasive that senior management consistently fails to understand the psychological dimensions of human performance.

Humans can bring intuition, creativity, insight, flexibility and common sense to safety issues, even if they have good and bad days. Furthermore, managers need to establish systemic protocols such as an independent auditing or prospective and retrospective HAZOP systems to identify and respond to failure of materiels, failure of safety systems, failure to discriminate signals, failure to monitor operating conditions, failure to utilise records, habituation to warning signals, failure to engage in or provide feedback, hazard identification, failure to employ many eyes, ignored warnings, and inattention.

Both human and systemic factors generate information significant to safety. This requires that people across the organisation (all staff) understand the importance of maintaining a low vigilance threshold and of paying attention to risk signals. It is essential that dominant coalitions realise they can not rely on their own error detection capabilities alone. Therefore, it is a competency to be valued by management in front line operators working in high-reliability organisations. The research suggests that information collected should be incorporated into a continuous organisational learning process that becomes the basis of training and cyclical refresher training programs both in management and safety. Such programs should be structured to ensure the lowest possible vigilance thresholds are maintained across the organisation.

HIGH-RELIABILITY DIAGNOSTIC QUESTIONS

Human performance and human competencies are intimately related. For example, this perspective helps us consider the importance of conceptual training and deep understanding through practice versus rote memorisation in learning the procedures needed to construct a 'working memory' to enable operation of a complex piece of equipment. Furthermore, it helps us interrogate issues in competency acquisition such as whether it may be better to learn a complex task through mastery of its components or by practicing the whole task together from the beginning.

This perspective on vigilance raises such questions as:

•If skills are forgotten when they are not used (salient working memory fades) then what sort of refresher training might be the most useful?

•How site specific and situation specific should training be?

•It also raises the problem of individual differences in verbal and spatial abilities and raises the question, should these differences be considered when training?

Finally, is it likely that packaged non-site specific, off -the-shelf, training packages can be sufficiently salient to ensure low vigilance thresholds? These questions should direct the reader to theories of organisational and adult learning such as those of Argyris and Schön (1996); theories of organisational development and change such as those of Cummings and Worley (1963); and the compelling theories of education concerned with individual differences and human intelligence such as Gardiner (1985).

1. Parliament of Victoria (1999). The Esso Longford Gas Plant Accident: Report of the Longford Royal Commission. Victoria.

2. Queensland Warden's Court (c1996). Report on an accident at Moura No 2 Underground Mine on Sunday, 7 August 1994: Wardens Enquiry conducted pursuant to Section of The Coal Mining Act, 1925, [Brisbane]

3. Staunton, J. H. (1996). Report of the Commissioner / Commission of Enquiry into the Relations between the CAA and Seaview Air. Canberra. 2v.

4. Department of Defence (1999). Report of the Board of Enquiry into the fire in HMAS Westralia on 5 May 1998.

14.COMPETENCY 4: JUDGEMENT: WEIGHING UP, TRADING OFF, AND DECIDING

THIS CHAPTER DELVES INTO THE COMPETENCY OF "JUDGEMENT," highlighting the cognitive process of weighing options, assessing risks, and making sound decisions, especially in complex or ambiguous situations. It explores the factors that can influence judgement, including ethical considerations, experience, and cognitive biases.

"Knowledge is the treasure, but judgment is the treasurer."

William Penn

WHAT IS HIGH-RELIABILITY JUDGEMENT?

Judgement means weighing up, trading off, prioritising and deciding – often in circumstances that make little sense or meaning1. Most decision models only indicate steps to either follow or eliminate or ask the decision maker to focus on several different choices and select between them.

A better way to decide is to pose the problem as a question or to frame the problem as a choice between two alternatives (Rowe et al,

(1992)). This makes understanding the differences between judgement and decision making easier because it forms a 'dichotomy', where acceptable alternatives exist simultaneously, making the concepts mutually exclusive.

For example, imagine you are a Minister charged with resolving the problem of commercial deforestation.

QUESTION

Should you keep the forests or employ the timber workers?

JUDGEMENT (the decision process, which considers variables such as discretion, the scale and scope of an action and its consequences, the frame-work and context, the best interests of the parties, intent, trade-offs, impact on organisations, people and the environment, taking account of rights, values, duties, codes of conduct, moral rules, human relationships, keeping promises and being able to rely on people doing what they say, non-malevolence, mutuality, and respect for property belonging to others)

Save the forests or employ the timber workers. Saving forests is good and so is employing timber workers. But timber workers cut down forests. Cut down forests destroys the resource for ever. Unemployed timber workers cost taxpayers money, and they are not skilled in other areas. If you fire them, they will move out of the area and destroy its infrastructure. Entire towns will close. There will be serious industrial relations and political consequences if you sack timber workers or cut down the forests.

DECISION

Retrain the timber workers as forest experts, forest conservationists, tour guides, and hospitality workers in the forests. Promote the area as a tourism destination and provide extensive bridging support. Build a tourism infrastructure.

DECISION OUTCOME

Save the forests and employ the workers, who will then pay tax rather than be a drain on the public purse and continue to live in the area ensuring its infrastructure endures. Politicians can align themselves with constructive decisions.

A decision is the endpoint in a series of activities primarily of a cognitive nature (Browne (1993:5)) and involves deliberate and considered thinking. Most managers do not distinguish between a decision and a decision process. The process (identified as 'judgement' in this book) involves much more than just making a choice between many alternatives.

Decision variables are those factors you have to consider that are changeable or that can take on different values or vary in some way. Judgement takes account of normal logical decision variables such as 'what costs less', but also goes further to consider finer grain variables such as discretion, the scale and scope of an action and its consequences, the framework and context, the best interests of the parties, intent, trade-offs, impact on the organisation and its people and the environment. Other factors having an impact on judgement include variables that often appear in codes of conduct and social system audits (i.e., under the Public Sector Standards Act, 1984), such as rights, values, duties, codes of conduct, moral rules, human relationships, keeping promises and being able to rely on people doing what they say, non-malevolence, mutuality, and respect for property belonging to others.

Because the mental ability to perceive and distinguish relationships and to act with discernment is central to this book (for example, fatigue may affect a pilot's judgement or discernment of distances), this competency is an underpinning capability in high-reliability management. The concept 'judgement' is more complex than first appears. There are several approaches a manager can take to understand the concept of 'judgement'. One pathway constructs an argument for the logic (i.e. syllogistic analysis) of judgement. Another approach considers the decision styles of managers (Rowe, 1992). Perhaps the most useful way is to start from the view that decision-making processes differ from one situation to another and from one person to another. Different Directors make decisions utilising different processes (Nutt, 1990).

For example, as Mech (1993) suggests, some directors are:

Results-oriented and impersonal, relying on facts and figures to make decisions.

Sensitive and responsive to the needs and feelings of others and make decisions cognizant of their impact on people.

Planners who rely on careful analysis before making decisions.

Creative, innovative, and take risks, depending more on intuition than on fact.

In that sense judgement emphasises individual cognitive competencies such as weighing up, trading off, prioritising, and deciding, using many of the mental skills outlined in the dictionary definition, such as: acumen, adjudication, appraisal, assessment, belief, censure, common sense, conclusion, condemnation, criticism, decision, decree, determination, disapproval, discernment, discretion, discrimination, estimation, evaluation, finding, good sense, intelligence, judiciousness, level-headedness, mind, opinion, order, outcome, perception, percipience, perspicacity, perspicuousness, prudence, reproof, result, ruling, sagacity, sentiment, shrewdness, understanding, upshot, valuation, verdict, view, way of thinking, wisdom, and wit.

It is not surprising that judgement is a trait associated with leadership. Good leaders can usually be relied upon to make good judgements most of the time. However, there are significant differences between leadership and management. They do not always occur at the same time and the same place and in the same person.

In high-reliability organisations, safety related 'judgement' is a managerial competency that involves intentionally weighing up equally weighted, but uncertain, alternatives (judging) and selecting the alternative that would be considered to result in a right or good decision (deciding). It is the capacity to assess situations or circumstances and draw sound conclusions.

This is different from 'satisficing' in which one sets lower levels for the various objectives that, if attained, will be good enough. The 'satisficer's' philosophy is that in real-world problems there are too many uncertainties and conflicts in values for there to be any hope of obtaining the optimal decision and that it is far more sensible to set out to do well enough to get the job done as efficiently as possible.

However, 'satisficing' cost lives in high-reliability situations. Judgement is critical to management decisions in high reliability organisations so that 'decisions' are the 'outcome' of the deliberation or 'judgement process' (weighing up, trading off and prioritising). In this book then, high-reliability 'judgement' infers intentional reasoning about uncertainty - seeking to discern the 'best outcome' as opposed to the 'good enough' outcome of the satificer.

JUDGEMENT, MEMES, ETHICS AND BALANCE

Good managerial judgement (weighing up, trading off, and deciding - often in circumstances that make little sense or meaning) results from using a range of management competencies plus experience. Hippocrates spoke of the role of experience in judgement in about

400BC in his writing on medical ethics. The notion is not startling or new. The core competency most closely related to 'judgement' is ethics, because of its deontological (duty) impost on decisions.

In essence one of the best and most succinct tests of a judgement is The Golden Rule (do unto others as you would have them do to you). This also resonates with Gunningham's (1999) observations regarding 'principle-based' compliance (competency eleven). Judgement also has an important memetic connection with each of the other competencies because the way an organisation judges safety issues conveys the organisation's attitude and that of its senior management into its mission and activities, no matter what it may have espoused as its mission.

Memetic means the survival of messages and meanings. The memes that, for example, allow an Australian citizen to be deported to another country or be illegally held in custody are related to operational level dissonance with the managerial level messages of racial purity coming from the most senior levels (ministerial and CEO).

These higher-level messages have memetic survival power because of their high-level sources and sycophantic shaping of the messages as they flow down through an organisation (such as DIMIA).

Senior and middle-level managers simply believe their interpretations of policy are correct. Their belief systems are shaped by the top-level memes they receive day by day in communications from the top. Therefore, if higher level management holds certain views they will inevitably shape action at operational levels of the organisation, no matter what policy or strategy is 'in place'.

Considered judgment is one of the very few tools available that can detect memetic factors that affect operations.

Kant's (1797) views of judgement amplify the Golden Rule and reflect David Godsell's (1993) observation that organisations have a deontological responsibility to society. Kant concludes that we must always act as belonging to a community and treat others with respect since we all have intrinsic worth. This principle can be seen in the efforts made by some professional bodies to fulfil their deontological role in society.

For example, the Institution of Engineers Australia Code of Ethics describes engineering as a: creative process of synthesising and implementing the knowledge and experience of humanity to enhance the welfare, health and safety of all members of the community.' This definition places particular emphasis on the implications of engineering technology on the community it services. All the members of the engineering profession, therefore, have an implied responsibility to address the social implications of the technology they provide. Bridges and buildings are much more than engineering commodities, they also have a social impact.

Gunn. et. al. (1986) describes the nature of an engineering practice that does not have any regard for ethical conduct:

'Engineers harness technology to achieve their (own) goals, Yet the history of recent technology is a history of the wasteful use of mostly non-renewable resources, aimed at satisfying short term human wants without regard either to future human needs or the rest of nature.'

If an engineer is faced with conflicting values in the decision-making process, ethical guidelines give a systematic approach to providing resolutions to such conflicts. It is for this reason that various engineering institutions, such as The Institute of Engineers Australia, have developed a 'Code of Ethics'.

A code of ethics that is put in place to govern any profession is a documented recognition of the responsibilities of all members of that profession to the general community. In addition, a code of ethics provides guidelines and factors to consider for the conduct of those members, should a situation arise that requires judgement.

Generally, a code of ethics covers obligations to society, the profession and other colleagues. In the 1994 publication Engineering Ethics and the Spirit of Community Service, Mair writes, in reference to an institutional code of ethics: 'Ultimately, it is used as an instrument of the profession to shape the conduct of its individual members.'

This confirms the relationship between judgement and ethics and suggests a strong connection to competency five, 'Balance', which emphasises psychological tenor, persistence and courage. Both Judgement and Balance require the ability to act with discernment. A discerning judgement should detect and consider both causes and consequences. Sound, discerning judgements should first 'do no harm' (Hippocrates, c400BC).

IDEAS ABOUT JUDGEMENT

This section engages with some useful ideas in cognitive psychology, since it is the science that explores how people reason, formulate judgements and make decisions. Cognitive psychology suggests that people make mistakes when they encounter complex problems. The distinctive finding is that everyday situations are often complex enough to confidently predict that mistakes will happen.

Knowing and thinking, or epistemology and logic, rely on a conception of 'judgement' (Brentano, 1874). However, knowledge and logic are not always reliable. For example, ideas that have evolved to seem true (at least to untrained minds) can in fact be false (Drexler, 1986). Naive human judgement (common sense) compared to judgement aided by scientific and statistical techniques, is very often wrong and, just as we suffer from optical illusions and blind spots, so we suffer from cognitive illusions and blind spots (Nisbett and Ross, 1980).

Memes show how people share systematic misunderstandings in organisations. Other cognitive experiments show that untutored people share systematic misunderstandings of elementary facts such as the direction a ball will move when whirled in a circle and then released, believing it will continue to travel in an arc rather than a tangent. This error is easily understood if one observes an Olympic hammer thrower in action. The hammer travels in a straight line out from the point of release, not in a curve or arc.

Learned medieval philosophers (who neglected to test their ideas against reality) evolved whole systems of science based on identical misunderstandings (McClosky 1983). The implication of these insights is that competencies underpinning high-reliability management, such as 'judgement', require specific training because they are often counterintuitive, and if they are left to ordinary humans to exercise in extraordinary circumstances, they may evoke dangerous memetic, rather than educated, responses.

In 1999, the Centre for the Study of Intelligence, at the Central Intelligence Agency, published research that was suggestive that once an experienced analyst has the minimum information necessary to make an informed judgement, obtaining additional information does not improve the accuracy of his or her estimates. Additional information does, however, lead the analyst to become more confident in the judgement, to the point of overconfidence. From a HRO perspective, the CIA observation that experienced analysts have an imperfect understanding of what information they use in making judgements is identical to the way prior information is used by safety system managers in the accident reports in this book. They are unaware of the extent to which their judgements are determined by a few dominant factors, rather than by the systematic integration of all available information. Managers actually use much less of the available information than they think they do.

Relevant to this book is the CIA's finding that if analysts have good insight into their own mental model, they should be able to identify and describe the variables they consider most important in making judgements. However, there is strong experimental evidence that such self-insight is usually faulty.

These experimental findings by the CIA should not necessarily be accepted at face value. For example, circumstances exist in which additional information does contribute to more accurate analysis

(Slovic, 1973). However, there also are circumstances in which additional information, contradictory information, decreases rather than increases a manager's confidence.

For example, this paragraph contains opposing views. How would you decide which view gives the most confidence? Human reasoning is susceptible to predictable errors; that is, some mistakes are made repeatedly by most people. Hence, cognitive psychology is a scientific discipline that has something useful to say to high-reliability managers, about managerial judgement. For example, Berner (1994:1792-6), observes that the diagnostic ability of an astute clinician is still much better than the performance of a sophisticated computer programmed with an encyclopaedic knowledge of medicine. On the other hand, Dawes (1989:1668-74) claims the judgements of psychologists that are intended to predict parole violations or those of university admissions committees that are intended to predict student performance are not much better than simple statistical models.

There are opposing views and dichotomies about most things. That is exactly what makes them amenable to judgement. It is not necessary to 'satifice' these opposing views with a decision to adopt one or the other. They need to be weighed.

A core problem relevant to managers in high-reliability organisations is that people are often poor at judging their own performance, even in the most ideal conditions. For example, studies done by McCarthy (1993:579-82) show that 85% of people believe that they are better-than-average drivers, which is even contrary to the laws of probability.

Cognitive psychology holds that the human brain is a finite organ with bounded capacity. We could all gain by having more memory or intellect, but this is not possible. Leape (1994:1851-7) suggests that although some weaknesses may be offset by technology such as computers, the core exercise of decision-making remains fallible because of human limitations and other pressures. Therefore, failures in judgement can confront any manager.

A paradox arises because managerial judgement is so valued that it verges on being silly. Durna (1995:248-51) makes the striking and useful analogy that grandparents often consider their own grandchildren to be distinctly attractive, even when no genetic link is present. In consequence, the grandparents' adoration makes it hard for them to compare their grandchildren fairly with other children, to hear negative feedback about their grandchildren and to discipline their grandchildren. It is fair to say that the same failures occur when managers make judgements about their own 'darlings'.

The wisdom needed to produce good judgement may be the same wisdom that is needed to recognise good judgement (Wu, 1991:2089-94). Faulty judgement can lead to self-fulfilling prophecies.

Redelmeier (2001:164), who researches in the field of medical and hospital safety, makes the analogous observation that most physicians are dependent on information based on the work of others. Their clinical judgement can be seriously faulty if it is based on erroneous charting of vital signs, reports of radiology studies, messages about biopsy specimens or other misinformation from a range of diagnostic testing sources. In an organisational setting reliance by management on information generated by other people and systems should commit managers to ensure that such sources are valued and valid.

A final concern is that judgement is a complement to, but not a substitute for, knowledge. An experienced CEO or manager who trusts only his or her judgement and never engages in retraining, for example, might be brilliant at diagnosing a recurrent safety problem but may never realise that it could have been prevented by simply installing computer sensors. Such a manager may not appreciate the limits of his or her judgement and may be unaware of a superior approach offered by new technology and new ways of examining issues.

CASES OF FAILURES OF HIGH-RELIABILITY JUDGEMENT

The process of 'judgement' is well supported by the intellectual discipline of Philosophy, epistemology and deontology (the philosophy of duty). The practical processes involved in judgement leading to an outcome is explored in the work of Sheeran (1992:16-17) who suggests that philosophy provides practical knowledge. It leads to action after knowledge has been acquired. This application of philosophy has practical consequences. For example, the issue of cascading effects applies in a practical way to accidents both before an accident where small events can cause consequential events, and after an accident where the accident itself can cause other accidents or have other serious consequences.

The Longford Gas plant accident came about after a series of events which cascaded into an explosion, and after the accident the state of Victoria experienced consequential loss of electrical power.

The organisation responsible was found to have failed in its practical exercise of its duty of care on several fronts. The judgement required to weigh up the cascading and increasing signals and information from the locus of a possible accident is critical to effective and timely intervention. The phenomena were also seen in the Westralia case, as seen in paragraph 12 of the report (Department of Defence, 1999), where smoke preceded the fire and the fire itself caused critical electrical cabling to fail (paragraph 13), which then caused emergency power circuits to fluctuate, resulting in loss of compass and communications (paragraph 15).

Westralia

[cascading effects]

12. A fire report was made to the bridge and emergency stations was sounded. A brief inspection of the main machinery space through the door of the machinery control room revealed thick black smoke and

flames. Visibility was severely limited. Four people escaped from the main machinery space into the machinery control room. Three of the personnel were injured and were initially treated by the ship's emergency medical organisation and later assisted by medical staff from SUCCESS, STIRLING, and the Sea Training Group.

13. The fire was intense, causing rapid smoke to build up and extreme heat. Despite some heroic but unsuccessful firefighting efforts, the atmosphere in the main machinery space soon became inadequate to support life. Electrical cabling on the deckhead over the fire was quickly damaged with a consequent loss of services, including some communications.

15. After the machinery control room evacuation, the emergency power circuits were subject to severe voltage fluctuations, probably because of fire damage in the main machinery space. Power to the gyro compass and the communications centre was lost.

This cascading series of failures in which each hazard caused another compounding hazard had followed from poor judgement in the commissioning of flexible fuel hoses which did not meet specifications. Considerable trust had been placed in an external agency, ADI Limited, to fit fuel hoses that met specifications. This trust was misplaced and demonstrated poor judgement and decision making on the part of the Navy Fleet Intermediate Maintenance Authority (paragraph 6 of the Board of Enquiry report).

16. [decision making, external agencies, misplaced trust] Prior to the ship sailing from Fleet Base West on 5 May 98, WESTRALIA had undergone an assisted maintenance period for about 6 weeks. During this period, members of the ship's company of WESTRALIA in conjunction with Fleet Intermediate Maintenance Authority and the ship's contractor, ADI Limited, carried out maintenance work. The work included the fitting of new flexible fuel hoses to the ship's main engines by a subcontractor under the direction of ADI Limited.

Finally, when a judgement was made to extinguish the fire using CO2 gas it was a significant failure of judgement because it failed to utilise prior knowledge about the flood of oxygen that entered the fire space when the engine room was opened to the air.

33. The Board cannot say whether the CO2 extinguished the fire or not. The decision to re-enter the main machinery space to fight the fire, after only fifteen minutes was, however, premature and showed a lack of understanding of the way in which a fire extinguishing system using oxygen depletion works. This lack of understanding increased the risk to the ship and the hose teams. (EXECUTIVE SUMMARY (1999:4)

This series of poor judgements could have been avoided if the competencies necessary to judgement had been in place. Lack of 'understanding' is a euphemism for poor judgement. This critical competency failed in each of the cases studied. For example in the loss of the Lake Illawarra, the Captain's judgement was impaired by a series of cascading events that confused him. The following six paragraphs from the Illawarra Enquiry (slightly condensed) demonstrate failure of judgement, the effects of conflicting evidence subverting competence, and the passage of hazardous cascading events.

Illawarra

[judgement, conflicting evidence, doubt about capability, cascading effects]

The evidence leads very to the conclusion that this increase to sea speed, so that the vessel arrived in the vicinity of Rosny Point, some 7 cables (approximately 1300 metres) from the Bridge, at a speed of 8 knots, (Pelc 1075, Bonnitcha 644-5), set the stage for the disaster that followed.

Asked why he stopped the engines, Captain Pelc said it was because his vessel was moving over the ground with greater speed than he had anticipated (1082).

The order "hard a-port" was given, according to Captain Pelc, in order to bring the ship back on to the lead line (1083). At that stage he was still confident he could "enter the main channel leads" and had given no consideration to aborting the exercise (1083, 1143), nor did he ever consider the possibility of going under any of the other spans (1208).

The following paragraph illustrates the capacity of cascading events to produce confusion, rendering the vessel out of control.

After ordering "hard a-port", the Master saw the ship was not responding at all. He asked the helmsman twice if the rudder has hard to port, and the helmsman said it was. He looked at the electric rudder indicator and noted that it indicated hard to port (1085). The ship was moving but he could not estimate for the Court what its speed was at that time (1085). It did not occur to him that the ship had lost steerage way. He thought it may have suddenly developed a steering malfunction (1085). He asked the helmsman "Is she answering?", and the reply was, it was not. At and from this point, our conclusion is that the vessel was, in the circumstances, out of control (see Question 13A (a)).

As the result of further poor judgement, the captain then caused a further hazardous cascading effect.

Being then about two ships' lengths from the Bridge (about 300 metres), or even less (1085-6), he ordered "full astern", then gave a double ring full astern. With that order executed, the bow of the ship began to swing to starboard and the stern to port (1088), under the combined influence of the astern motion of the propeller and the 'hard aport' position of the rudder; whilst the ship still moved forward at an increasing angle to the Bridge. The Master ordered the shipwright on the forecastle to drop both anchors. He saw the shipwright standing on the port side of the forecastle and thought that he dropped the port anchor (1088). The ship struck. The Master's impression was that the port side of the ship struck a glancing blow on one pylon only. The roadway collapsed in the centre and fell on the ship, and the pylon fell. The bow of the ship had struck on an angle of about 30 or 40 degrees. The collapse of the roadway and the pylon occurred within seconds afterwards (1090), and the ship started to sink quickly (1090).

The Enquiry found that Captain Pelc was confused and exercised poor judgement resulting in poor seamanship, from which flowed the chain of events that resulted in the accident. The Enquiry suggested that he could have avoided the accident if he had judged the overshooting vessel had sufficient inertia (steerage way) to warrant aborting the maneuver. Rather than do this he proceeded to make the situation unrecoverable by deciding to stop the engines, leaving the vessel without steerage.

Poor seamanship on the part of Captain Pelc consisted primarily in approaching too close to the Bridge at too fast a speed before attempting to align the lead lights. It was a combination of those two factors that set off the disastrous chain of events; although the collision could probably have been avoided had the Master chosen to abort the exercise of passing under the Bridge when he found the vessel overshooting the leads for the second time - that is, to the east. But he then compounded his previous errors of navigation by stopping the engines, which caused the ship to lose steerage way: an event that he ought to have anticipated, should have recognised when it happened, and should then have reacted to more quickly.

The Lake Illawarra accident was preventable had the captain's 'judgement' been exercised at a higher level. The point here is that circumstances can overwhelm judgement so that a satisficed decision is called on to resolve a problem. Managers, ships captains, aircraft captains and military officers all prize their 'decisiveness'. However, decisiveness often means simply 'satisficing' with little capacity for judgement, in situations requiring consideration of many factors.

Complexity and urgency add also deplete the capacity to exercise judgement.

Many factors can impair judgement, for example, inadequate training (paragraph 13.30 of the Longford Royal Commission Report, 1999) causing failure of prior knowledge and an unsafe working environment amplified by lack of appropriate operating procedures and failure of responsibility by senior staff (paragraph 14.12), as is shown in the following examples from the Longford case. Both paragraphs show poor judgement on the part of ESSO.

Longford

[judgement and training]

13.30 Esso also relied upon the evidence of Luke Musgrave, the Longford gas restoration project manager, to support its contention that operators were adequately trained in appropriate responses to the loss of lean oil circulation. He gave evidence that he had knowledge of the consequences of the loss of lean oil flow and said that he acquired that knowledge from discussions with operators, reading the Red Book and from some courses that he attended. (Ch 13 Longford Report:197)

[practically preventable, ethical implications] ,

The failure of Esso to provide a safe working environment on 25 September 1998 resulted from its having failed to take plainly practicable measures. In order to provide a safe working environment, there could and should have been appropriate operating procedures to deal with the loss of lean oil circulation, cold temperatures and the shutdown and start-up of the plant. Furthermore, the operators and supervisors could and should have known of and understood the real hazards confronting them on the day. (Ch 14 Longford Report:225)

Judgement can be seriously impaired by the priority of production and by judging safety to be a cost in economic terms as is seen in the following example from the Moura case.

Moura

[economic factors]

The view that the Moura explosion stems from the priority given to production has much more to recommend it. Moura was a mine whose economic viability was in doubt and there was pressure to maximise production. As counsel for the miners put it in his final submission, `BHP ran a dangerous race against time to extract all of the coal from 512 [panel] in accordance with the plan'.

DIAGNOSTIC TOOLS TO IMPROVE HIGH-RELIABILITY JUDGEMENT

The evidence from the cases suggests that mistakes are frequently made in managerial judgement. Flawless intellectual reasoning, constant vigilance, diligent checking for errors and fool-proof environmental safeguards would require superhuman skills. This observation suggests that, theoretically, it is important to the mastery of this competency that recognition of the tight correlation between foresight tools, personal vigilance, discerning judgement, and deontological ethics is made to offset the range of factors which can impair judgement and decision making under uncertainty.

Because judgement in matters of safety is deontological (duty and obligation) in nature and the responsibility of senior management, it has a higher priority than production and it can not be passed off to the regulator.

The most salient attributes of judgement almost exactly mirror the findings of Eraut and du Boulay (2001) concerning making holistic and balanced decisions in situations of uncertainty and complexity.

Descriptors of poor judgement in both findings included:

•* not integrating all the data

•* attending to fine detail, the small print", but missing the big picture

•* choosing an inappropriate management plan

•* overvigorous intervention

•* not taking into account conflict between people and systemic information and feedback

•* being competent in all the important aspects of the job, but failing to make a sensible decision on a particular site-specific case as a whole

•* making decisions on current evidence alone and disregarding prior knowledge.

Good judgement descriptors included:

•* incorporating lessons from prior learning

•* discerning the key features and deeper layers of a problem in a more complex way

•* going beyond the guidelines

•* actively examining assumptions

•* intuitive but rationally assessing expertise

•* making small responsive approximate decisions and readjusting (fuzzy logic)

•* being prepared to do nothing.

Situations where judgement was called for included:

•* decisions based on fuzzy logic and partial information in situations too complex to fully understand

•* ill-defined situations that are complex diffuse and muddled

•* high risk situations

•* situations combining technical - systemic and human - psychological aspects

•* deciding what to tell key staff and how to put it

•* diagnosing phenomena and adjusting safety thresholds

•* deciding between maximum interventions and minimum interventions (or doing neither)

•* balancing cost and safety

Other aspects of judgement described in the literature concern:

•* ethical issues

•* the effect of a practitioner's feelings and emotions about a particular case-these could concern the event situation, their own behaviour, the actions of other professionals or the organisation (Fish and Coles, 1998)

Hopkins (1999) ground breaking studies of the Australian setting identified other factors that can compromise decision making and the ability to make sound judgements regarding safety, such as the structural problem inherent in the dual role of some regulators to both promote and police an industry at the same time. This was also a weakness revealed in the Seaview case where the CEO had a level of control over the regulator. Hopkins points to a useful solution adopted in Britain when this phenomena became known:

There is also a sense in which the very structure of government implicitly gives priority to production. I refer to the location of mine inspectorates in government departments whose primary function is the promotion of the mining industry. As we saw, this undermines the ability of inspectorates to impose safety standards on mines.

This problem was identified in the Piper Alpha report and led to a recommendation to relocate the offshore inspectorate within the general occupational health and safety organisation in Britain, to ensure its independence from the industry it was supposed to regulate. This same structural problem is inherent in the regulatory regime for offshore petroleum production in Australia: safety is the responsibility of a government department whose primary concern is to facilitate production.

Safety inspectorates in Australia's extractive industries need to be relocated to reduce the risk that safety will take second place to production (Hopkins:133)

THINKING ABOUT JUDGEMENT

Evidence from each of the cases examined in this book revealed that sound judgement was needed and lacking in early accident scenarios when accidents could have been prevented. 'judgement' requires intentional effort and the highest level(s) of expertise by CEOs and managers. Accordingly, courts and commissions of Enquiry should give guidance by defining judgement either as an advanced level of a necessary competence or as managerial expertise that goes beyond competence, because the hardest problems to solve in high-reliability organisations are the ones where no one recognises that anything is wrong.

Consequently, managerial judgement deserves just as much scrutiny as any other component of a manager's responsibilities. Managerial judgement should be framed by an organisation's deontological responsibilities to society as well as its more immediate stakeholders. Therefore, management decisions should be ethical and discerning.

Because judgements concerning safety are often made in circumstances that make little sense or meaning, the capacity to weigh, trade off, prioritise and decide to constitute a more complex skill set than at first appears. This competency demands cyclical refresher training and furthermore it must be set against the quality of information other people and systems provide. Finally, if managerial judgement fails then legal compliance imposts must be sufficient to save lives and ensure adequate vigilance and deployment of foresight systems in high-reliability organisations.

HIGH-RELIABILITY DIAGNOSTIC QUESTIONS

Book (Reason, 1991) suggests that human judgement is susceptible to predictable errors. People make mistakes when they encounter complex problems. Therefore, it might provide managers with necessary insights to discover what factors can influence bring about error prone judgements and better decisions in safety critical situations. The author's own HyperRESEARCH analysis of the cases reinforces and confirms Reason's view that human judgement is susceptible to predictable errors, and raise questions such as:

Do these identified issues adequately frame the issue or issues?

What mental metaphors do managers use to conceptualise safety system management issues?

Can managers be taught skills that enable sound, discerning judgement under uncertainty?

To what extent do missing data, conflicting information, limited time and long-term trade-offs influence judgement in matters of safety?

Do factors such as cascading effects in operational systems become amplified by poor decision-making skills?

Managers might also examine the boundaries they put on a problem. What aspects of the situation do managers leave out of consideration? If salient material is left out of consideration, then what implications might follow, such as doubt about one's capabilities and poor ethical decisions and how is success measured?

Accountability issues which relate to regulatory frameworks are also important and raise questions such as, what is the exact role of regulatory agencies and, do other people other organisations in our industry think about this question differently from the way we do? Related questions also need to be considered, such as the consequences of failure to conform to guidelines, in response to economic factors and the pressure of production.

Finally, any consideration of judgement should raise concerns about responsibility. Managers, Directors and Governments should intentionally consider the deontological issue of duty of care, since principles and codes and regulatory policies do not provide specific guidelines for every conceivable set of circumstances. Principles require judgement, which depends on character, moral discernment, and a person's sense of responsibility and accountability.

It follows as night and day, as life and death, that if senior management hold certain views, they will have powerful memetic force and inevitably shape action at operational levels of the organisation, no matter what written policy is in place or what strategy is espoused. In high-reliability organisations, failure to discharge this high-level responsibility adequately can cause otherwise preventable fatalities. Deliberate disengagement from this responsibility of duty of care is psychopathic.

1. Fischoff, Slovic & Lichtenstein, 1978; Hayek, 1945

2. Browne, 1993; Cooke and Slack, 1984; De Michaelis, 1996, Gilligan, 1983

15.COMPETENCY 5: BALANCE: TENOR, CONSONANCE, EMOTIONAL INTELLIGENCE, MATURITY, COURAGE, PERSISTENCE

THIS CHAPTER EXAMINES THE COMPETENCY OF "BALANCE," EMPHASIZING the importance of emotional intelligence, psychological resilience, and a measured approach to decision-making in high-pressure environments. It discusses the challenges of maintaining composure and making rational decisions under stress.

"You can't control someone else, but you have total control over your own actions and emotions. The important thing is that you clearly define for yourself what you want and need and then do those things first."

Sheperis

WHAT IS HIGH-RELIABILITY BALANCE?

Psychological balance (loss of centering on organisational and individual purpose and values), courage (acting morally in the face of coercion and fear) and integrity (educated moral judgement) in making decisions about safety are not possible in dysfunctional organisations focused on the financial bottom line or where personal or group power is exercised inappropriately.

Balance is a competence anchored in Australian National Training Authority (ANTA) guidelines. The ANTA Elements of Competency and Performance Criteria include analogous concepts to those used in this book. Balance appears as a specific unit of competence in several competency requirements, in much the same way it is used in this book.

For example, in the Public Sector competency unit, PSPETHC601A/02, it is constructed as a competency in which the participant will demonstrate they can, *Balance competing public interests*. Its performance criteria include *Consideration of relevant facts is comprehensive, and weightings given to competing interests are unbiased and defensible* (implying fairness and honesty devoid of self-interest and focusing on the 'consideration' process). *Decision-making processes are transparent and accountable and reasoning / grounds for decisions are documented in accordance with policy and procedures* (implying that the decision making or judgement 'process' steps can be scrutinised). *Advice to government regarding policy decisions relating to the public interest, is objective and impartial* (implying equity). *Where staff indicate conflicts of interest, action is taken to resolve the situation in accordance with policy and procedures* (implying concern with codes of conduct).

Balance infers a sound mental and psychological tenor or state of mind of someone with good judgement. Mental soundness is often equated with mental health. Balance, as used in this book, is associated with cognitive consistency or consonance, and imbalance with cognitive dissonance. It has close resonance with the work on emotional intelligence and leadership by Goleman (1995), Boyatzis, et al (1999), Boyatzis (2000), Cherniss (2001), Sala & McBer (2001), Boyatzis, et al (2000), Sala (2000), McLelland (1973). Hien (1999) defines emotional intelligence as a form of intelligence relating to the emotional side of life, such as the ability to recognise and manage one's own and others' emotions, to motivate oneself and restrain impulses, and to handle interpersonal relationships effectively.

As a synonym for emotional intelligence, it is important not to confuse the meaning given to 'balance' in this book with the organisational management term meaning 'work-life balance'. However, one might argue that in this case balance is also concerned with reconciling conflicting demands or pressures. The 'process' of resolving these can result in cognitive consistency or cognitive dissonance.

Goleman (1998) suggests that emotional competence, or balance, is a learned capability based on emotional intelligence that results in outstanding performance at work. Goleman suggests that our emotional intelligence determines our potential for learning the practical skills based on the five elements: self-awareness, motivation, self-regulation, empathy, and adeptness in relationships. Our emotional competence, he claims, shows how much of that potential we have translated into on-the-job capabilities.

Goleman's dimensions of emotional competence are:

- Independent (each contributes to job performance);
- Interdependent (each draws to some extent on certain others with strong interactions);
- Hierarchical (the emotional intelligence capabilities build upon one another);
- Necessary, but not sufficient (having emotional intelligence doesn't guarantee the competencies will be demonstrated);
- Generic (different jobs make differing competence demands.

These are significant, both conceptually and in practice, to understanding the concept of 'balance' as it is used in this book. 'Balance' embraces these variables.

The HyperRESEARCH data analysis revealed the following examples of how the concept of 'balance', cognitive consonance, or emotional intelligence, is congruent with the sources cited above, and as it is used in this book.

HyperRESEARCH Balance Descriptors

conflict of interest, defect reporting, diligence and propriety, dispassionate discourse, institutional timidity, integrity.

BALANCE, ETHICS, ETHOS AND HABITUS

This competency relates to competencies eight (salience of the particular situation - understanding relevant task, particular and site specific incident factors) and nine (particular performance, managerial actions in a high-reliability setting, stress, conflict, disaster management, risk management.

Bordieu's theory of 'habitus' is a resonant concept when considered in relation to competencies one–ethics; and six–organisational ethos, which examine the data from the perspective of values and how they influence decisions and judgement (competency four).

Foresight (competency two) is also compromised under a dysfunctional habitus since it mainly relates to the 'attitudinal stance' and balance of managers and the organisations they shape.

Cognitive consistency and balance resonate through each of the competencies and connect the major theoretical concepts, such as 'prior knowledge', 'habitus', 'autopoiesis', 'memes', and high-reliability theory.

IDEAS ABOUT BALANCE

Socrates made reference to the negative impact that organisations had on the individual. Argyris (1955) in his early work, and in (1996) in his discussion of Model I and Model II learning (theories in use), suggested we organise in ways that endanger individuals' psychological balance. Adam Smith in 1776 stated that business-people "seldom gather together except to conspire against the public interest". The idea is also echoed in the concept of habitus. Habitus plays a central role in Bourdieu's (1972/1977, 1980/1990, 2000/2004) "generalized economy of practices", which specified both the social conditions of emergence of economic actors and systems of exchange and the concrete way they encounter, propel, or thwart each other.

It also salient to recall, in the context of 'balance', that Australian directors have a number of potent and purposeful powers that create conflicts of interest and the opportunity to serve their own interest ahead of the company, its shareholders and stakeholders and to entrench their position, status and influence to serve their own interests (Turnbull, 2002). Corporations governed by a single (unitary) board have absolute power to manage their own conflicts of interest (Turnbull, 2000). If such Boards govern high-reliability organisations, then potent and purposeful psychological balance can be expected to be at risk.

CASES OF FAILURES OF HIGH-RELIABILITY BALANCE

The five cases offer examples of all the 'balance' variables: conflict of interest, defect reporting, diligence and propriety, dispassionate discourse, institutional timidity, integrity. However, the Seaview-CAA case has been selected to illustrate how these variables appear in an accident sequence because the Commission of Enquiry1 report provides both a logical sequence and a clear understanding of the issues as part of an unfolding accident scenario, making them accessible to the reader.

It is important to frame the examination of the following data by an understanding that both the operator and the regulator failed to prioritise safety because their principal driving force was to keep aircraft flying for profit by ensuring certification, not primarily to address the safety issues.

Hence, this loss of critical balance confirms the links between organisational and human pathology. For example, since the Commission was able to examine other cases, its perspective on the role of the regulator extended beyond Seaview Air. The Commission was, therefore, in a position to observe the regulatory system in operation with CAA officers unconnected with Seaview Air. There was a considerable gap between the rhetoric and the reality.

Serious breaches in the past that reinforce Turner's (1997) premise of prior knowledge, including fraud in the renewal of an instrument rating, were never referred to prosecution. The Commission found that the CAA was afflicted by an institutional timidity against taking strong action for transgressions by the aviation industry, reinforcing Goleman's (1998) view of psychological competence.

<u>CAA</u>

[institutional timidity]

The institutional timidity of the CAA

The CAA in its submissions accepted the validity of that observation. It said this:

"To the extent that outside pressures (legal, political, industry and managerial) affected the ability or resolve of officers to take decisive and forceful action may be termed as "institutional timidity", then that expression is probably an accurate description of an environment that existed at that time in which officers may have been wary of making particular decisions." (Executive Summary:3)

The loss of balance on the part of the CAA was a direct consequence of a conflict of interest and a loss of integrity because the government required the CAA to both act as an enabler of the aviation industry and its policeman. The Commission suggested that Mr Paull's lack of diligence was due to systemic failure in the regulator, and it compromised his ability to carry out his duty as an agent of the regulator. Goleman (1998) would characterise this as an example of emotional incompetence; La Porte and Consolini (1991:19-47) would suggest that as a high-reliability organisation, CAA management failed to prioritise both performance and safety as organisational goals and failed to gain consensus among its staff and relevant organisations that these goals are unequivocal.

[loss of integrity, conflict of interest] Evident throughout was an approach by the CAA to unsafe practices or breaches of the law by operators. It is a problem that arises through the application of the policy of "graduated response".

[loss of integrity, conflict of interest] Mr Paull presented as an opportunist who enjoyed too much the company of operators, and saw matters too readily from their viewpoint, rather than the viewpoint of public safety. Mr Paull appeared not to have appreciated the need for some distance between (himself as) the regulator and the regulated. His dealings with Heliscene and Solitary Island Helicopter Service showed an insensitivity to the possibility of a conflict of interest. The closeness of his relationship with each operator inevitably compromised his ability to act as a regulator.

Loss of integrity and conflict of interest resulting from the dissonance caused by the Government's requirements resulted in failure of due diligence and acts of impropriety. In terms of the core premise of this book (Turner, 1997) that prior information cannot be captured and utilised and is lost is again seen to be salient (i.e. 'the CAA ignored warning after warning').

[diligence and propriety] The CAA was under an obligation to conduct surveillance of Seaview Air to determine its health or otherwise. In three years it did very little and discovered almost nothing.

Worse, the CAA ignored warning after warning. It failed to act on intelligence communicated repeatedly to it. The upgrading process to RPT suffered as a result. The CAA processed the upgrading with only minimal attention to its own guidelines. The absence of surveillance, for instance, was consistent with a lack of diligence on the part of Mr Paull, or his having accepted, unreasonably, what were worthless assurances and glib explanations given by the operator. Mr Paull's lenient treatment of Seaview Air was, in part, the product of a systemic problem in the CAA arising out of the policy of graduated response.

Mr Paull failed to charge Seaview Air for the chief pilot interview, and he lied about his reasons, though ultimately it was not for benefiting Seaview Air corruptly. It was a lack of diligence which so characterised Mr Paull's performance of his duties. He knew the rules, and he pushed them to their boundaries, and sometimes was in breach, but always ready with an excuse. Thus, when he came to supervise Seaview Air, such were his own personal standards that he lived so close to the edge of "legality" that he was ready to accept that standard in Seaview Air, and willingly accepted their excuses and assurances for their deficiencies without question and without adequate investigation. (Executive Summary p43)

Mr Paull allowed himself to be compromised by the receipt of significant benefits from CareFlight, and, with the fax machine and the CB Radio, requested those benefits. He must have appreciated that this was wrong. There was no CAA officer he knew of who had received such benefits. Instead: These matters were not revealed to his superiors by him. He was aware of the Code of Conduct. (Executive Summary p41)

. . .

The Commission alleged many serious deficiencies in Seaview Air and observed that these defects had been reported so often (many being corroborated by information already available to the CAA), that an investigation by the CAA, rather than by Mr McIver, ought to have been undertaken at once. Specific guidance was available as operational and breach manuals; however, vital information was rendered ineffective, both by an inadequate information processing system (technical) and by a culture (social) that neutralised it.

Several manuals were in use within the CAA providing guidance to officers how they should respond to a breach. Reading these manuals, one would expect officers of the CAA earnestly to consider prosecution or suspension when a serious breach was uncovered. Indeed, if action were not taken in such circumstances, one would expect questions to arise about either the diligence of the officer, or his or her relationship with the operator. (Executive Summary:3)

Central to Turner's (1997) thesis is the premise that the information needed to prevent an accident is already known within the organisation and is not heeded - as a result people die or are injured - this failure can therefore be pathological. Organisations and their safety systems seem to reflect the personalities (balance) of their top executives, a premise that also finds support in the literature suggested in (Kets de Vries, 1984). The author also suggest that the CAA failed as high-reliability organisation by placing the entire weight of the regulatory role on Mr. Paull, since the theory suggests that that organisations that are good at disaster avoidance, systemically mobilise as many pairs of eyes as possible to scrutinise critical information. This maximises the likelihood that the organisation will respond effectively to signs that things are going wrong. It was an absurdly benign and dangerous failure of diligence and propriety to regard Seaview Air as suddenly becoming competent simply because there was a new chief pilot.

For example;

[defect reporting, diligence and propriety] It was not until September 1994, for instance, that Seaview Air ultimately corrected the problems associated with the absence of a system in respect of life jackets and life rafts.

[defect reporting - courage, multiple factors compromising integrity] The shortcomings were:

•• overloading.

•• cheating on maintenance releases.

•• failure to record defects.

•• operating an unauthorised RPT service; and

•• a "culture" of pilots and their attitude to regulation.

The areas in which Mr McIver did not set a good example to his pilots, were:

•• it seems that on occasions he flew overloaded and tolerated a degree of misstatement ("fudging") in documents recording the weight of passengers and freight; and

•• though he urged pilots to record defects in maintenance releases (in accordance with CAR 50), he appears not to have done so himself.

On 2 October 1994, the day of the Seaview Air crash, Mr McIver recorded Mr Green's weight on the manifest of VH-IBF as 77kg (the standard weight), when it was obvious that Mr Green was considerably more (92kg).

The task Mr McIver inherited as chief pilot required pilots to change habits that had been formed over many years. Such a task was formidable. Mr McIver's only hope of succeeding was if he were to demonstrate implacable opposition to overloading, and to demand integrity in the completion of documents. Regrettably, he seems to have done neither. (Executive Summary:24)

. . .

Both aircraft had numerous defects (16 Class B items), none of which was noted on the maintenance releases, as they ought to have been. (Executive Summary p37)

DIAGNOSTIC TOOLS TO IMPROVE HIGH-RELIABILITY BALANCE

Managers do not randomly construct or reconstruct their personalities, emotions, needs, perceptions, and ways of reasoning. They do so to devise and maintain practical organisational activities or habitus. Much of the concern about balance then must lie with the unconstructed and less than competent managerial personality. The work of Bordieu (1997, 2000, 2004) and Kets de Vries (1984), is salient here because the Seaview/CAA case data identifies serious concerns about specific dysfunctional behaviour such as institutional timidity at an organisational level of analysis, and integrity and courage at an individual level of analysis.

The literature confirms this, in relation to cognitive consistency and cognitive dissonance and habitus points to the complexity behind these characteristics. In the organisations studied (and demonstrated with the CAA example), there was little success in integrating individual human beings, with all their varied abilities, interests and needs, into organisations, and require them to both reflect *on* an incident and reflect *in* an incident, while demanding that they focus on economic performance at the same time. This points to either a need for separation of these tasks or training to better prepare managers to achieve this delicate balance.

THINKING ABOUT BALANCE

Bourdieu (1975, 1972, 1977, 1980, 1990, 2000, 2004), states that a socially constituted set of understandings guide perception, thinking, emotions, motives, needs, imagination, and behaviour. The socially constituted set of understandings that form the core of our cultural psychology is called a habitus, a term that Bourdieu borrowed from Marcel Mauss (1934), who also considered the concept of 'capacity' (or competence) as the self-reflexive and knowing aspect of habitus, showing how this is an essential feature of the agential self. The roots of habitus are found in Aristotle's notion of hexis, elaborated in his doctrine of virtue, meaning an acquired yet entrenched state of moral character that orients our feelings and desires in a situation, and thence our conduct.

In Bourdieu's words, the habitus is a socially structured, and structuring structure. It is a structure of understandings about the nature of things that structure psychological phenomena, and which is itself structured by social practices. The habitus is a social product in that its 'dispositions are durably inculcated by the possibilities and impossibilities, freedoms and necessities, opportunities and prohibitions inscribed in the objective conditions' (Bourdieu, 1975, chap. 2; 1990a:76-86; 1990b, chap. 3).

Therefore, if the organisational habitus is unbalanced, it will have a dysfunctional 'disposition', as has been seen in the text data for each of the underpinning competencies and an accident potentiating dysfunctional behaviour results. As is seen in the next chapter, the dysfunctional effect also influences organisational factors.

Bordieu's theory grounds the book data when applied to reported data from other incidents. For example, The New Scientist (12 August 2000) described concerns about Concorde's tyres breaking up, which could lead to catastrophic problems, including uncontrolled fire and multiple engine failure. Both figured in the crash outside Paris when an Air France Concorde smashed into a hotel two minutes after taking off from Charles de Gaulle airport, killing 113 people. These 'engineering' concerns were reported to the Confederation of European Aerospace Societies in Cambridge in 1999. From a 'contextual' perspective we can say that the factors that could produce an incident were known to the organisation before the incident occurred, as Turner (1976, 1997) determined. The data required to exercise *foresight* was available to management prior to the accident but failed to evoke managerial decision support because *judgement* was framed by a habitus of commercial priorities over safety.

A study commissioned by British Airways was very detailed and should have triggered a system response. It looked at problems that could arise with the engines and examined the history of previous failures to calculate the odds of each event occurring in the future. It divided the consequences into five classes, ranging from 'trivial' to 'catastrophic'. The latter included 'non-containment of high-energy debris, engine separation, uncontrolled fire [and] multiple engine failures'. The analysis identified 152 separate risks, including 55 'significant' risks inherent in the design of the Rolls Royce Olympus engines, but it showed that Concorde's engines did not fall short of the safety standards required for airworthiness certification by the Civil Aviation Authority in Britain and its counterparts in France and the US. British Airways emphasised the CAA had not required it to improve the plane's engines, so it decided not to do so. The factors needed to trigger a response were below the threshold of concern. It is unquestionably dysfunctional when managerial cognitive consistency prevails in hazardous situations and renders them paradoxically 'normal', as suggested by Perrow (1984), to satisfy commercial needs over safety requirements.

British Airways gave the appearance it intended to exercise consonance when it commissioned the risk analysis of Concorde's Olympus 593 engines. However, the motive is not altruistic or related to customer safety. The dissonance revealed by New Scientist was that it wanted certification to keep the 30-year-old supersonic plane flying until 2012 for commercial advantage. Concorde's engines had remained relatively reliable over the previous 10 years, with each engine being shut down about once in every 600 transatlantic flights because of mechanical faults. It can be confidently claimed that *habitus (the culture of the organisation and managerial intent)* was directed toward profit rather than safety priorities and that such priorities shaped management's agenda or capacity for 'balance'. New Scientist reports that a quarter of the 'significant' risks identified in the risk analysis required design changes to engine parts and half of the risks were said to require 'further analysis'. However, the principal driving force was to keep the planes flying for profit by ensuring certification, not primarily to address the safety issues3.

Evidence from each of the cases examined in this book reveals that managers failed to exercise sound judgement, often in the lead-up, during, and after an accident. Managers failed to heed warnings from human and organisational sources prior to accidents, ignoring prior knowledge. They often acted with in a state of confusion and with less than the required level of integrity and courage needed to effectively deal with an incident as it unfolded; and they often sought to blame others, such as front-line staff after the accident.

They did not show a psychological balance at each critical stage of an incident. The inference is obvious that if a manager making potential life or death decisions cannot do so in a state of psychological balance (for whatever reason) then that manager will influence and be influenced by the culture of the organisation. If the organisation has been rendered dysfunctional then dysfunctional decisions can be expected to follow.

The problem of balance becomes amplified when one considers managers are not automatons or computers. They have particular motives, values, fears, experiences and expectations that also come into play in the decision process. More importantly, they function in organisations that are cultural or social settings that also frame cognitive consistency and hence balance.

Therefore, when critical decisions need to be made, managers look for some consistency among their own experiences and memories. But what if there is some inconsistency? The Asch study (1956) showed what happened when there is a serious inconsistency between one's own experiences (and the beliefs based on them) and those reported by others, and that people under pressure are inclined to perform badly. But suppose the inconsistency is among the manager's own experiences, beliefs or actions? Many social psychologists believe that this will trigger some general trend to restore cognitive consistency - to reinterpret the situation so as to minimise whatever inconsistency may be there.

According to Festinger (1957), this is because any perceived inconsistency among various aspects of knowledge, feelings and behaviour sets up an unpleasant internal state - cognitive dissonance - which people try to reduce to restore balance. Decisions made in a state of cognitive dissonance can not be 'safe' decisions because of the complex cognitive and emotional influences at play, such as:

••anxiety (apprehension in response to perceived threat),

••incident cognition (perception, knowledge, memory and judgment about oneself and the problem at hand),

••conflict (antagonistic pressures forcing the manager to make a decision in the presence of simultaneous mutually exclusive priorities, such as 'safety versus cost'),

••consonance (congruence with personal and organisational values),

••dissonance (when two cognitions are inconsistent with each other such as, to close the hatch to snuff out the fire and kill the four seamen or fight the fire with the hatch open and put the entire vessel and all the crew at certain risk),

••recognising and managing personal and organisational defence mechanisms (coping behaviours that come into play such as media spin to protect organisational reputations versus honesty and candid reporting),

••forced compliance (balancing rewards an punishments and regulatory requirements) and other issues such as the relevance of information coming from the systems involved and how to manage the motivational factors.

Then again, once a decision is made it is the beginning, not the end of conflict (Festinger, 1957). Depending on the magnitude of the dissonance it is not difficult to visualise intense incident scenarios in which reality and perceptions are distorted to make rapid adjustments to try to restore cognitive consistency and balance between all the inconsistent factors, which itself further compounds the situation, making sound decisions impossible.

HIGH-RELIABILITY DIAGNOSTIC QUESTIONS

For managers to reflect on factors that engage with safety and factors that subvert safety at the same time, raises the proposition that if this is not feasible then managers who think they can perform this mental task must be delusional. Then the questions arise concerning the support that should be available for decisional support from enabling systems in organisations, such as human resources and information systems. For example:

- Can a manager make informed, courageous, balanced decisions regarding safety in dysfunctional or information poor situations?
- Furthermore, can managers who are dysfunctional themselves or have other priorities, make balanced decisions about safety?

This chapter suggests that if the underpinning competencies are absent or compromised by other factors, such as the primacy of production, then they can confidently be characterised as dysfunctional. Dysfunctional high-reliability organisations exhibit impaired balance (loss of centering on organisational and individual purpose and values), failure of courage (acting morally in the face of coercion and fear) and compromised integrity (educated moral judgement). For example, where organisations focus on the commercial drivers or where personal or group power is exercised inappropriately the role of the regulator and legal sanctions becomes critical to safety by forcing organisational change in organisations that have a record of accidents, where dysfunctional habitus (culture) has been shown to be a factor. Dysfunctional organisational cultures are created by dysfunctional managers, not staff, and they lead to dysfunctional managerial decisions that potentiate accidents. They close themselves off from their stakeholders and it becomes difficult to establish a culture of safety.

1. Staunton, J. H. (1996). Report of the Commissioner / Commission of Enquiry into the Relations between the CAA and Seaview Air. Canberra. 2v.

2. British Airways commissioned the risk analysis of Concorde's Olympus 593 engines because it wanted to keep the 30-year-old supersonic plane flying until 2012. The risk analysis was done by the airline in conjunction with Rolls-Royce, which built Concorde's engines, and BMT Reliability Consultants of Fareham, Hampshire.

3. The risk analysis was done by the airline in conjunction with Rolls-Royce, which built Concorde's engines, and BMT Reliability Consultants of Fareham, Hampshire.

4. Asch wanted to investigate whether people could be influenced by what other people did. He did this in a very simple way by having a single subject make a very simple decision. Normally, this would be a very simple task, but the single subject found him/herself outnumbered by seven other people who deliberately make the incorrect choice. Asch demonstrated that people could easily be made to follow others despite overwelming evidence that what they were doing or saying was wrong.

16. COMPETENCY 6: ORGANISATIONAL ETHOS: OPEN OR CLOSED [AUTOPOIETIC] ORGANISATIONAL CULTURES

This chapter explores the concept of "organisational ethos" and its influence on safety culture. It examines how organisational structures, leadership styles, and communication patterns can foster or hinder a climate of safety, highlighting the importance of transparency, accountability, and a shared commitment to risk management.

"All men dream: but not equally. Those who dream by night wake in the day to find that it was vanity; but the dreamers of the day are dangerous men, for they may act their dream with open eyes, to make it possible."

(T. E. Lawrence)

HIGH-RELIABILITY ORGANISATIONAL ETHOS

Morphogenesis

Definition- literally, the "coming into being" (*genesis*) of "form" (*morphe*) is important to understanding the ethos in high-reliability organisations in that it engages the concept that organisations are more than the sum of their parts; there is something within them that is holistic and purposive, directing their development toward certain goals. Aristotle argued that a tree had the organising power of a tree. The matter of a tree would be organised as a tree.

The scientific world recognises the tendency of things to follow patterns we call laws of nature. Sheldrake's (1991:83) dubious, but intriguing, theosophical view of organising fields, he calls 'morphic resonance' enables visualisation of an organising process governed by an ethos. According to Rupert Sheldrake's theory, a radio would tune into events from outside it. If the radio is turned off the events are not turned off, the events keep on happening. The voices do not come from the radio itself. By analogy, neither functional nor dysfunctional values can be turned off if they exist in the atmosphere (ethos) of an organisation, they have organising force.

In analysing organisational ethos, its most obvious dysfunctional manifestation is a tendency to 'autopoiesis', which is defined as a process whereby a system becomes self-referential and closes itself off from the outside world. An autopoietic system is operationally closed and structurally static with no apparent inputs and outputs. The CAA (described in the data analysis s6.1.5) is perhaps the most obvious example. It mishandled issue after issue and consequently came under attack in parliament, the aviation industry and the media and closed itself off as best it could with obfuscation, denials and refusal to cooperate along with individual hubris among managers as they tried to put a positive bureaucratic 'spin' on events as did BHP after the Longford explosion.

Each of the cases was subjected to HyperRESEARCH analysis and the process revealed many descriptors of organisational ethos. These are congruent with the morphogenic organising power of the collective mind of the dominant coalition. It revealed a tendency for dysfunctional organisations to shift to autopoietic behaviours (refers to a self referential system capable of producing and maintaining itself by creating its own parts). These descriptors are listed in the panel below.

HyperRESEARCH Organisational Ethos Descriptors:

administrative politics, autopoietic behaviour, corrupt management, cultural factors, culture of denial, dominance of CEO, dominant coalition, erroneous management paradigm, failure to notify safety concerns, favoured treatment, ignore legislation, improvised safety standards, legislative framework, management interference, managerial dysfunction, misplaced reliance on SSM, management neglect, management speak, decision making, priority of production, regulator arrogance, regulator incompetence, safety as a cost, sacrifice of safety for economic reasons, standards sacrificed, systemic management failure, wages and conditions, written reports ignored

ETHOS, CULTURE, VIGILANCE AND FORESIGHT

The cascading consequences of ethos:

The systemic nature of the ethos (competency 6) determined the capacity to construct a culture of safety (competency 7), that depends on psychological balance (competency 5), judgement (competency 4), vigilance (competency 3), capacity for foresight (competency 2), and the ethics of its dominant coalition (competency 1). The direct sequence of connections to each of these high-reliability competencies is through the previously developed conceptual interplay of the theories of habitus, memes, autopoiesis, reflective practice, and prior knowledge.

IDEAS ABOUT ORGANISATIONAL ETHOS

Having the capacity to diagnose and manage the ethos of the organisation has been shown in this book to be one of the core failings of the dominant coalition, as was seen in several perspectives considered earlier, notably Turner's (1978, 1997) 'misinformation' or theory of 'prior knowledge'; Reason's (1990) 'latent errors' and Kletz's (1994) 'organisational memory failure'; Perrow's (1984, 1999) theories of 'normal accidents'; and Bordieu's (2004) theories of 'habitus'; and Roberts (1990) view that failure-tolerant managers create hazardous conditions in their pursuit of downward pressure on costs and increasing shareholder dividends.

Theories of autopoiesis and enactive cognitive science claim that certain self-organising biological systems can close themselves off from their environments and abandon symbolic representations and instructional interactions to polarise an altered reality (Maturana et al, 1980; Varela, 1979 & 1991). These theories can provide useful inferential insights into how accidents might happen in high-reliability organisations.

'Autopoiesis' suggests that certain organisations might close themselves off from their stakeholders to protect the internal 'actors', management. Under such conditions key players ignore warnings, deny events, and lie to cover-up errors. These two theories amplify Bourdieu's (1975, 1977, 2004) theory of 'habitus' which states that a socially constituted set of understandings guide perception, thinking, emotions, motives, needs, imagination, and behaviour.

Morgan discusses the morphogenic dimension of autopoiesis while considering the form, function, and character of enterprises suggesting that 'autopoietic systems are closed loops: self-referential systems that strive to shape themselves in their own image' (Morgan, 1986: 242). Von Krogh and Roos (1995) apply principles from autopoietic theory in laying out a schema for corporate knowledge building. Mingers (1994) points to similarities between autopoietic theory, and sociologist Anthony Giddens' (1984) to structuration theory.

Giddens' theory of structuration (Gauntlett, 2002) notes that social life is more than random individual acts, but is not merely determined by social forces. Giddens suggests that human agency and social structure are in a relationship with each other, and it is the repetition of the acts of individual agents which reproduces the structure. This means that there is a social structure - traditions, institutions, moral codes, and established ways of doing things – but it also means that these can be changed when people start to ignore them, replace them, or reproduce them differently. Put simply, management determines structure and all structural values. If management becomes dysfunctional so does the organisation. These two theories also resonate with Bourdieu's (1975, 1977, 2004) theory of 'habitus'.

Whitely (1999) sees the usefulness of autopoiesis as a metaphor for reflective thinking about organisations contemplating change. The issue of how autopoiesis can or should be applied to social systems is an ongoing topic of debate (Zeleny, 1980; Benseler, Hejl & Kock, 1980; Zeleny, 1981; Ulrich & Probst, 1984; Mingers, 1994). These authors tend to indicate that there are two primary approaches in applying autopoiesis to social systems. The first applies the formal aspects of autopoietic theory to the social system itself (e.g., organisation; autopoiesis).

The second derives an explanation of the social system from the phenomenological aspects of the theory (e.g., the observer; communication, hence memes).

In this book the theory is best understood when both the organisational and communication factors are considered together: autopoiesis + memes = explanation for many of the issues the various Commissions of Enquiry discovered that lead to failures which resulted in fatal accidents. For example, the issue of the failure of prior knowledge is explainable in light of a purposive, dysfunctional system that devalues and subverts information that might point to an impending accident.

Von Bertalanffy (1980) claims that an autopoietic or 'closed system' is one where behaviour is entirely explainable from within, essentially a system without input. Systems may be variously closed to new ideas, to information, and/or to organisation. Systems closed to energy or new ideas are 'autark', systems closed to information are independent, and systems closed to organisation are 'autonomous'. The output has nothing to do with whether a system is closed. Systems without output are non-knowable through observation from the outside. Organisations such as the Navy and the CAA are almost unknowable from the outside and therefore meet this criteria.

Evidencen makes it clear that autopoietic organisations such as the CAA attempt to organise the environment to enable the organisation's self focus. Morgan (1986: 244) calls organisations like this 'egocentric', suggesting they often do not understand their own complexity as '[they] draw boundaries of narrow definitions around themselves and proceed to advance the self-interest of this narrow domain.'

To such autopoietic organisations, the future is a projection of the present. Changes are only welcomed when needed to keep the status quo. Change is imposed, something that upsets the equilibrium, and often this change must come from outside. This indicates the critical and often interventionist role required of the regulator where safety is put at stake by an organisationally egocentric predisposition.

The change literature comments on the challenges and difficulties of implementing change and confirms this reaction by both management and workers (Kanter (1984); Dunphy & Stace (1992); Ulrich et al (1997). Therefore, it is unlikely that concerns of outsiders, such as for safety, will cause a self-referential, autopoietic organisation to voluntarily change. Intervention, rather than concern, is required to bring about change. Maturana (1981) suggests that invariance in an organisation is the essence of an autopoietic system and such a system cannot undergo an evolutionary change. Therefore, this book suggests that it is the ultimate responsibility of the regulator to understand the culture of the organisations under its purview where such characteristics have become institutionalised and intervene where appropriate.

CASES OF FAILURES OF HIGH-RELIABILITY ETHOS

Each of the organisations discussed in this book had a distinct, purposive organising ethos, which was shown by the Commissions of Enquiry, to have contributed to each fatal accident. It existed much as background dissonance in each of these dysfunctional organisations and was amplified (tuned into) by the accident scenarios as they unfolded. Some of these failings were subtly autopoietic. For example, there is evidence that disconnected managers used deception and cunning to further their own ends (creating an organisational ethos where the end justified the means).

The HyperRESEARCH analysis revealed considerable disconnection between an organisation's espoused position regarding its organisational obligations and the reality revealed by tuning in to its actual behaviour (as suggested in Whitely, 1999 - chapter 4, s4.8), with the clarity brought to bear by a Royal Commission. As an example, paragraphs 13.38, 39, and 40 of the Longford Commission showed that although the Longford operation had excellent best-practice manuals, their actual practice did not align with the safety guidelines outlined in those manuals. The evidence suggests that the manuals were a cynical exercise in obfuscation to 'appear to be in compliance' with safety requirements.

Longford

[dangers of disconnection between espoused values and actual practice and need for simplification]

13.38. Evidence was given that OIMS was a world class system and complied with world's best practice. Whilst this may be true of the expectations and guidelines upon which the system was based, the same cannot be said of the operation of the system in practice. Even the best management system is defective if it is not effectively implemented. The system must be capable of being understood by those expected to implement it.

13.39 Esso's OIMS, together with all the supporting manuals, comprised a complex management system. It was repetitive, circular, and contained unnecessary cross referencing. Much of its language was impenetrable. These characteristics made the system difficult to comprehend both by management and by operations personnel.

13.40 The Commission gained the distinct impression that there was a tendency for the administration of OIMS to take on a life of its own, divorced from operations in the field. Indeed, it seemed that in some respects, concentration upon the development and maintenance of the system diverted attention from what was actually happening in the practical functioning of the plants at Longford. (The Esso Gas Plant Accident, Report of the Longford Royal Commission. 1999)

Paragraphs 13.38-40 show that the OIMS system (operations integrity management system) became self-sufficient shelf decorations, using jargon like 'world's best practice', without effectively putting these guidelines into action. It can reasonably be inferred that this was a way 'management' could impress and mislead both the parent company, Exxon, and the regulator.

The recurring problem with management jargon and management speak' is their dangerous propensity to take on memetic force and become a mantra endowed with sufficient power to create an autopoietic entity, an organisational ethos serving its own ends.

Such an entity can be as small as a department or a management group, or as large as an organisation. It also has ethical implications in the sense that while espousing a high moral tone to engage in necessary action, management both cannot carry out these actions and obscures its own inaction in a language that requires forensic unravelling to understand.

This is of particular concern when this obfuscatory language finds its way into glossy manuals governing the safety operations of high-reliability organisations. Not only does it hinder actual operations, it also makes training virtually impossible. This creates a propensity whereby dissonance is set up, which then results in dysfunctional paradigms (mental models of an organisational world) governing actual behaviours by the organisation.

Erroneous management paradigms can guide a person to unsafe behaviours in hazardous, stressful conditions where reflex rather than reason takes over. Often, the edge of the rut can be mistaken for the horizon in such constrained, autopoietic paradigms. Perrow (1999:9) points out that 'mariners had quite reasonable explanations for their actions; it is just that the interaction of small failures led them to construct quite erroneous worlds in their minds, ...and these conflicting images led to collisions.' The paradigmatic force can be subtle and framed by erroneous perceptions and expectations, as in the Court of Marine Enquiry: ss Lake Illawarra (1975:8) example that follows.

Illawarra

[erroneous management paradigm]

The Master's reason for charting a course instead of steering by landmarks, he said, was that he expected bad weather and poor visibility. Normally he would have steered by landmarks in these pilotage waters, starting at about the place where a pilot would be picked up, between White Rock Point and Crayfish Point. When the weather and visibility improved instead of getting worse, the Master did not adjust his navigation to his usual practice of steering by landmarks. (Commission Report p8)

This perfectly sensible but entirely erroneous mental model in the mind of the Master is not dissimilar to the erroneous mental paradigms used by senior decision makers in each of the cases. For example, in the Longford Royal Commission (1999:13.71), a more serious mental model is described. It ignored the effects of hot condensate transferred down the line.

Longford

[erroneous management paradigm]

13.71 Importantly, in considering the impact of the modification on the transfer pipeline, the 1992 study identified condensate carryover into the absorption oil system as a potential outcome of high levels of condensate in the absorbers. It did not, however, examine the effect of condensate carryover on vessels downstream from the absorbers in GP1. This was because of a conclusion reached by those involved in the study, that condensate carryover was "not a new phenomenon" and that it should "...be handled in the same way as it is handled now". The study noted that no follow-up action was required.

These assumptions can have the effect of creating altered realities in dominant coalitions leading to thwarting safety system tests to identify latent systemic problems. For example, in the Executive Summary of the Seaview Report, Staunton, J. H., (1996:22), the Commissioners observed that administrative politics played a role in subverting safety.

CAA

[administrative politics]

Mr Roser directed the Head of the Directorate of Aviation Safety Regulation, Mr Macionis, in these forthright terms:

"Please have the history, the current operations and the above issues of Seaview independently audited and reviewed as a matter of absolute priority and provide a report to me on the findings, plus any actions you propose to have taken as a result of the investigation."

Mr Macionis referred the issue to Mr Abberton, Acting Regional Manager, North East Region. Mr Abberton was furious at not having been consulted. He was determined to thwart the Enquiry.

Neither Mr Macionis nor Mr Abberton examined the Seaview Air files to determine the position. Neither asked that someone independent, with technical expertise, do so. Mr Abberton simply solicited a response from Mr Paull, the person who was the subject of the accusations. Mr Paull, predictably, denied the allegations. Soliciting his denial was hardly a substitute for an independent audit.

Mr Macionis thereafter assured Mr Roser that an independent audit was not necessary. Mr Roser accepted that assurance. An opportunity, therefore, was lost. It was lost, moreover, for reasons connected with administration politics, and unrelated to the merits of Mr Roser's direction. (Executive Summary p22)

The report identifies further evidence of the regulator's internal failure to carry out its role because of a failure in the organisational ethos that the CAA previously purported was one of safety. It bears highlighting that each of the people identified in the Commission report are CAA employees.

<u>CAA</u> [managerial dysfunction] Twice Mr Roser had asked Mr Macionis to investigate allegations against Seaview Air (18 April and 9 May 1994). On both occasions Mr Macionis had failed to investigate. He had simply referred the issues to Mr Paull, who had provided a rebuttal. The rebuttal had been accepted without an independent

check and passed on to Mr Roser. That was not good enough. (Executive Summary p27)

The processing of the Operations Manual demonstrated, first, the dysfunctional nature of the Coffs Harbour Office, where the Flying Operations Manager and the Airworthiness Manager plainly could not agree. (Executive Summary p29)

Hence, the play of organisational politics and the exercise of organisational and personal power was sufficient to create an ethos in which precedence was given to the interests of the dominant coalition, and the systemic traps and tests needed to overcome this powerful force were not in place.

The internal problems revealed by the Seaview and other fatal crashes pointed to a dysfunctional ethos and demonstrated how a dysfunctional ethos can permeate into every corner of an organisation and diminish many critical competencies related to safety or critical mission. For example, the damaging effect on vigilance in the CAA as the result of dysfunctional systems operating in the dysfunctional habitus described above can be seen in the following sequence of accident precursors:

CAA [managerial dysfunction, systemic management failure] Officers and Flight Service Officers. Many other errors were brought about by a distinct lack of concentration or inattention by both, including:

- Failure to notice for some minutes that VH-SVQ had disappeared from the radar screen.
- Failure to recognise that VH-SVQ was in controlled airspace when the pilot announced a significant descent.

• Failure to ask the pilot whether his operations were normal.

• Failure to carry out a communications check for an unacceptably long time after the position report of VH-SVQ was due.

Management problems were also evident. Shift supervisors manipulated shifts or were late. Airspace positions were closed when they ought to have been open, it being the weekend of the Bathurst Motor Races. There were local "Sydney practices", which were not the best practices, in what needs to be a disciplined environment. Pilot breaches were not reported; non-procedural expressions were tolerated; and departures from procedural requirements were almost commonplace. What was most extraordinary was a television set being present in the flight service area, broadcasting the Bathurst races. Its presence had been permitted earlier by a manager. It was connected to a permanent aerial wall jack and was tolerated by later shift managers. One officer, near the television, denied that his many and serious errors had been caused by the presence of the television. If it was not the cause, then his lack of concentration, and that of other officers had no apparent cause other than a lack of diligence. (Executive Summary p47)

One dimension of an unhealthy organisational ethos, or habitus, in the CAA is the evidence put forward by the Commission of regulator arrogance. The characteristics of autopoietic behaviour are many and often quite subtle. The propensity for paranoia and the memetic reinforcement gained from evidence from the environment can alter perceptions of responsibility and drive the organisation inwards on itself in a self-protective mode. Behaviours that manifest this inclination include the likelihood that anyone from inside bearing 'bad news', or more 'whistle blowing', will be severely punished, either by losing their jobs or career path opportunities. Therefore, people at the safety interface are often disinclined to be the 'bearer of bad tidings' since there is often a tendency to 'execute the messenger'. For example,

. . .

CAA [regulator arrogance] In its submissions, the Authority has failed to extend to Mr Hoy the apology for his treatment that he deserved. Indeed, the submissions disclosed the same irritation with Mr Hoy that was the root cause for his warnings having been ignored. That attitude, in the Commission's belief, signifies that the lesson of these events has not been learned, notwithstanding the acknowledgment of timidity. [Executive Summary p22]

The durability and expression of the core high-reliability competencies identified in this book are reliant on a sound organisational ethos. However, since the source of a healthy organisational ethos derives mostly from the influence of the dominant coalition and, in particular, the CEO. If the CEO is dysfunctional the core competencies cannot be expressed. For example, persisting with the CAA case, the lapses identified above can be traced back to the dominance and exercise of power by Mr Green and his innate propensity for dysfunctional and unethical behaviour (ie the pressure he applied to others to break rules and put productivity ahead of safety).

CAA [dominance of the CEO, wages and conditions, pressure to break rules, priority of production] Mr Green, as the proprietor of Seaview Air, was a dominant figure. His pilots were all young men. They had entered general aviation in the hope that one day they would fly for one of the major airlines. That ambition required the accumulation of experience and flying hours. Jobs were in short supply. Mr Green regarded his pilots as being lucky to have a job. They so regarded themselves. He was, therefore, in a position of significant dominance so far as the pilots were concerned.

That dominance manifested itself in two distinct ways:

• First, Mr Green offered wages and conditions considerably less advantageous than those provided by the Pilots (General Aviation) Award. That award was, for Seaview Air, the law. Mr Green was bound by it. Yet he regarded it as irrelevant to his company. His pilots were prepared nonetheless, to accept his conditions. Indeed, they were eager to do so, because they were anxious to keep their jobs.

• Secondly, Mr Green was in a position (as he acknowledged) to put pressure upon pilots to break or bend the rules, to his financial benefit. It was plain that he applied such pressure. (Executive Summary p4)

The evidence is strong that Mr Green did not exercise a level of responsibility congruent with the power he exercised. Somewhat similar dysfunctional relationships also played a role in the accidents discussed in the other cases, in the Longford and Moura cases. In the Longford case, Management in Melbourne, at head office, ordered a cost cutting reduction of supervision at Longford, which included the transfer of its engineers to Melbourne. This reduction of supervision at Longford, described in the Longford Royal Commission Report (1999:13.36), including the transfer of engineers to Melbourne, necessarily meant a reduction in the amount and quality of the supervision of operations there. There was a correspondingly greater reliance by Esso on the skill and knowledge of its on-site operators.

LONGFORD 13.136 [priority of production] Had there been surveillance by qualified engineers, there would have been an opportunity to detect and correct the operating practices which led to the accident on 25 September 1998. The failure to conduct the HAZOP study for GP1 and the reduction of supervision at Longford, including the transfer of engineers to Melbourne, were a result of Esso's desire to control its operating costs.

. . .

This reduction in supervision to achieve cost cutting goals related to production was compounded by the dysfunctional behaviour of senior staff left on site at Longford, which resulted in failure of critical hazard related 'prior information', as suggested by Turner, (1978, 1997).

13:30 If Musgrave acquired the knowledge, which he said he did, he did nothing as plant manager to ensure that the written operating procedures contained instructions to be followed in the event of loss of lean oil circulation.

The change in supervisor responsibilities left operators without structured operational procedures to follow in the event of specific hazardous events. This amplification of contributing factors was behaviourally endorsed in the framing of the Longford ethos during regular on-site visits by senior management whose actions provided clear memetic cues to the sort of behaviour head office expected (paragraph 13.33 demonstrates low managerial concern for hazard identification).

13:33 Monthly visits to Longford by senior management failed to detect these shortcomings and were therefore no substitute for essential on-site supervision.

This consistently poor hazard identification was compounded even further by the actions of an external assessment team, who appear to have provided a 'management speak' assessment of hazard at the Longford plant. The management speak 'power words' that are used in such compliance reports to convey dynamic organisational processes to managers, whom the report writers believe want to hear such hyperbole, are underlined in paragraph 13.36 below. these words can be taken out without changing the meaning. This propensity for memetic falsehoods is extant in most organisations and covers the incompetence of poorly qualified audit or human resource staff who feel the need to 'Harvardise' their language. Everything must be 'dynamic' or 'powerful', or 'extensive'. Not only are these clues to potential hazards, they are also dangerous 'belief system' memes that can shape the ethos or habitus of high-reliability organisations. It is relevant to note that this audit report would not have been called for except that it was required for compliance purposes.

13.34 Element 11 of the ECI Guidelines, which were translated into Esso's OIMS Systems Manual, required a "process that measures the degree to which expectations are met" and regarded that requirement as essential "to improve operations integrity and maintain accountability". That meant that Esso's OIMS were required to include a system to ensure that these guidelines were met and, in particular, that Esso's operations were assessed at predetermined frequencies to establish the degree of compliance.

13.35 An external assessment was carried out by a team under the leadership of Wayne Achee in March and April 1998. A report of the assessment was prepared and sent to Sikkel. The report acknowledged that the assessment was required by element 11 of the ECI Guidelines to determine the extent to which Esso was meeting the guidelines and the requirements of its individual management systems. The report noted that the assessment team had concluded that Esso had successfully applied OIMS and had a high level of management involvement and participation, presumably in that process.

13.36 The report further noted the following achievements:

There was a common set of operating manuals, references and records which were identified and in place at all sites.

There was an extensive set of operations and maintenance procedures which were updated at specified intervals as changes occurred.

There was a good understanding of and high discipline in safe work routines and procedures.

There was a structured and disciplined process in place for shift handover for offshore and onshore operating sites.

There was a comprehensive incident reporting, investigation and analysis system which was well understood throughout the organisation. Esso personnel were well disciplined in following their procedures.

Near miss reporting was actively encouraged by management and supported by Esso personnel.

The Longford Royal Commission (1999:13.37) observed that these (and other) observations of the assessment team appear inconsistent with the Commission's findings concerning the failure of Esso to implement its own systems, in relation to risk identification, analysis and management, training, operating procedures, documentation, data and communications. Paragraphs 13.107, 13.108, and 13.67 of the Report point to similar failings in critical aspects of hazard prevention (log book entries and handover procedures, and management speak).

13.107 Shift handovers and logbook entries were used ineffectively In the lead up to the accident on 25 September 1998. Moreover, laxity in the implementation of the handover requirements seems to have escaped scrutiny by management.

13.108 Logbook entries were not subjected to any examination either by Longford plant management or by management in Melbourne. They do not appear to have been used by management as a means of monitoring process conditions at the plant nor were they passed on to any person or group in Melbourne for plant surveillance purposes.

13.67 However, OIMS Element 2 did not identify any procedures for risk assessment associated with management of change. The only reference to this topic was in the following terms: "Production Technology operate within a management of change procedure which is consistent with the EAL management of change philosophy."

The Commission also observed (paragraph 13.18) that the collective experience of those present at GP922 on 25 September 1998 was more than 200 years at Longford, and yet no one recognised the hazards associated with the plant conditions which culminated in the explosion and fire.

Appropriate supervision of operators to ensure adherence to basic operating practices was a responsibility of Esso management. The investigation of the events leading up to the accident revealed a number of occasions when operators failed to adhere to rudimentary operating practices. These included failures to monitor plant conditions, respond appropriately to alarms, report process upsets to supervisors and undertake appropriate checks before adjusting process variables. Had there been an ethos in place where operating practices been more closely monitored and supervised by Esso management, these departures from appropriate operating practices would have been detected and remedied.

Finally, the problem of ethos is inherent in the regulatory regime for offshore petroleum production in Australia, where safety is the responsibility of a government department whose primary concern is to facilitate production. This situation is like that pertaining to aviation.

In discussing the Moura case Hopkins (1999) observed that the mine operator, BHP, had experience of previous mine disasters, the most recent being the explosions at Moura No. 4 in 1986 and at Appin in NSW in 1979. It is BHP as an organisation whose memory was defective. However, at the time of the Moura accident the economic viability of the mine was in doubt and there was pressure to maximise production. Counsel for the miners put it in his final submission, 'BHP ran a dangerous race against time to extract all of the coal from 512 [panel] in accordance with the (management) plan' (Hopkins, 1999:134).

There was a habitus and ethos of denial at Moura which served to nullify warnings of impending disaster. Compliance requirements demanded that production could continue at top speed only if the mine was understood to be safe. This requirement consequently generated an elaborate set of dysfunctional beliefs that provided this reassurance. For example, the routine practice of allowing men underground when a sealed panel was going through the explosive range involved a sacrifice of safety. Shift production reports were prepared at a higher level in the management structure than shift safety reports. Substantial financial incentives were paid for production but none for the diligent management of catastrophic risk. This led to a situation where safety did not pay for relevant decision makers (Hopkins (1999).

DIAGNOSTIC TOOLS TO IMPROVE HIGH-RELIABILITY ETHOS

This capacity for an organisational ethos to morphogenically shape purposive dysfunctional management behaviours and systems highlights the critical ability needed by management to engage in assumption surfacing and verification to test for dangerous but entirely plausible mental paradigms and persistent memes, both in management and operations. Such assumptions are often the source of cycles of mistrust and subsequent autopoietic tendencies. Organisational cultures in HROs need to be responsive to stakeholder concerns and inputs to avoid autopoietic responses to a crisis. Power relationships, such as that engendered by fear and bullying, and direct and indirect discrimination, need to be proactively and unambiguously driven from the workplace by the dominant coalition to overcome tendencies to autopoiesis and to engender lower barriers to safety, quality, productivity and innovation.

THINKING ABOUT ORGANISATIONAL ETHOS

In the early 1980s, only two years after joining the company, the CEO of Beech-Nut Nutrition Corporation found evidence suggesting that the apple juice concentrate, supplied by the company's vendors for use in Beech-Nut's "100% pure" apple juice, contained nothing more than sugar water and chemicals. The CEO was under extraordinary pressure to turn the ailing company around. Eliminating the inventory would have killed any hope of turning the $700,000 profit promised to Beech-Nut's parent, Nestle.

A number of people in the corporation, it turned out, had doubted the purity of the juice for several years before the CEO arrived. But the ethos created by the 25% price advantage offered by the supplier of the bogus concentrate allowed operations to meet cost-control goals. When a member of the book department voiced concerns about the juice to operating management, he was accused of not being a team player and of acting like "Chicken Little." His judgment, his supervisor wrote in an annual performance review, was "coloured by naiveté and impractical ideals."

This propensity to ignore the advice of front-line operators and to label them as 'whistleblowers' or 'troublemakers' is present in every case examined in this book. It confirms the premise of 'prior knowledge' developed by Turner (1978, 1997). No one else at Beech-Nut seemed to have considered the company's obligations to its customers or to have thought about the potential harm of disclosure. No one considered the fact that the sale of adulterated or misbranded juice is a legal offence, putting the company and its top management at risk of criminal liability. In 1987, the company pleaded guilty to selling adulterated and misbranded juice. Two years and two criminal trials later, the CEO pleaded guilty to ten counts of mislabeling. The total cost to the company - including fines, legal expenses, and lost sales - was an estimated $25 million.

Such errors reveal a culture that is insensitive or indifferent from ethical considerations, or one that lacks effective organisational systems or is plainly focused on the 'bottom line'. The media followed the somewhat similar cases examined in this book. For example, The Canberra Times (Sat. Oct. 7, 1995) carried an article by Mike Taylor in which he states: 'The Seaview tragedy claimed a dozen lives, the Monarch crash claimed seven lives. Based on evidence given to the Commission of Enquiry into Seaview's relationship with the CAA and on the submissions of the Counsel assisting the Coronial Inquest into the Monarch crash, which occurred two years earlier, the CAA had little to be proud of. What has become clear in the evidence given to both forums is that a culture of distrust had evolved within the organisation - a culture borne of radical and poorly targeted restructuring; a culture borne of jealousies and internecine warfare.'

The same phenomenon was evident in the Challenger disaster where a belief evolved that O-ring malfunction was normal and acceptable. This belief served to disguise the fact that safety was being sacrificed so that launch schedules could be met. Safety did not pay in the Moura accident data. Moura was not unusual in this respect: Bhopal and the Herald of Free Enterprise were two other disasters where it seemed that safety did not pay for the integrity of relevant decision makers.

Whiteley (1999), identified eight markers of autopoietic organisations. Her eight factors are important because they provide strong triangulation support for the observations deduced in this book using a different book methodology (chapter 4, s4.8).

1. Conflict between organisational reality and the espoused organisational environment.

2. Predisposed to stability and stable structures

3. Rules and Policies linked to stability

4. Hierarchical structure and decision-making

5. Tends to view the environment as stable and unchanging

6. Lack of openness to change

7. Ineffective focus of change

8. Staff, Knowledge and Communication

Deficiencies within the culture of the CAA led to serious problems in airlines operating regular public transport services not being addressed. For example CAA officers had known for months that both Seaview and Monarch Airlines were cutting corners on aircraft maintenance and it was also well known that each was in breach of regulations. The factors identified in the Seaview crash as accident contributors were previously identified in the Monarch crash from which the CAA appeared to have learned nothing. Its response after Monarch was to close itself off from scrutiny as best it could. It behaved autopoietically and failed to incorporate the lessons of the Monarch crash. The situation was so bad that the Minister split the organisation into two. The Civil Aviation Safety Authority (CASA) was formed to handle safety, and Airservices Australia was formed to handle commercial operations.

The Longford and Lake Illawarra cases also demonstrated the dangers of disconnection between espoused values and actual practice, where priority of production constructs dangerous paradigms.

The state of mind of the organisation and the way it sees itself at any particular time is framed and constructed against the views its stakeholders believe the organisation values. This ethos tends to percolate from the dominant coalition downwards. These coalitions place value on certain artefacts, espouse certain beliefs, and behave according to a set of underlying assumptions (mostly related to the priority of production). This drives their behaviour, which then acts as a driver of organisational ethos. 'Prior knowledge' of accident conditions tends to be ignored when there is a conflict between commercial priorities and a commitment to safety. It is imperative that an organisational ethos must never be allowed to develop where safety is seen by the dominant coalition as a cost item rather than an investment. Systems should be in place to manage crises so that an incident becomes a learning experience, not a reason to withdraw. An accident is not a reason to 'circle the wagons'; it is an opportunity to learn.

HIGH-RELIABILITY DIAGNOSTIC QUESTIONS

This book raises many questions concerning the role played by organisational management and the regulator in building an ethos of safety. For example,

•If assumption surfacing and verification are essential to test for dangerous mental models and persistent memes in management and operations, what role should the regulator play in enforcing this process?

•How can organisational cultures in HROs be responsive to stakeholder concerns and inputs to avoid autopoietic responses to a crisis?

•What role should the regulator play in driving fear and bullying, and direct and indirect discrimination, from HROs to overcome barriers to safety, quality, productivity and innovation?

•Is this task solely the responsibility of management?

•What if management themselves are the source and cause of these problems?

The state of mind of the organisation and the way it sees itself at any particular time is framed and constructed against the views employees believe the organisation values. For example,

•How can management place value on safety as an investment rather than a cost, espouse positive beliefs about safety, and demonstrate they behave according to a set of cognitively consistent underlying assumptions if these values are at odds with their real agenda and behaviour?

•If 'prior knowledge' of accident conditions tends to be ignored when there is a conflict between commercial priorities and a commitment to safety how can managers deal with these financial pressures?

. . .

Other questions that might indicate autopoietic tendencies include:

•Is there a hierarchical structure and top-down decision-making?

•Does the organisation see that it is hierarchical?

•Does it favour internal promotions only?

•Does the organisation tend to view the environment as stable and unchanging?

•Is its system of values grounded in 'old' world practices?

•Does the organisation demonstrate a lack of openness to change?

•Does it not recognise when there are problems, or does it persist with bad decisions?

•Is it aware of the variety of cultures within it?

•Is it inclined to highlight the barriers to change rather than possible adaptation to future?

•Is the focus for change blurred and ineffective?

•Is it possible to name and bring to the surface the faulty and subversive assumptions and memes which govern practices in relation to hanging on to old benefits, perceptions of roles in relation to clients and customers, and the organisation's reputation?

1. Morphogenesis asks, 'How do complex living organisms arise from much simpler structures such as seeds or eggs?' 'How does an acorn manage to grow into an oak tree, or a fertilised human egg into an adult human being?' A striking characteristic of living organisms is the capacity to regenerate, ranging from the healing of wounds to the replacement of lost limbs or tails. Organisms are more than just complex machines: no machine has ever been known to grow spontaneously from a machine egg or to regenerate after damage.

17. COMPETENCY 7: CONSTRUCTING A CULTURE OF SAFETY: CULTURE OF SAFETY, WAYS OF SEEING, PERSISTENT IDEAS - 'MEMES'

THIS CHAPTER FOCUSES ON THE COMPETENCY OF BUILDING AND sustaining a robust safety culture within organisations. It explores the role of leadership in shaping perceptions, attitudes, and behaviours related to safety, emphasizing the importance of communication, training, and continuous improvement.

"A company's culture is the 'water' in the fishbowl. It's the environment in which your employees swim, and it can either nourish or poison them depending on what senior management puts in the water."

Edgar Schein

WHAT IS A HIGH-RELIABILITY CULTURE?

Persistent ideas and ways of seeing can be readily understood if one grasps the concept of the 'meme'. The concept of a 'meme' is simply a cultural equivalent to the biological entity called the 'gene'. In this cultural context it is applied to persistent ideas which seem to survive in a particular communications niche, such as an organisation (echoing 'the survival of the fittest'). Organisations can take on characteristics all their own, and a relationship with the organisation develops which is 'parasocial' because it takes place between constructed personalities - organisations and humans. We tend to seek out elements of identity in the organisations we belong to and in which we work. The nature of parasocial communications is always captured and understood through its ethos and through its memes. 'Meme' is a term coined by the Darwinian biologist Richard Dawkins (1976 and 1989) to describe self-replicating cultural elements. Each of the organisations studied in this book failed in its intention to value safety as a persistent way of seeing and consequently set itself up for catastrophic failure by not understanding the powerful memes at work that subvert safety.

Turner (1997:49) points out that, 'A way of seeing is also a way of not seeing.' A problem defined may well mask an unseen problem. The clarifying factor is the extent to which assumptions about the 'way of seeing' are embedded in the psyche of the organisation and reinforced by the language and values used to transmit them, which in turn points to the distinctive relationship that exists between autopoiesis and memes. For example, where a culture is attempting to preserve the status quo based on patterns of shared assumptions that are based on the need for feelings of security and internal equilibrium, these 'ways of seeing' can be conveyed, in covert and overt communications and mantras that act as instructions embedded in human brains (Blackmore, 1999; Brodie, 1996) Examples of these 'ways of seeing' include:

•"That's just a matter of opinion." - devaluing others views reinforces the idea that 'we know best. So we will not entertain perturbating 'ways of seeing'.

•"What would they know anyway." - diminishes the experience of others.

•"We do it this way for the sake of consistency." - it saves confrontations and thinking.

The following descriptors all share a common thread. They point to aspects of the state of mind, mental stance, or habitus, of the organisation and the way it sees itself at any particular time. They are memetic constructions/instructions, and they are suggestive that an individual in an organisation is para-socially influenced by others, who are themselves influenced para-socially by the organisation and its perceived values (not its espoused values). Every new idea coming into an organisation is weighed against the views the organisation is perceived to value and is embraced or rejected accordingly. For example, action plans and administrative procedures; modes and quality of communication and constraints on upward communication; attitudes such as contempt for regulations, the disinterest and failure to train and retrain that causes failure of organisational memory; the failure to provide a safe environment and the failure to capture and utilise critical hazard related information; the malaise that under-utilises expertise, are all organisation specific and come about because of the carriage and influence of memes. The descriptors that follow are related to the construction of a culture of safety and its failure.

HyperRESEARCH Constructing a Culture of Safety Descriptors

action plan, administrative procedures, communication, complex management system, compliance, contempt for regulations, cultural attitude to regulation, failure of organisational memory, failure to provide safe environment, failure to utilise information, first order attribution of cause, hierarchy of knowledge, incident reporting system, knowledge management, lessons from previous accidents, maintenance documentation, post hoc forensic recording, motivation, pseudopsychology, resolute intervention, self congratulatory discourse, shared beliefs - memes, under-utilised expertise, upward communication

. . .

This organisational 'state of mind' or 'attitudinal stance' tends to percolate from the dominant coalition downwards. This process is usually in the form of a self-propagating idea, phrase, 'meme', or manner of thinking that circulates from person to person, so that all perceptions and cognitive processes are to some extent shaped and filtered by this way of thinking or 'ethos'. It is unlikely that dysfunctional management will result in a well-balanced, sound ethos.

CULTURE, ETHOS, ETHICS, BALANCE AND JUDGEMENT

The factors revealed in examining this competency are diagnostic of the state of mind of the organisation and the way it sees itself. Ideas are weighed against the perceptions people believe the organisation values. This organisational cognitive consistency or 'state of mind' is shaped by the dominant coalition. These values take on the force of self-propagating ideas, phrases, 'memes', or manner of thinking that spiral outward and downward from person to person and all perceptions and cognitive processes are to some extent shaped and filtered by this way of thinking or 'ethos'. The collection of images, ideas, examples and actions that managers draw upon becomes the substance of their managerial repertoire. Organisations having an ethos with poor ethics (competency one), poor judgement (competency four) and dysfunctional cognitive capabilities (competency five) are unlikely to construct and maintain a culture of safety.

Competency 6, ethos, is a necessary antecedent to the capacity to construct a culture of safety (competency 7), which in turn is dependent on psychological balance (competency 5), judgement (competency 4), vigilance (competency 3), capacity for foresight (competency 2), and the ethics of the organisation's dominant coalition (competency 1). Each of these high-reliability competencies build on one another, and ther is also a powerful interplay of the theories of habitus, memes, autopoiesis, reflective practice, and prior knowledge.

The salient thread connecting all of these core competencies is 'communication and messaging in an organisational setting', which can frame assumptions that then guide actions and decisions regarding constructing a habitus of safety. Certain messages persist and take on and make sense of assumption sets. For example, 'the cultural attitude to regulation' is an echo of the problems we saw in the competency dealing with ethos, (competency 6), and with the need for foresight, (competency two), and with vigilance, (competency three). The following data also illustrates the strong relationship of this competency with ethics, competency one.

IDEAS ABOUT ORGANISATIONAL CULTURE

Evidence from each of the cases examined in this book reveals that there was a conflict between commercial priorities and a commitment to safety. This resulted in an organisational culture where safety was seen by the dominant coalitions as a cost item rather than an investment. Perhaps one of the clearest examples was the Civil Aviation Authority (CAA) Directorate of Aviation Safety Regulation (DASR) head, George Macionis, who was quoted in the media reacting to events (the Monarch, MiG-15, and Nomad crashes, and the new air traffic control configurations that lowered possible intersect conflicts between light and commercial aircraft, known as TAAATS [The Australian Advanced Air Traffic System] and AMATS [Airspace Management and Air Traffic Services]). He said that the CAA would compartmentalise the safety-related compartments into one compartment. His language, strategies and assumptions all subverted the construction of an organisational ethos needed to ensure safety. Organisational culture cannot be deliberately compartmentalised at a CEO's whim or directive. Marcionis' solution is no solution since it would guarantee to bury the problems under even deeper layers of bureaucracy. The press claimed at the time that the CAA demonstrated how some of these 'compartments' were failing safety (monitoring and surveillance), even to the point of describing the CAA as 'out of control'.

Several orthodox writers in organisational and management theory are concerned about its language (Burrell & Morgan, 1979; Griffin et al, 1998; Zohar & Marshall, 1994), which has been characterised as mechanistic, rational, transactional, if-then, controlling, and also that the language used plays an active part in shaping a world in its own image (Morgan, 1986; Hayles, 1994; Black, 1962). This is significant because the language of an organisation can amplify or mitigate memes. It requires little imagination to visualise the effect on an organisation of the meme for 'priority of production' amplified, for example, by the organisational and management theories suggested by Sun Tzu in the 'Art of War' (Clavell, 1910, 1981; Wee Chou Hou, 1991). Meme theory suggests that dangerous pathogenic messages can survive in certain conditions (organisations) and alter meanings sufficiently to reconstruct human behaviour compliant with these robust messages. Under such conditions ethical behaviour can be severely compromised.

This view is congruent with that of Schein (1993) who says we can simplify the notion of organisational culture by looking at three levels – firstly its artefacts, the visible behaviours and processes such as language, socialisation rules, documents and office layouts - the things you first notice when you first enter an organisation. Secondly, its espoused beliefs, the stated strategies, the purpose, and its philosophies - often traceable back to the founder or CEO of the organisation. Thirdly, the underlying assumptions which drive behaviour, the unconscious, taken-for-granted values and perceptions which are always there but rarely considered because 'that's the way it's always done around here'. Each of these were found to be dysfunctional in the cases that follow.

CASES OF FAILURES OF HIGH-RELIABILITY CULTURE

Examples of memetic dysfunction (dysfunctional instructions embedded in the organisational brain) are evident in the case data that follows, (Blackmore, 1999). One organisation saw itself as immune from accidents (as in the Longford case). Another set about confusing individual memory of an accident by evoking memes and demonstrating that organisational cultures mirror the neurotic state of mind of the organisation's top executives (in the Westralia case).

Paradoxically, orthodox management and administrative procedures often contribute to the dangerous meme set in an organisation's communications network because they do not adequately explain and illuminate critical high-reliability communications issues such as assumption surfacing and the consequential organisational 'state of mind'. They do not recognise unexamined assumptions because they are memetic (virus-like) and largely invisible. Procedures that place administrative reliance on manuals, for example, can lead to a sequence of misinformation where prior knowledge is not utilised because it does not appear in the manual, or it is in the manual and not implemented. This was seen in the Esso Gas Plant accident at Longford. The Commission points to the problems of management working from a set of seriously deficient and erroneous orthodox assumptions which proved be pathogenic. The Commission observed that: 'Reliance placed by Esso on its OIMS for the safe operation of the plant was misplaced.' The Commission observed that the accident on 25 September 1998 demonstrated that important components of Esso's orthodox system of management were either defective or not implemented. Paragraph 13.42 of the Longford Royal Commission Report (1999) goes on to say:

Longford [communication, knowledge management, administrative procedures, documentation, failure to utilise information, failure to utilise information learned from previous accidents] 13.42. If the implementation of OIMS by Esso was to be measured by the adequacy of its operating procedures, they were deficient and failed to conform with the ECI Upstream Guidelines or with the OIMS Systems Manual. If it was to be measured by reference to the actions and decisions of those persons who were attempting to resolve the process upsets on 25 September 1998, they were also deficient. The deficiencies were in the manner in which Esso dealt with the acquisition and retention of knowledge. This involved its training system, its operating procedures, its documentation and data system, and its communication system. (Report of the Longford Royal Commission. 1999 p200)

Esso management had identified what sort of orthodox risk assessment management needed to be done at Longford. As the Commission points out, they were either not implemented or were defective.

It ought to have been obvious through the Longford plant's knowledge management system that separate procedures were required under normal circumstances and in a period of change. For example, paragraphs 13.46-48 of the Longford Royal Commission report show that 'planned hazard prevention' was addressed in a range of orthodox operating procedural manuals and knowledge management requirements. However, many of these were simply not implemented or were.

Longford [knowledge management, hazard identification] 13.46The highest level required planned hazard identification and risk assessment to take place in various circumstances. These assessments embraced Periodic Risk Assessments (PRAs) which were to take place at intervals specified by RAMS; Quantitative Risk Assessments (QRAs) which were detailed risk studies carried out as needed to assess specific major hazard risks; and triggered risk assessments which were scenario-based assessments prompted by the happening of particular events.

13.47 At the next level there were hazard identification techniques to be used by employees and management in the course of operations.

These included the use of check lists, analyses based upon the question "what if?" and hazard and operability (HAZOP) studies, either prospective or retrospective, conducted when the need appeared to identify particular hazards involved in the operation of the plants.

13.48 At the lowest level there were hazard identification "tools" to be used by operators to identify hazards and mitigate risk on a daily basis. These tools, or techniques, primarily comprised "step back 5x5' (stepping back 5 paces and pausing for five minutes to reflect upon likely hazards) and task analysis. (Report of the Longford Royal Commission. 1999:201-202)

The orthodox knowledge management system failed. The issue is not one of the existence of the tools needed to ensure safety but an enduring mental model that subverted the use of these tools.

This theme echoes the primary premise of this book suggested by Turner (1978, 1997) that prior knowledge exists within and organisation and if heeded could prevent accidents, for disasters are eminently preventable. For example, the Moura accident was found by the Commission of Enquiry to be a 'carbon copy' of previous accidents (Braithwaite 1985:34-8). Curiously the organisation concerned was also BHP. For example, the Moura No.2 underground coal mine explosion occurred because vital information was rendered ineffective, both by an inadequate information processing system (failure of prior knowledge in particular) and by a culture that neutralised it. The culture systematically discredited indicators that something might be wrong (Hopkins, 1999).

The Commission found that if BHP had learnt and applied the lessons of those earlier disasters the most recent in the series would not have occurred. If BHP had attended to the lessons of earlier coal mine explosions, eleven men would not have lost their lives at Moura in 1994. The lessons of Moura must be learnt once and for all, so that this totally avoidable industrial carnage stops.

. . .

there was no enduring intention to manage safety at Moura and in the Longford example, and here lies the central focus of this competency. Critical HAZOP exercises would have been diligently carried out if the organisation took safety seriously. BHP has a long record of such accidents. One of the four workers seriously burnt in a gas explosion, at BHP Billiton's iron plant in Port Hedland on 19 May, 2004, died in Royal Perth Hospital with burns to his lungs and 95 per cent of his body. Hours after the gas explosion, a 19-year-old Westrac apprentice died from head injuries at the company's mine site near Newman when he was struck by heavy equipment. Another worker was killed earlier in May at the company's Nelson Point facility. Earlier, the Iron Baron had foundered off the Tasmanian coast, spilling hundreds of tons of oil and threatening wildlife.

This disconnection between espoused values and actual practice is always diagnostic of underlying persistent ideas (memes) about how things should be done in an organisation. Hopkins (1999) suggests the whole problem can be summed up as one of organisational inattention. The attention of the organisation was simply not focused on the control of catastrophic risk. It is not difficult to detect these latent pathogens during a rigorous audit. What presents to the organisational consultant or psychologist is evidence of actual hazard management practices. These can be examined for memes. It is also possible to make a clear connection between organisation attitudes, actual practice and the role of the regulator. The regulator (even an internal one) should have resolutely intervened and insisted on these prospective HAZOP procedures being carried out. Hopkins (1999) observes that such organisations:

...must be rigorously audited to ensure that they are working as intended. Auditors must find ways of pulling the triggers to see if what is intended to happen really does happen. Moreover, someone must audit the auditors to ensure that they are doing their job thoroughly. There is an important role here for the inspectorate. Inspectorates must also be willing to enforce the requirements of safety management plans and be prepared to prosecute when they find serious cases of non-compliance with plans that are supposed to be in operation.

The problem is confounded by administrative procedures set up to deal with change that simultaneously focus on the 'bottom line'. There is an echo here of Turner's (1978, 1997) premise that risk is increased in an atmosphere where the 'priority of production' supersedes concern for safety. Soucek (1993) makes the point that different circumstances require different competencies. The following paragraphs from the Longford Royal Commission Report (1999:13.65-68) suggest that risk assessment procedures based on orthodox management principles do not prevent accidents. They make the point that change (both long term and short term) requires a risk assessment of the change and it is management's responsibility to ensure that such a risk assessment encompasses change itself and the consequences of change. It should be diagnostic of potential hazards that organisational memory does not inform situational risk accompanied by change.

Longford

[administrative procedures, change can result in invalidation of prior risk assessments]

13.65. Attached to and forming part of Element 7 was Esso's Management of Change Philosophy dated August 1993 (the philosophy). In the philosophy, Esso recognised that change was "necessary and desirable" as part of the operation of a facility but also recognised that "changes potentially invalidate prior risk assessments and can create new risks, if not managed diligently".

. . .

[risk assessment requirements specified]

13.66. The philosophy contained management of change procedures to be followed in undertaking, amongst other things, any modification or addition to an existing facility. These procedures required any permanent change to an existing facility to be accompanied by a risk assessment of the change, consistent with the procedures in OIMS Element 2, "Risk assessment and management". The primary purpose of such an assessment was to determine the impact of the proposed change on the safe operation of the facility.

[risk factors not converted into operational procedures and also masked by 'management speak']

13.67. However, OIMS Element 2 did not identify any procedures for risk assessment associated with management of change. The only reference to this topic was in the following terms: "Production Technology operates within a management of change procedure which is consistent with the EAL management of change philosophy."

[espoused values subverted by poor compliance, contempt for regulations, cultural attitude to regulation, failure of organisational memory, failure to provide safe environment, failure to utilise information,]

13.68. Moreover, Esso management neither made any attempt to define the breadth or scope of any risk assessment study to be undertaken to comply with management of change procedures - OIMS Element 7 (Management of change) nor OIMS Element 2 (Risk assessment and management) (Report of the Longford Royal Commission. 1999)

. . .

The critical organisational change process occurring at the time of the accidents did not seem to be taken into account in relation to safety. Slovic (1973) cautions against overconfidence. It seems that BHP-Esso's management were otherwise preoccupied. BHP understood the paradox that change increases risk and at the same time invalidates any prior risk assessment.

In spite of all the lessons learned, risk is situation specific. Reason (1991) made this clear in *Human Error* when he observed that managers should not ignore the situation-related factors. This is discussed in more detail in the next competency, which examines how we might better understand the salience of the particular situation and its context (awareness of organisational and incident factors peculiar to particular hazardous environments)

Manipulation of memes is all too easily accomplished by the dominant coalition in an organisation, in the immediate aftermath of an accident. Paragraphs 51 and 52 of the Westralia Enquiry point to the capacity for behaviour after a catastrophe to be both autopoietic and have the ability to shape witness and employee behaviour through very subtle meme-based manipulation. All that is needed is the ability to confuse or cloud individual memory by evoking resonating appeals to prior meme-based triggers such as 'loyalty' to the service. The level of psychological skill needed to do this is minimal. Kets de Vries (1984) suggests that organisational configurations (cultures) seem to broadly *mirror* the psychodynamic neurotic configuration of the top executives. So, if top executives feel the need to mask their own errors or role in causing or contributing to a preventable accident, this is one tool at their disposal. It is subtle and can be seen at work in the Westralia case ((Department of Defence, 1999) in the debriefings that occurred after the accident where evidence was possibly contaminated.

Westralia

[pseudopsychology, motivation, self-congratulatory discourse, shared beliefs post-hoc forensic recording]

51. An informal 'de-fusing' was undertaken through the CO addressing the ship's company on return to Fleet Base West on the evening of the incident. An information session was conducted for the whole ship's company at STIRLING on 6 May, and group 'de-briefing' was conducted at STIRLING on 7 and 8 May. This de-briefing focused on each individual's recounting of their activities and was done in groups of about 30 personnel who had shared similar experiences on the day. The feedback from ship's company was mostly favourable, although some felt it was of little use and others attended against their will.

52. There was some suggestion that de-briefing conducted before personnel had had the opportunity to record their recollection of events, may have exacerbated the process of 'contamination' of evidence that can occur through witnesses discussing matters among themselves. (Westralia Executive Summary p10)

There is a strong attitudinal element running through much of the material coded from the various commissions of Enquiry. These extracts continually point to a cultural attitude to regulations, as is evident in the Westralia data in paragraph 61 of the Enquiry. The 'errors' referred to in paragraphs 51 and 52 above involve an attitude to regulations that had been subverted by a 'she'll be right' meme. Whatever brought about the acceptance of inventory acquisition outside regulations had evolved with implicit permission from higher up in the chain of command or it would not have occurred.

[cultural attitude to regulations]

61. The new flexible fuel hoses were fitted by a subcontractor to ADI Limited during March and April 98. The flexible fuel hose change to the main engines was a configuration change which bypassed the prescribed processes. It was not approved by appropriate authorities

and did not comply with Lloyd's Register of Shipping requirements. (Westralia Executive Summary p11)

The RAN later placed the blame for the faulty hose with the contractor. It seems to have escaped their notice that if ordinary Naval regulations had been complied with the accident would not have happened, because the contractor would have supplied to specifications.

Memetic dysfunction evident in the case data illustrates that organisational cultures mirror the neurotic state of mind of the organisation's top executives and that orthodox management and administrative procedures often contribute to the dangerous meme set. Critical assumptions can be ignored and unexamined when invisible, virus like, memes shape an organisation's 'way of seeing'.

Commission reports into fatal accidents point to the problems of management working from a set of seriously deficient and erroneous orthodox assumptions, which proved be pathogenic, resulting in a range of dysfunctional behaviours such as, prior knowledge not being utilised, and implicit permission from dominant coalitions that it is acceptable to bypass safety regulations. People and evidence can also be manipulated by dominant coalitions who have the authority and influence to evoke memes, such as the 'loyalty meme', so top executives can mask their own errors or role in causing or contributing to a preventable accident and pass the accident off as 'systemic failure'.

DIAGNOSTIC TOOLS TO IMPROVE A HIGH-RELIABILITY CULTURE

An organisation's 'way of seeing' determines its capacity to construct a culture of safety. A range of limiting factors related to an organisation's propensity to autopoiesis can be detected in its values and behaviour. These subversive factors can be diagnosed by analysing the organisation's meme content along with its espoused and actual behaviour along several specific dimensions. Once diagnosed these factors can be turned around to enable the organisation to construct a culture of safety. It is an error of interpretation of orthodox management principles to attempt to construct a 'culture of safety' simply by imposing change. It becomes apparent in analysing the case reports above that accidents were associated with organisations in a 'process of change'. Blackmore (1999) pointed out that dysfunctional instructions can be embedded in the organisational brain, and that the configuration, or way of seeing', an organisation adopts is largely a mirror of its dominant coalition.

Therefore, the key to high-reliability and safety appears to be to purposively configure an appropriately focused 'safety' culture, rather than simply change organisational structures (which most organisations call 'change'). Changing structure amplifies complexity as problem elements of an organisation simply change their geography and do so under pressure - which itself tends to further complicate factors related to safety; signalling the need for management to be even more vigilant and focused on safety, and guard against unexamined assumptions entering the organisation as memes that may mirror their own neuroses.

THINKING ABOUT ORGANISATIONAL CULTURE

Organisational failure extends into the most sophisticated of high-reliability organisations. For example, it was reported on the internet on June 8, 2004, that such were the worries about the Beagle mission to Mars, ahead of its launch, that one leading member of the European Space Agency (ESA) said that he had wondered whether it might have been better cancelled. Professor David Southwood, Director of Space Science at ESA, said the Enquiry had found that "no single event led to failure and no single individual made a bad decision. However, failure was institutional (systemic). We were working in a system which wasn't right, where the organisational structures weren't right, and people didn't have the right level of empowerment, authority or resource."

Professor Southwood1 had absorbed the dominant coalition's meme of the priority of a launch deadline. When he started his job in the summer of 2001, he examined the Beagle 2 project and initially decided that it should not take place at all. "By the autumn I had accepted (the meme) that Beagle was going to go," he said. "Maybe I should never have accepted that. But frankly I would have had to have been a different person for me to take that final decision."

As in the NASA example above, other examples serve to confirm the case data findings. In the Westralia case the Coroner found that the accident was preventable. The Kursk accident was found to be the result of a failure to construct a culture of safety. The Russian Navy conducted its affairs with complete disregard to prior knowledge and ethics in an environment that mirrored the values of its dominant coalition.

Westralia Coronial Enquiry

When Western Australian Coroner Alistair Hope released the findings from the WA CORONERS INQUEST - HMAS WESTRALIA FIRE, in December 2003.2 he severely censured the Navy for ignoring expert advice, using wrong procedures which bypassed safety checks, and not adequately monitoring work carried out by defence firm ADI (Australian Defence Industries). ADI later faced charges that it contravened section 19(1)(a) of the *Occupational Health and Safety (Commonwealth Employment) Act 1991*.3 Coroner Hope said the tragedy could have been avoided.

These behaviours are all characteristic of 'ways of seeing' and point to a culture where 'safety' is espoused at the 'senior officer' level but needs to be reconstructed at this level so that the necessary values are transmitted as positive memes to the workface rather than the ambiguous ones seen in the book data.

Safety cannot be consistently constructed through issuing orders. It has to be a 'top-down' value set.

The Naval Board Enquiry gave the impression that Midshipman Megan Pelly, 22, had disobeyed a lawful command when she ran into the engine room at the time of the blaze, had panicked and "contributed to her own demise". However, Coroner Alistair Hope ruled that Pelly and the three other sailors were ordered into the engine room and died in circumstances where they faced great danger while trying to save the ship and their fellow navy personnel. One can only construe that the Naval Board was more intent on reducing damage and embarrassment to the Navy than in providing an accurate assessment of what happened on the ship.

The Bulletin, Bell (2003), reported that 'there were concerted attempts by Navy personnel to deliberately withhold key information from the BOI, sufficient to suggest that the Enquiry itself was little more than a sham.' He reports that a four-year investigation into the circumstances surrounding the fire, and the Enquiry into it, uncovered the following developments:

* A second former crew member of the Westralia has claimed she was encouraged to withhold information from the BOI if asked about the nature of her work on flexible fuel lines the night before the ship sailed. This work had involved bending the hoses back and forth.

* A retired former warrant officer has claimed that in order to reassure crew members that their bending of the hoses had not caused the fire, the navy secretly made a video showing a length of flexible hose being bent back and forth and then passing a pressure test.

Bell (2003) points out that although flexible hoses should never have been fitted to the Westralia, no mention was made in any BOI evidence that crew members had been bending the hoses back and forth or in half in an attempt to fix the Westralia's fuel leaks the night before it sailed. The Coronial Enquiry found that former RAN marine technician Melissa Munday claimed she was told by a senior officer to lie to the BOI if she was asked about attempting to fix the leaking fuel lines or using shifting spanners to carry out that work. When asked if she had told the truth to the board of Enquiry, she replied: "No I did not. We were told if the ADI lawyers ask you if you worked on the fuel line, to say no because we were unqualified. If you are asked if you used shifting spanners to repair the leaks, say no. I was told to keep my mouth shut about [the fact that] the fuel lines that burst were the ones that we all had a go at bending backwards and forwards. 'Be careful what you say', we were told both individually and as a group. We were told not to say too much about the fuel lines, or anything that wouldn't look good. "We were told that we had to keep in mind that the RAN was who we were working for, and we were told the Navy had to be looked after" (Bulletin, Vol 121:20).

Curiously, in spite of this and other witness testimony, the Coroner found no evidence that the Navy had misled a board of Enquiry (BOI) or pressured witnesses to lie. However, such witness statements and other revelations made at the Coronial Enquiry tends to confirm the finding that the meme responsible for acceptance of inventory acquisition outside regulations had pathogenically evolved with implicit permission from higher up in the chain of command or it would not have occurred.

The Navy pleaded 'systemic failure', however, implicit permission from individual senior officers created the attitude that it was acceptable to bypass safety regulations. It also confirms theoretical views, such as Kets de Vries (1984), who suggests that organisational configurations (cultures) broadly *mirror* the psychodynamic neurotic configuration of the top executives. So, if top executives feel the need to mask their own errors or role in causing or contributing to a preventable accident, they have the authority, influence and motivation to do so.

Severe consequences followed this accident. One of the people giving evidence to the Coronial Enquiry was the mother of Matthew Liddell, aged 29, a survivor of the Westralia fire who committed suicide. Dulcie Liddell said her son, a marine technician who suffered smoke inhalation in the fire, later suffered severe depression and post-traumatic stress disorder. This death and others prompted a Senate Enquiry into military justice and mistreatment of Australian Defence Force personnel after The Australian published a series of stories on military suicides last year (Meade, 2004).

The Kursk

Another salient example of failure to construct a culture of safety where the subsequent 'way of seeing' resulted in an organisation's safety culture being subverted by its dominant coalition is the sinking of the Russian submarine, the Kursk which sank in the Barents Sea on the 12 of August 2000 as the result of two explosions. 118 men were lost. Christine Middap (2000) reported that the context of the accident is set against a long history of cultural malaise in the Russian Navy. The ability of the crew to deal with emergencies was questioned after evidence of drug use among sailors, lack of navy training and theft of military equipment. In November 1999 an admiral and several senior officers were charged with selling warships for personal profit. Others had sold warships for scrap metal. In one incident conscripts on an island in the Far East starved to death when their rations failed to arrive. It is reported that conditions on Russian ships are so bad that it is common for seamen to sell vital operating equipment to survive. The issue of compliance and other competencies, such as prior knowledge and ethics are also at play in this in this incident.

Middap also suggested that rescue submersibles rely on second-hand batteries. Her important claim in terms of this book is that authorities were aware of this when they steadfastly refused the offer of high-tech Western equipment for rescue of the sailors. Russian Navy officials admitted that batteries on one of the unmanned rescue vessels, the Priz, last for only two hours even though a single rescue operation takes four or five hours. The rescue submersibles were fitted with old batteries for reasons of economy. The Priz almost succeeded in locking on but had to return immediately to the surface because its batteries were flat.'

This mishap further demonstrates the central tenets (managerial failure to address prior knowledge, competencies, compliance) of the book' argument. It also signals the critical nature of *ethical* practices in hazard situations. Navy officials were prone to unethical behaviour in which they exercised scant concern for the welfare of their sailors and lied about the time that the accident occurred and then spent the next week offering conflicting accounts, half-truths and long silences (McMahon, 2000). The Defence Minister, Igor Sergeyev, denied responsibility, would not accept outside help, blamed a collision with another vessel for the accident, and persisted with a line of secrecy and misinformation while men died at the bottom of the ocean (tapping was heard from inside the hull for two days - Monday 12 and Tuesday 14).

These examples triangulate well with the book findings indicating the characteristics of such cultures (for example, the Royal Australian Navy, and BHP and its subsidiaries) that exhibit a dysfunctional 'way of seeing', discussed in the Literature and Case data sections of this competency. However, these factors can be turned around to create a culture of safety if diagnosed early enough.

Evidence from each of the cases examined in this book revealed that even in healthy cultures there is a tendency to 'blame and shame' which ignores the fact that failures often arise from levels of complexity that human beings cannot cope with rather than irresponsibility or wickedness. The research revealed that many individuals and organisations simply cannot assimilate and apply the vast amounts of technical knowledge they may need, and regulatory demands may just add to the knowledge burden. Fox (2000) suggests that this accounts for the increasing interest in 'decision support', 'workflow' and other computer technologies to help deliver complex services.

Another compelling perspective to emerge from the data is that the greater the pressure on 'performance' the more demotivated and likely to habituate hazards front line operational staff become. Sennett (1998) re-iterates the critical importance of people working within an organisation and identifies the 'performance versus loyalty' paradox. He suggests that organisations offering less loyalty to their workforce, while depending on their ever-increasing productivity, face managing a workforce demotivated and alienated by the environment within the organisation.

Relatively stable government organisations such as the CAA and the Australian Navy are prone to the development and persistence of memes, many of which are dangerous and destructive. It is possible to identify and replace dangerous memes, provided they are recognised and the impetus comes from the dominant coalition. However, the literature suggests it is just this group which is usually the source of the most dangerous memes and is most persistent in holding on to them (Blackmore, 1999). Memes are most easily detected and audited in the communications and corporate symbols which characterise an organisation.

Deeply entrenched memes are revealed during periods of change (Blackmore, 1999; Brodie, 1996; Dennet, 1993). Change forces an organisation to rediscover its foundations. The elaboration to structure and form becomes more pronounced the further up the structure one goes. The carriage of memes into daily operational usage subverts examination of assumptions and therefore the capacity to examine organisational foundations. This results in superficial change, where only the names on the doors are changed.

Organisational memes make it difficult to make the deep cultural changes to values, which are essential to turn around unsafe organisations. To remind the reader of one of the examples of memes discussed in the Literature Review, language such as 'that's how we do things here' is a simple phrase but a deadly meme with a powerful cultural force acting as a direct counter to the examination of core assumptions. Such memes signal a persistence of vision or way of seeing the world of the organisation. The fact that such mindsets are reinforced by orthodox management practices renders them difficult to unravel. Insiders are often blind to these factors because they are immersed in them.

While working as a management consultant the author became aware of many phrases which have memetic force and signal cultural malaise in an organisation. These phrases signal acceptance of unexamined assumptions and fear. They get in the way of thinking and learning. They prefigure resistance to change, uncertainty about the future, dislike for fellow employees, mistrust of authority, and distrust of outsiders, and are therefore diagnostic.

The CAA for example, did not like or trust the government, the International Civil Aviation Organisation, the Airlines, or the Bureau of Air Safety Investigation, nor did it welcome public scrutiny. It tended to close itself off from these stakeholders.

Examples of corrosive phrases often found in the communications channels of organisations such as the CAA are:

"We've always done it this way."

"It's too expensive."

"Not in the budget."

"Realistically..."

"In principle I agree, but..."

"Too much paperwork."

"It's not our policy."

"This needs more study."

"They won't do anything about it anyway."

"They don't care."

"They don't want to know."

"We have enough complications already."

"There are no clear answers."

"That's just a matter of opinion."

"That's just your opinion."

"What would they know anyway."

"We do it this way for the sake of consistency."

"Redundancy is built in."

HIGH-RELIABILITY DIAGNOSTIC QUESTIONS

To examine and turn around an organisation's 'ways of seeing' in regard to safety one needs to ask diagnostic questions, those that point to relationships with other competencies. For example:

1. Is there conflict between organisational reality and the espoused organisational environment? Does the organisation preserve the status quo whilst espousing new values? Are the new values, such as putting safety first, modelled at the level of the dominant coalition? Is there evidence that management values provoke conflicting drivers such as operational efficiency and customer relationships which tend to be elitist, when the dominant coalition espouses collaboration?

2. Is the organisation predisposed to stability and stable structures? Has it constructed stable structures and implemented quality systems which don't fundamentally change the way it does things, which then results in making the organisation more rigid and less flexible? Is its structure layered and inappropriate to its purpose with rigid staff classifications?

. . .

3. Are its rules and policies linked to stability, or the flexibility needed to 'detect safety signals'? Is the organisation inclined to introduce systems, rules and procedures to enhance predictability? Has it gone too far by moving towards autopoiesis from a chaos environment or is there, perhaps, a strong push to standardise procedures?

4. What is the relationship and impact of the organisation on its staff, acquired knowledge and communication? For example, if it is an autopoietic organisation is there evidence that makes it clear that it does not perceive its impact on staff, customers and other stakeholders.

This chapter suggests that if dysfunctional managerial behaviour is allowed to shape the habitus of a high-reliability organisation by subverting the 'intention' or capacity to establish a culture of safety, then the organisation will evolve dysfunctional 'ways of seeing', and allow the introduction of dangerous persistent ideas - 'memes' - that will mitigate the organisation's systemic capacities for managing safety. It will result in disabling an ethos of safety, if one already exists, and it will subvert the creation of such an ethos, thereby reducing its hazard management capabilities. Creation of such a habitus or culture, reinforced by immobilising self-preservation memes, will drive the organisation to close itself off from its stakeholders.

A culture or ethos of safety does not appear by happenstance or government legislation. It is constructed and nurtured by the dominant coalition and shaped over time by example and deep and enduring cultural values. Turning around a workforce lacking in trust, commitment, and stability becomes a critical priority for managers of organisations where safety should be paramount. The implication for meme management and the management of dysfunctional and often autopoietic organisational configurations becomes critical in high-reliability organisations. However, it must begin with the dominant coalition because the messages and the morphology are connected and shape the organisation's capacity to perform its core function.

1. http://science.newsfactor.com/story.xhtml?story_title=Organisational-Failures-To-Blame-for-Loss-of-Beagle----Enquiry&story_id=24191&category=innv

2. The WA Coroner convened an inquest at the West Australian Coroners' Court on April 28, 2003 to enquire into new evidence which was alleged to have emerged following the Board of Enquiry. This coronial inquest was separate from the Board of Enquiry (BOI) conducted in 1998 by Navy. Several legal matters arose in connection with the fire on HMAS Westralia on 5 May 1998, including Commonwealth v ADI Limited, a claim in tort, contract and under the provisions of the Trade Practices Act 1974.

3. WA Court Of Petty Sessions, Friday, 27 February, 2004.(Comcare, Australian Government, Feb. 2004)

18. COMPETENCY 8: SALIENCE AND CONTEXT: ORGANISATIONAL AND INCIDENT FACTORS PECULIAR TO HAZARDOUS ENVIRONMENTS

THIS CHAPTER EXAMINES THE COMPETENCY OF RECOGNIZING AND adapting to the specific context and nuances of each situation. It highlights the importance of situational awareness, flexibility, and the ability to tailor responses to the unique challenges and risks of each environment.

"We make guilty of our disasters the sun, the moon and the stars, as if we were villains by necessity, knaves, thieves and treachers by spherical predominance."

King Lear, Act1 Scene2

WHAT IS HIGH-RELIABILITY SALIENCE?

This chapter examines the set of competencies considered most relevant to managerial capacity to perform in high-reliability organisations. As in the two previous chapters it adopts the framework of the modified grounded theory approach set out in sections 4.2 and 4.3 of the Data Analysis chapter: interpretation of the concept as it is used in this book followed by a consideration of the relationships between the competency under consideration and the other key competencies. The chapter then poses a set of generative questions and a review of the literature salient to the concept and complementary to the main literature review. An elaboration of the insights revealed to theory is attempted and other data from the book is then used to ground the theory.

This chapter emphasises the managerial need to understand the salience of a particular situation rather than have a generic, 'off the shelf' approach to hazard management. It also identifies the need to perform in a particular setting and the capacity to bring together skills from different areas of expertise.

The capacity to adapt and adapt again, and the need to value intuition are central to the capacity to perform. Mitroff (1993) captures this notion when he observes that military planners are prone to anticipating future strategies and tactics without considering how the enemy will adapt to minimise the effectiveness of those strategies. This is the problem-solution, one step process, that is congruent with the human tendency to simplify. It fails to anticipate the problems that *result* from the original solutions.

The issue of trust in one's intuition, as well as that of others such as front line workers, is critical to understanding the competencies outlined in this chapter. Siu (1978) said that the, 'does it add up?, 'does it sound OK?, and 'does it feel right?' questions CEOs pose for themselves cannot be adequately addressed by rational or scientific knowledge. Only intuition can address the second and third questions. Siu's proposition is more profound than first appears. This begins with experiential brain patterning, which then becomes an operational schemata, accessed by a huge index established through expertise, using intuition. It is far more than a hunch because each person with operational experience in anything has a unique set of patterns that informs his or her intuition in a crisis (Mitroff, 1993).

It's relevance for the following three competencies is that front line expertise in unbounded, unstructured hazardous situations that don't present as problems that have structured solutions, may be largely unconscious and should not be discounted by managers. Operational intuition should be valued. Competencies that are salient to the situation, appropriate to the setting, and bring together a multidisciplinary schemata of problem-solving perceptions may not be available to central office dominant coalitions.

Salience of a particular situation is marked by safety specific insights into that particular situation (understanding relevant task, particular and site-specific incident factors). This insight must also necessarily precede competency nine, 'performance in a particular situation'. The competency demands that a person in a particular situation has the technical and human skills needed to interpret signals from the situation that may indicate real and potential hazards. Salience is a psychological 'way of seeing' in a particular situation.

Factors identified under this competency indicated the need to both foresee, identify and react to accident conditions, active failures in progress, and cause and effect phenomena, to be able to understand and interpret detailed operational and procedural guidelines, and to possess the diagnostic skills necessary to identify systems failures. The various Commission of Enquiry determined that there was evidence of a range of shortcomings that fall within this core competency. The following descriptors indicating understanding of situational salience were derived from the HyperRESEARCH analysis of the five cases:

HyperRESEARCH Salience of a Particular Situation Descriptors

accident conditions, active failures, cause and response, cause immediate, cause of accident, detailed guidelines, diagnostic failure, failure to enforce regulations, falsifying maintenance reports, falsifying records, poor information verification, inadequate information gathering, insufficient information, perfunctory inspection, inconsequential and sub-standard auditing, signifi-

cant reliance on personal experience, a dangerous reliance on oral communication, and a failure to identify critical situational risk factors

SALIENCE, ETHOS, FORESIGHT AND CULTURE

Understanding the salience of the particular situation is closely related to foresight, competency two and related to organisational factors such as ethos, competency six, and competency seven, constructing a culture of safety. If lessons have been learned from previous accidents then future accident scenarios ought to be reasonably foreseeable, at the same site or closely related sites. This competency is necessary to competency nine because performance in a particular situation or setting requires prior understanding of its salience. Both are necessary to competency ten because the schemata needed for multidisciplinary performance require a clear grasp of both salience and setting.

IDEAS ABOUT SALIENCE

Each high-reliability operational site and interface carries within it a large set of potential accident factors. Reason (1990) calls these factors 'latent errors'. Reason and Maurino (1995) observe that major accidents occur when latent errors, arising mainly in the managerial and organisational spheres, combine adversely with local triggering events (weather, location etc) and with the active failures of individuals at the sharp end (errors and procedural violations).

The latent failures at Moura, for example, were seen in the deficiencies in communications. The local triggering event was the heating, and the active failures were the failures of individual managers to apply their minds diligently to the possibility that a heating event might be occurring at the time of the explosion.

These factors were almost identical to the accident conditions at Longford. The company had apparently learned nothing from the Moura experience. Reason's analysis would suggest that actions or inactions of individuals were a part of the chain of events that led to disaster, but he would also conclude that focusing on these active failures of individuals is not as useful from the point of view of accident prevention as focusing on the salient latent or organisational failings involved.

This book suggests that part of the cause of accidents and the inability to make situation salient insights into possible accident scenarios is because there is an unhealthy anxiety about the loss of power at the highest levels of many high-reliability organisations. Writing about Sagan's (1993, 1996) perspective on High-reliability Theory and expressing his concern that power elites impose risks on the many for the benefit of the few, Perrow (1999: 369) says, 'the issue was not risk, but power'. Schein (1994) suggests that part of the problem is the inability of managers to acknowledge their own vulnerability and uncertainty and hence to become learners in their organisations. He suggests that this dangerous myth portrays the lone problem solver as hero and that this is amplified by the additional cultural force of 'rugged individualism'. Perrow points out that operators cannot exercise initiative in a decentralised site while at the same time having to comply with centralised rules and guidelines.

Schein cites Karl Deutsch (1996) who said, "power is the ability not to have to learn anything." Deutsch's observation about not learning tends to reinforce the case data that suggests that this competency, understanding the salience of a situation, is readily obscured by those who in fact have the power to act to mitigate accident conditions, for example, by adapting generic site experience or centralised manuals to the present one. According to Schein the competition-based work hierarchy then ultimately becomes the main source of security and status, and higher level managers can be expected to act in a more decisive and controlling manner to express that status.

The problem seems to be that managers either experience managerial inertia (Mitroff, 1993) or ignore prior knowledge (Reason, 2000) and previous experience (Hopkins, 1999) or apply it with hubris in an ill-considered one-size-fits-all manner (Mitroff & Pauchant, 1990; Mitroff & Linstone, 1993), much as they also pull training and technical manuals off the shelf to apply to all situations. These all act as barriers to learning (Turner, 1997). Hopkins (1999:58) points out that, 'The question that management posed for itself that Sunday afternoon was not, should the men go down (into Moura no 2), but what should be done if the men expressed any concerns *about* going down.' Management saw an industrial relations issue not a problem of safety.

This competency demands intellectual application and a certain vulnerability, since learning is involved. The vulnerability needed to learn seems to be at odds with the dominant coalition's reluctance to learn. Again, the data points to psychological factors as contributors to fatal accidents where managers act with superior attitudes and often with arrogance (Kets de Vries, 1984) to dismiss safety critical information readily available from the organisation (Mitroff, 1998). Where people are just another resource, rather than a prime factor of concern to management, creating a learning culture from such a set of assumptions becomes very difficult. Hence insight brought about by critical knowledge just does not find its way into decision making.

A significant problem is the dangerous attitude evident in the orthodox risk management literature, which emphasises the organisation's interests in relation to risk assessment by reducing consequences to a frequency count. This quantisation of a disaster's impact has the effect of making an accident nothing more than an annoyance for management. It creates the inference that a formula contains *all* of the consequences, when significant effects on stakeholders and victims are not necessarily accounted for. For example, Ridley (1999:24-25) states:

Once a list of risks within a company has been compiled ... the risks may be put in order of priority in terms of when control action is required, i.e. immediate; short term; medium term; long term on the basis of a ranking of the risks relating to their relative impact on the organisation. Such an assessment should take account of legal, humanitarian and economic considerations. The fundamental equation in any risk assessment exercise is:

Risk magnitude = Frequency (how often?) X Consequence (how big?)

Low frequency, low consequence risks should be retained (i.e. self-financed) within the organisation. Examples include the failure of small electric motors plate glass breakages, and possibly motor vehicle damage accidents (via retention of comprehensive aspects of insurance cover).

Low frequency, high consequence risks should be transferred (usually via insurance contracts). Examples include explosions, and environmental impairment.

High frequency, low consequence risks should be reduced via effective loss control management. Examples include minor injury accidents; pilfering; and damage accidents.

High frequency, high consequence risks should (ideally) be avoided by managing them out of the organisation's risk portfolio. If this appears to be an uneconomic (or unpalatable) solution, then adequate insurance i.e. the risk transfer option must be arranged.

Ridley goes on to develop a risk rating equation based on the risk magnitude equation above in which a multi fatality is allocated 50 points. The inference is, 'insure or transfer the risk'.

There is little in the above quotation to suggest that prevention might be a possible alternative. This arises from the notion that a hazard is not a risk. Hazard is the danger; risk is the likelihood or mathematical probability that an accident will occur. This orthodox approach can induce organisations to assess risk, not necessarily hazard. Essentially, it encourages senior coalitions to gamble with the lives of others while at the same time purporting to account for 'humanitarian' factors.

CASES OF FAILURES OF HIGH-RELIABILITY SALIENCE

The weight of the literature examined is suggestive that not only are notions of hazard, risk, incident, accident, and near miss misunderstood, but that they are site specific, and not likely to be resolved during a crisis by 'head office'. It is critical that learning from prior experience and all other sources needs to be decentralised and adapted to the specific situation where hazard resides.

Mitroff (1998:59) developed a theory that argues for a four dimensional perspective on a problem (a safety related problem) to include the scientific and technical aspects of the problem and the factors that influence it and flow from it; the existential, taken for granted aspects of meaning and purpose; the interpersonal, psychological and social aspects ; and the systemic, dynamic and consequential aspects of an accident. This analysis follows from correct identification of the type of problem at hand, its scale and scope options, a stakeholder analysis, and the management of paradox. Mitroff identifies what he calls the 'one fundamental flaw' to which all serious errors of management can be traced, and that is solving the wrong problem precisely. He blames orthodox management literature for this problem of muddled thinking based on wrong assumptions since it implies managers already know what their most important problems are. Therefore, orthodox management literature is itself a cause of the failure to learn.

The following HyperRESEARCH case extracts illustrate these concerns (salience and orthodox management skills). For example, in the Longford case a range of situation specific issues were raised by the Commission, such as the actual site specific conditions that were salient at the time; the actual on site cause and the responses to the accident conditions; the failure to diagnose latent conditions manifested in hazard signals; the failure to gather and correctly interpret information; and the failure of audits and inspections to reveal situationally specific potentiating accident conditions.

Longford

[accident conditions, active failures, cause and response, cause immediate, cause of accident, detailed guidelines, diagnostic failure, failure to enforce regulations, information verification, information gathering, insufficient information, perfunctory inspection, auditing, situational risk factors]

13.139 The actual procedure for the reporting of incidents was set out in another Esso manual called the Safety Management Manual (SMM). In its introductory paragraph, the SMM stated:

"All incidents, no matter how minor, are to be reported immediately to the worksite supervisor. All incidents are to be recorded on the hard copy Esso Incident Form, regardless of whether the Profs reporting system is used".

The Commission observed that these critical terms were defined in the Safety System manual (SMM). Longford Royal Commission Report (1999:13.140) states, 'Incident' is an unplanned event that caused, or could have caused, injury or damage to personnel, property or the environment which, in the case of injury, involved an Esso employee or contractor, and in the case of damage to property, occurred at a place controlled by Esso or involved Esso property. Paragraph (13.141) states that a 'near-miss' is '...an unintended or unwanted event or circumstance which under slightly different conditions would have resulted in an incident'. Therefore, a 'near-miss' would qualify as an 'incident' for the purpose of SMM incident reporting requirements.

Using a system somewhat similar to Ridley's (1999) impact assessment formula cited above (Risk magnitude = Frequency (how often?) X Consequence (how big?)), the SMM also contained a classification system for ranking incidents according to their seriousness or potential seriousness (13.143). In theory this was to ensure that appropriate resources were directed to investigation and follow-up. Incidents which were classified as serious had to be accompanied by a critical evaluation of all related OIMS systems and critical equipment, to detect weaknesses in such systems or equipment and to ensure preventative action was taken. However, in practice, the Commission found that (13.144) 'the obligation to report incidents was construed narrowly both by Esso management and by operations personnel.'

Process upsets were rarely, if ever, the subject of an incident report, unless they were accompanied by injury to persons or damage to property. Consequently, process upsets that may have signified to qualified and experienced personnel that defective equipment or inappropriate operating conditions or unsafe operating practices were common, were not brought to their attention. The Longford Royal Commission (1999) observed that this resulted in learning opportunities that were lost.

13.146 A pertinent example of such a lost opportunity was the failure of operations personnel to report the cold temperature incident which occurred on 28 August 1998. (Longford Report 198-222)

The critical issue of misinformation and its conjoint interplay with the problem of a failure of prior information (Turner, 1997), was also identified by the Commission (1999:13.96-98) in relation to log books, highlighting the following issues: information verification, information gathering, insufficient information, perfunctory inspection, auditing, reliance on personal experience, reliance on oral communication, and situational risk factors.

13.96 The other method of communication upon handover was through the control room log. This log was kept on the control room desk. Panel operators were required to record in it "the activities that have taken place in their operating areas, during the shift". Those activities included changes made during the shift to key process parameters and the results of such changes, any process or machinery problems encountered, any safety systems or devices defeated (including bypasses in the outside areas) and any controllers that were being operated in manual and the reason why.

13.97 In practice, however, operators did not keep control room logs in accordance with the stated requirements. An examination of the GP1 control room log revealed that entries were usually short and often contained only limited process information. There was inconsistency in the way entries were made and m their subject matter. Process issues, if referred to, often received only scant attention. Standing on their own, log entries were often confusing and incomplete. On frequent occasions, panel operators made no log book entry at all at the conclusion of a shift.

13.98 The log book entries made by the GP1 panel operators leading up to the accident on 25 September 1998, did not contain any reference to the abnormal process conditions occurring in Absorber B. These conditions had been occurring almost constantly from the afternoon of 23 September until the accident.

Verbal communications also failed. The Commission reported (13.94) that the night shift operator, Olsson, should at least have told Ward (the GP1 operator:13.19) about the almost constant occurrence of the Absorber B high level alarm and the TC913 alarm and the fact that such alarms were still active at changeover. The inference is that Ward placed reliance on Olsson's personal experience and oral communication concerning any specific situational risk factors. Olsson did not express concern regarding the continuous alarms.

13.101 At the commencement of the day shift on 25 September 1998, the outgoing GP1 panel operator had an obligation to tell the relieving operator, not only about the cold temperatures in Absorber B, but about the off-scale levels of condensate in that vessel. Both of these conditions had existed for some time. Indeed, the purpose of the handover procedure as a communication tool was to ensure that important process information was passed on. In the same way, Olsson's logbook entries at the conclusion of his shift could have been, and should have been, more informative. They should also have made reference to these matters.

13.103 Had Ward's attention been directed to these matters he may well have taken steps to see that the temperature and level of condensate in Absorber B were more appropriately managed.

The Commission made the point that Ward would not have directed Rawson to close the TRC3B bypass, as he did at 7.30 am, if he had had proper information. On the contrary, it is likely that he would have given Rawson (an area operator with 18 years experience:

13.21) a direction to open rather than close it. The Commission was inclined to the view that Longford was a preventable accident.

13.104 Had the shift handover communications been in accordance with the requirements laid out in the LWMM, reference would certainly have been made to the abnormal conditions in Absorber B and to the fact that the level of condensate in that absorber was still out of control. Similarly, had the control room log book been entered in a proper way, it would have made reference to these matters.

13.105 It may also be observed that the process difficulties experienced during the night shift were also known to the night shift supervisor, Wijgers. He had, during the course of the night shift, spent time with Olsson in the GP1 control room endeavouring to deal with the high levels of condensate in the slug catchers. However, at the change of shift Wijgers made no mention of the abnormal conditions of Absorber B to the relieving supervisor, Visser.

. . .

13.106 As shift supervisors were not primarily responsible for process matters, their obligation to pass on at handover information regarding process upsets was different from that of operators. However, given the degree of Wijgers' personal involvement with the process difficulties experienced on the preceding night shift and his knowledge of the abnormal conditions in Absorber B, he should have passed on this information to the incoming supervisor, Visser.

The 'cause real' for the accident then seems to fall back to management. With examples of poor log bookkeeping, substandard handovers, misinformation, poor verbal communications, the Commission found that these issues all escaped scrutiny by management.

13.107 Shift handovers and logbook entries were used ineffectively In the lead up to the accident on 25 September 1998. Moreover, laxity in the implementation of the handover requirements seems to have escaped scrutiny by management.

The logbooks were not examined in any way by management, nor were they used to monitor the conditions of the process.

13.108 Log book entries were not subjected to any examination either by Longford plant management or by management in Melbourne. They do not appear to have been used by management as a means of monitoring process conditions at the plant nor were they passed on to any person or group in Melbourne for plant surveillance purposes.

The issues identified in the Longford case above (misinformation and communications) of information that should be factually captured and recorded for organisational learning purposes reaches its ultimate deontological demise when the records are falsified for compliance purposes, such as recording correct weights for overloaded aircraft and falsifying maintenance reports, as in the CAA [Seaview] case.

. . .

<u>CAA</u> [falsifying records] Mr Green also directed his pilots in 1992 to create certain documents. The documents were then backdated in order to falsely represent to the CAA that they were the documents used for various flights undertaken by the company. Again Mr Green's denials have been rejected by the Commission. (Seaview Executive Summary p5)

The aircraft was seriously overloaded, and the documentation associated with the flight sought to disguise the overload. (Seaview Executive Summary p31)

[falsifying maintenance reports] Maintenance is a significant overhead. It is required to be undertaken periodically (usually every 100 hours). It is dependent, therefore, upon the accurate recording by pilots of the aircraft's hours in service. There is a temptation to cheat. Mr Green could not resist that temptation. He himself cheated, and he encouraged his pilots to do likewise. Flight times were either understated, or sometimes not recorded at all. (Seaview Executive Summary p5)

DIAGNOSTIC TOOLS TO IMPROVE HIGH-RELIABILITY SALIENCE

A vigilance regime should signify previous incidents, 'near misses', and accidents as important information from which it is possible to learn. These opportunities to learn enable higher awareness of potential accident factors but do not necessarily deal with local triggering events and salient, but very particular and different, factors from those previous incidents. Auditing for potential salient factors must be deliberate and informed by previous events, but at the same time must be situation specific and develop largely from a 'clean slate'.

THINKING ABOUT SALIENCE

The mine that exploded in 1994 (Moura No. 2) had not had a previous explosion, however two adjacent mines had. Hopkins (1999:137) reveals that the mine operator, BHP, had experience of previous mine disasters. There was Moura No. 4 in 1986 and previously at Appin in NSW in 1979. As an organisation, BHP's memory was defective because decentralised responsibility for disaster prevention to mine sites had no central capacity or expertise with respect to disaster prevention. This is an example of an organisation running multiple hazardous operations expecting each one to independently learn the lessons the organisation itself should have noted as 'significant' and disseminated.

On 19 December 2003, news.com.au (The Australian) reported that a two-month naval Enquiry found the May 5, 1998 fire started on board the Westralia after newly-installed flexible fuel hoses burst and sprayed diesel fuel onto hot engine parts. This Enquiry was followed by a coronial Enquiry and the West Australian Coroner, Mr Hope concluded that a "series of mistakes and systemic deficiencies" had led to the fuel hoses being changed from solid metal to a flexible type. The mistakes were very serious mistakes, as the hoses were to be installed close to the indicator cocks that were known to be extremely hot and a possible ignition source. The use of flexible fuel hoses to replace pipes in the close vicinity of an exposed heat source capable of igniting diesel without any engineering assessment of their fitness for the purpose was an outrageously bad error." Mr Hope said.

The loss of 193 lives in the Zeebrugge ferry disaster on 6 March 1987 (the Herald capsized) identified one of the key factors in the accident was pressure to produce annual dividends for shareholders (Crainer 1993). P&O's declared policy was to comply with the standards laid down by current legislation. However this 'minimal' compliance failed to protect the lives of customers and employees. It was a clear example of the failure of this competency since managerial focus was on financials rather than people. Money was more salient than the particular conditions on the ferry. The Zeebrugge Enquiry found that simple design modifications such as the addition of simple indicator lights would have told the captain whether the bow doors were shut and bulkheads would have slowed the vessel's capsize. The risk was well understood by management but they ignored it. Crainer observes that:

Ferry operators repeatedly claim that they are 'dedicated to safety'. However, this usually means they have satisfied whatever regulations have been forced upon them by bodies whose track record is one of belated response rather than foresight. In general terms, the capsize of the Herald demonstrated the need for strong and consistent managerial involvement in all aspects of safety. Responsibility for safety must be taken (and be seen to be taken) by the board of directors.

Procedures need to be appropriate for the hardware and written for the specific application. (In the case of the Herald, procedures were 'lifted' from other ferries with visor bow doors, ignoring the fundamental difference of a ferry with clam doors.) (Crainer 1993:158)

Evidence from each of the cases examined in this book revealed that the salience of the particular situation was not appropriately appreciated. This lead to erroneous assumptions being made that resulted in fatal accidents. For example, the Westralia engine room fire occurred because hoses that were neither the correct ones that were required to have been fitted in that particular situation nor the immediate response to the actual fire and its intensity were understood. The culture of the Navy allowed what should have been clear indicators that something might be wrong in purchasing the hoses to go unremarked and unchallenged. The actual fire and its development also showed that the Navy and its staff were not adequately prepared or trained to deal with the events that developed in that particular situation.

. . .

Schein (1994) offers a useful insight into this kind of thinking and the operational assumptions of such dominant coalitions.

Human history has left us with a legacy of patriarchy and hierarchy, and a myth of male dominance and superiority based on the male as the warrior and protector. One can think of this as almost a state of "arrested development" in the sense that we have very limited models of how humans can and should relate to each other in Organisational settings. The traditional hierarchical model is virtually the only one we have. One consequence of this set of historically based cultural assumptions is that managers (who are mostly male) start with a self-image of having to be completely in control, decisive, certain, and dominant. Neither the leader, nor the follower wants the leader to be uncertain, to admit to not knowing or not being in control, to embrace error rather than to defensively deny it.

Organisations that manage operations in different parts of the country (or globe) should take responsibility for acquiring sound accident prevention knowledge and for disseminating it to each site. Paradoxically, each site is different and requires appropriate adaptations of knowledge and, hence, site specific risk auditing. This is congruent with Turner's (1997) theory that misinformation and energy cause accidents. It is also congruent with Reason's (1990) theory that latent errors reside in the managerial spheres of organisations and combine with local triggering events to cause accidents. It also resonates with Dawkins (1989, 1999) theory that memes survive to effect communications and cultures in organisations.

HIGH-RELIABILITY DIAGNOSTIC QUESTIONS

Because psychological balance is critical to shaping the habitus of a high-reliability organisation to 'intentionally' establish a culture of safety, then organisational 'ways of seeing' shape the 'memes' that will effect the organisation's systemic capacities for managing safety. Such questions require insight gained both from the previous generic information and the particular site-specific information. Therefore, questions directed to salient information and an ethos of safety become important. Such questions include:

•To what extent is previous experience of a generic nature salient to decisions made regarding a specific site? Is the necessary insight possible in an ethos of power, hierarchic decision processes, where organisational learning is limited by managerial hubris?

•Are there gender related psychological factors involved in limiting the opportunity for insight into the signification of salience in incident scenarios?

•To what extent do task orientation, preference for hard numbers, preoccupation with financials and short-run orientation all conspire to obscure latent errors and make insight into potential accidents difficult?

•Because creating an environment for learning is a long-range task, to what extent are managers able to plan for critical people and learning processes and knowledge systems in particular or site-specific situations?

19. COMPETENCY 9: PERFORMANCE IN A PARTICULAR SETTING: STRESS, CONFLICT, AND UNFOLDING DISASTERS

THIS CHAPTER EXAMINES THE COMPETENCY OF RECOGNISING AND adapting to the specific context and nuances of each situation. It highlights the importance of situational awareness, flexibility, and the ability to tailor responses to the unique challenges and risks of each environment.

"Reliability is the precondition for trust."

Wolfgang Schauble

WHAT IS HIGH-RELIABILITY PERFORMANCE?

This book suggests that stressful conditions test competencies where particular managerial actions in a high-reliability setting (where stress, conflict, disaster management, and risk management are persistent factors) require skills and competencies that may be different from the competencies required in a similar setting or at a different site within the same organisation. Soucek (1993) suggests that different circumstances require different competencies. Performance in specific situations is mitigated by human competency limitations or slippages such as active failures of individuals who simply fail to perform a competency adequately. Examples listed in the panel below include, careless navigation, irrational reasoning, limited operator knowledge, unanticipated interaction of multiple failures and failure to prepare escape routes. Perrow (1999) suggests that there is an 'overriding importance of the context into which the subject puts the problem'. Other examples of descriptors of the competency include communication downwards, which invariably results in failures of procedures. Individuals who only get the 'approved managerial' view of critical systems and processes are unlikely to grasp the whole of system picture. Inadequate supervision often results in inappropriate and inadequate responses to information. Information overload inhibits performance that is amplified by specification failure resulting in critical processes and machinery operating outside safe limits.

HyperRESEARCH Performance in a Particular Setting Descriptors

active failures of individuals, careless navigation, communication downwards, escape routes, failure of procedures, failure to grasp whole of system picture, inadequate supervision, inappropriate response, inadequate response, information overload, irrational reasoning, limited operator knowledge, operating outside limits, specification failure, unanticipated interaction of multiple failures.

PERFORMANCE, ETHICS, FORESIGHT, VIGILANCE, JUDGEMENT AND BALANCE

Performance by managers and operational staff in particular settings is closely related to the ethos of an organisation and all of the previous competencies. This competency indicates the need for individuals in particular hazardous situations to deal with stress in a framework where ethics, foresight, vigilance, judgement and balance are required. These are not possible without an appropriate and supportive organisational ethos and an understanding of the salience of the situation in which they find themselves.

IDEAS ABOUT PERFORMANCE

Eraut (1994) claims that what makes people competent in a particular job depends on them being able to meet the requirements of that job. Hence, competence in a job is defined as the ability to perform the tasks and roles required to the expected standard. Using Eraut's definition, a manager found to have failed in a critical capability would be considered incompetent and ought not to hold that job. While this definition also applies to front line operators and can form the basis of a charge of incompetence (ie against Captain Pelc in the Lake Illawarra case), it has already been established that human operator error is far more complex than at first appears. Almost always 'operator' error occurs for reasons that can be traced back to management. This attribution can be applied to a manager at any stage in their career, not only to the newly qualified. The actual competency standard expected could be expected to vary with experience and responsibility and should take into account the need to keep up to date with changes in practice. However, it also leaves open the question of who will decide what is to count as competence when different people have different expectations.

Reason (1990:184-185) cites Rasmussen's (1980) studies of 200 cases where the author identified 'operational problems'. Rasmussen's range of errors of significance to this book and this particular competency are human factors in which failure to carry out particular actions signified a failure of critical performance in the particular situation. They are related to preventative and corrective tasks such as surveillance testing, removal and restoration of equipment, checking, supervision, post-maintenance testing and modifications. The particular error types that Rasmussen identified were all seen in the case data and can be characterised as performance failures: absent mindedness, familiar association, low alertness, omission of essential isolated acts, mistakes among alternatives, strong expectations, side effects not considered, latent conditions not considered, manual variability, poor spatial orientation. Paradoxically, these are also characteristic of a poor understanding of the particular situation, competency eight.

The evidence of poor competency sets points to poor professional development. In most professions training results in a steadily increasing range of competence, accompanied by gradually decreasing levels of supervision; and the process of expanding one's range of competence continues after completion of training through a range of professional activities that may well include cyclical refresher training. Therefore, one would conclude that throughout this period the principle holds good of not undertaking work for which one is not competent without appropriate supervision, whatever one's status. However, the bookcases demonstrate that managers still function beyond their competencies and do so without any serious checks and balances, other than those imposed by the regulator, which is often itself found to be seriously incompetent. In the case of safety related situations these managers also operate with poor information while under stress, resulting in compromised, if not dangerous, performance of their jobs. Rethans (1990) points out that many bookers have failed to appreciate this distinction between competence and performance. He also noted that only one of the eight studies he reviewed was able to show that competence was a significant predictor of performance. It was not due to measurement deficiencies, as claimed, because it was a behavioural problem rather than a psychometric problem.

CASES OF FAILURES OF HIGH-RELIABILITY PERFORMANCE

Autopoietic organisations and other culturally homogenous settings result in people seeing problems the same way (Mitroff (1993), so maintaining cultural homogeneity in a high-reliability organisation is dangerous, and yet, paradoxically, it is important to generate shared understandings of potential accidents. Active failure of individuals identified in the Longford Royal Commission Report (1999) focus on the exchanges between individuals on the night of the accident. Each in turn failed to perform to a high level of competence in a particular setting. Other competency shortfalls were also indicated, such as limited operator knowledge and inappropriate responses. However, these all point to poor training and failure of 'particular site' managerial responsibilities, rather than a responsibility on the part of operators.

Longford

[active failures of individuals, failure of procedures, failure to grasp whole of system picture, limited operator knowledge, inadequate response, inappropriate response, unanticipated interactions of multiple failures]

13.94 Most significant was the content of the handover discussion at the commencement of the critical day shift on 25 September. There were shortcomings in the exchange of information that took place between the night shift operator, Olsson, and his relieving panel operator, Ward. Olsson identified problems which he had experienced during the night with the rate of condensate coming into the slug catchers from offshore. He also made reference to cold condensate temperatures which he had experienced in Absorber B and to problems which he had experienced in controlling the temperature of this absorber throughout the shift. He made no reference, however, to the off-scale, high condensate levels in Absorber B, or to the frequent occurrence of TC9B interference with level control, both of which he had experienced during the night. Nor did he make any reference to the frequent incidence of alarm warnings acknowledged by him during his shift. These warnings had accompanied the high condensate levels and the TC9B override. Nor did he convey to Ward the fact that the alarms for high Absorber B condensate levels and TC9B interference were still active at the change of shift, indicating not only that the levels were still high, but that level control had still not been regained by the time of the change. (Longford Report p211-212)

[inadequate supervision, operating outside limits]

13.33 These failures were not confined to operators or to any one shift. Indeed, the evidence suggests that some of the failings were so prevalent as to have become almost standard operating practice. These practices could not have developed or survived had there been adequate supervision of day-to-day operations by Esso management. (Longford Report p199)

Justice Staunton's report on the CAA/Seaview case (1999), stated that wrong assumptions led the regulator to credit Seaview with maintenance it never carried out and lied about. The ability of Mr Paull, the regulator's agent, to perform with competence in that role, and in that particular setting, was profoundly diminished and because of this he entertained a mode of irrational reasoning and made entirely inadequate responses to his direct experience.

CAA

[irrational reasoning] The limited nature of the documentation examined was entirely consistent with a perfunctory inspection. Mr Paull did not believe, for instance, that it was necessary to investigate whether Seaview Air was cheating on times recorded in maintenance releases. Mr Paull believed it would have been foolish to cheat, given that the aircraft were flying across oceans to Lord Howe Island and given that Mr Green had his own maintenance facility.

Mr Paull was living in a fool's paradise. Mr Green, at this time, and throughout, was cheating on maintenance releases, even though that may have been foolish. On the flight on 6 September 1992, when Mr

Green flew Mr Paull to Lord Howe Island for the periodic inspection, Mr Green recorded 4.7 hours for the 6.5-hour flight, even though Mr Paull had been sitting beside him. (Executive Summary p6)

Illawarra

In relation to shipping and maritime accidents Perrow (1999) points out that unlike Aircraft, where pilots have the backup of co-pilots, ships masters do not. This tradition of the sea is apparently continued to enable shipping companies to pass blame and insurance risk to human error triggered by individual masters. The IMCO (United Nations Intergovernmental Maritime Consultative Organisation), which governs these matters is, according to Carter (1978), described as a forum dominated by shipowners who want to minimize their capital outlay and operating costs despite the greater risk of chronic pollution and accidents. Costs for accidents are simply passed along to clients and insurers. Hence the extraordinary pressure of 'turn-around' time is placed on ships masters, almost always with punitive fines for missed deadlines, no matter the reason.

It is common (*normal*) for sea captains to decline tugs and pilots if they can ensure shorter turnaround times, because of the covert and overt pressure on them by owners to do so. Perrow (1999) points out that the economics of the maritime system itself conspires to induce errors. He points to evasion of costs and responsibilities by owners and shippers. According to Lloyd's List (21 May, 1981), 2: 'the results of such regimes not infrequently lead to "a ship" beneficially owned on one country, owned by a company resident in another country, registered under a flag of a third country, managed by a company in a fourth country, but on long term charter to interests in a fifth country and even sub-chartered to interests in a sixth country.'

When the Lake Illawarra accident happened there was not a deeply understood scientific grasp of the nature of large keels in Hobart harbour. Therefore, issues such as, 'bottom effects', 'bank effects' and 'hull effects' (suctions created by water having to pass through shallow or narrow spaces) were not well understood. The findings against Captain Pelc seem onerous if one contemplates that his 'capacity to perform in Hobart harbour' failed him due to the pressures that may have been on him to turn his ship around. These more likely causes were not well understood and the Enquiry found him to be personally guilty of careless or negligent 'navigation'.

[careless navigation]

We are quite satisfied that it has not been established that Captain Pelc is incompetent within the meaning of Section 372 of the Navigation Act. On the contrary, all the evidence indicates that, apart from the events of the evening of 5 January 1975, he is a well-qualified, competent and capable Master.

However (keeping in mind the warning given in Spain's case supra, at pp. 658-9, not to be wise after the event in imputing negligence), we are of opinion that Captain Pelc was, in relation to this casualty, guilty of misconduct in the form of careless navigation (Lake Illawarra Enquiry p14).

Longford

[cause immediate, cause of accident, diagnostic failure]

15.6 Notwithstanding the matters mentioned above, the conclusion is inevitable that the accident which occurred on 25 September 1998 would not have occurred had appropriate steps been taken following the tripping of the GP1201 pumps. When efforts to restart those pumps proved unsuccessful, it should have been realised immediately that cold temperatures would ensue downstream from the absorbers and render vessels not designed to operate at low temperatures dangerous. Had this been realised, steps could and should have been taken to isolate the outlets of both rich oil and condensate from the absorbers in order to prevent those cold temperatures from developing in the ROD/ROF area. Those who were operating GP1 on 25 September 1998 did not have knowledge of the dangers associated with loss of lean oil flow and did not take the steps necessary to avert those dangers. Nor did those charged with the supervision of the operations have the necessary knowledge and the steps taken by them were inappropriate. The lack of knowledge on the part of both operators and supervisors was attributable to a deficiency in their initial or subsequent training.

Not only was their training inadequate, but there were no current operating procedures to guide them in dealing with the problem which they encountered on 25 September 1998. (Longford Report p234)

DIAGNOSTIC TOOLS TO IMPROVE HIGH-RELIABILITY PERFORMANCE

Stressful conditions test managerial competencies. Communication downwards results in individuals who require an overall operational view of critical systems and the ability to process the 'whole of system' picture, but often they do not have such a picture. Operational staff should take a broad and authoritative view of their duties. Supervision should result in appropriate and adequate responses to information. Performance can be enhanced by limiting information overload, where specification failures occur. This can often result in normal processes becoming critical. Achieving this balance is a management responsibility, since management also have a responsibility for overall organisational competence.

More books should focus on the conditions that influence managers' performance. Whatever the standard of performance at the end of training, the expectation must be for continuing improvement and this largely depends on the manager's attitude towards quality improvement and lifelong learning. This attitudinal component is essential because cyclical refresher training that makes performance salient in a particular setting not only includes site-specific skills but also the core values of managing in that organisation at that particular place. These are learned largely through discussion, site-specific problem-solving exercises, workshops and practical experience. An arrogant manager or CEO who found training 'beneath them' would have great difficulty with this and the higher stages that involve dealing with these values, which are likely to require at least some formal instruction in addition to opportunities for practice and formal feedback. Integrative skills, or applications of the values and characteristics, are gained by acquiring experience in realistic site-specific settings.

THINKING ABOUT PERFORMANCE

Hopkins (1999) observes that a normal or system accident, as Perrow defines it, involves the unanticipated interaction of multiple failures of various of the system components. Where a system is complex, in that its components can interact in unexpected ways and where it is tightly coupled, such that multiple failures can occur so quickly that there is not sufficient time to analyse and react to what is happening, then system accidents, he says, are virtually inevitable.

It is clear that the Moura explosion cannot be analysed in these terms. The system was not complex in the above sense. On the contrary, there was nothing at all surprising or unexpected about the sequence of events; the process was quite foreseeable and had given rise to disaster on two occasions in Queensland in the recent past. The system was not tightly coupled, according to Perrow's definition (Perrow, 1999:4). Events unfolded slowly and resolute intervention at any point could have averted disaster and saved the mine. Perrow himself acknowledged that coal mine disasters could not be explained by his theory and the analysis here confirms his conclusion.

. . .

The mine that exploded in 1994 had not previously experienced an explosion, although two adjacent mines had. This mine therefore had no direct experience or memory to draw on. BHP management should have learnt from the disasters in adjacent mines, which was salient to this site. As indicated in paragraph 7.1.7, there were relatively recent explosions at Moura No. 4 in 1986 and at Appin in NSW in 1979. BHP's management had decentralised responsibility for disaster prevention to management at individual mine sites and retained no central capacity or expertise with respect to disaster prevention. BHP as an organisation failed to engage in organisational learning and therefore failed to develop a corporate memory and retain the lessons of the various disasters.

Reason's (1990) theory of latent and active errors asserts that major accidents occur when latent failures, arising mainly in the managerial and organisational spheres, combine adversely with local triggering events and active failures of individuals at the operational interface (such as human errors and procedural violations). The latent failures at Moura identified in this book were largely organisational, cultural and ethos failings, especially the deficiencies in communications. The local triggering event was the heating, and the active failures were the failures of individual managers to apply foresight, vigilance and judgement, which would have made it clear that a critically unsafe heating could happen, at the time of the explosion when the actual failure process was in train.

The Moura and Longford cases both demonstrate the applicability of Reason's assertion that actions or inactions of individuals are a part of the chain of events that lead to disaster. Reason counsels caution, however, and concludes that focusing on active failures of individuals is not as useful as focusing on the latent or organisational failings involved. It is salient that both enquiries focused on the organisational factors and did not preoccupy themselves with the role individuals played in the Moura and Longford accidents.

Hopkins (1999) makes a strong claim that the Moura accident demonstrated key organisational failures - hence management failures. The Moura case showed that many of the competencies suggested by this book were involved:

C9. There was no adequate system for communication of decisions down the mine hierarchy.

C7. There was no adequate system of communicating information about warning signs up the hierarchy. In particular, people at BHP headquarters had no access to such information.

C7. There was no feedback mechanism to ensure that those reporting hazards or warnings were notified of what action, if any, was taken.

C6. There was a hierarchy of knowledge which led to a misplaced reliance on personal experience and on oral communication and a tendency to ignore written reports.

C5. The system for communicating production figures was more developed than the system for communicating safety information.

C6. There was a norm at the mine that unless warning signs were verified and confirmed they could be ignored.

C6. There was a series of beliefs at the mine, amounting to a culture of denial. One belief, in particular, `normalised' the evidence-that is, it reinterpreted the indications of abnormality as lying within the bounds of normality.

C7. There were no specified actions that were mandatory when warning signs were detected.

C7. No one was identified as responsible for critical, safety-relevant decisions.

C6. The system of auditing by the company was thoroughly inadequate.

C5. The mine was using the wrong safety indicator - the lost time injury frequency rate. This provided no indication of how well catastrophic risk was being managed, it just showed time lost due to injuries.

C8. There were no incentives for mine managers to concern themselves with disaster prevention.

C6/7 BHP had decentralised responsibility for the control of catastrophic risk, along with all other aspects of safety, to the mine level. It had no corporate expertise in disaster prevention, despite its history of mine explosions.

C11. (Compliance) The law does not in practice hold the company or its senior management legally accountable for disaster prevention in the mine.

C5. Coal mines inspectorates are hamstrung in their enforcement efforts by their position in mining departments.

Evidence from each of the cases examined in this book revealed that stressful conditions test managerial competencies. Different settings demand competencies which may be different from site to site in the same organisation. The book showed that performance in specific situations is mitigated by human competency limitations or slippages such as active failures of individuals who simply fail to perform a competency adequately. For example, careless navigation, as in the case of the Lake Illawarra; irrational reasoning, limited operator knowledge, unanticipated interaction of multiple failures as in Moura and Longford; and failure to prepare adequate escape routes as in the Westralia case. Communication downwards invariably results in failures of procedures, because individuals who need an overall operational view of critical systems and processes are unlikely to grasp the whole of system picture if they are simply subject to orders, as in the Zeebrugge case.

The Moura and Longford enquiries involved the same company (BHP) and indicated the clear need for salient performance management, which suggests overall organisational learning and specific site learning is needed in similar situations. Achieving this balance is a management responsibility. The Zeebrugge case confirms this. The last person to leave the car deck on the night of the disaster didn't check that the doors were closed or close them himself. The Zeebrugge Enquiry (Sheen, 1987) found that, 'He took a narrow view of his duties and it is most unfortunate that he took this attitude.'

There is a delicate balance between giving too much freedom and requiring people to stick rigidly to tightly defined job descriptions. The Herald of Free Enterprise (off Zeebrugge) disaster poignantly demonstrated the need for employees to be able to exercise their own judgement where it is salient to safety. P&O's managers, however, ignored the earlier concerns of employees regarding the haste to depart. The Enquiry also found that P&O management's inability to collect and communicate vital information was a telling reflection on their training, sensitivity and knowledge of the business they purported to manage. They failed to demonstrate any significant performance capabilities salient to the situation they were managing.

HIGH-RELIABILITY DIAGNOSTIC QUESTIONS

The case data point to the importance of trying to assess communications weaknesses because dysfunctional managerial behaviour can shape the habitus of a high-reliability organisation site resulting in a disabling ethos of safety, thereby reducing the site's hazard management capabilities. Questions need to be directed at the creation of such a habitus or culture, and its immobilising memes that lead to questions such as:

•What conditions outside normal operational parameters are likely to require special skills and competencies?

•Are there existing conditions that are pointing to accidents?

•Who is responsible for translating vigilance signals into operational defences?

•Is managerial performance enhanced or constrained by regulations?

•What can be done to simplify systems that are more complex than they need to be?

•What attitudes frame acceptance or denial of responsibility?

•To what extent can organisational learning and competency enhancement serve to eliminate unanticipated interactions of system processes and prevent multiple failures of processes and components?

•Are there definable differences between operational sites in the one organisation and how are they similar and different?

20.COMPETENCY 10: MULTIDISCIPLINARY PERFORMANCE

BRINGING TOGETHER SKILLS FROM DIFFERENT DOMAINS

"Knowing is not enough; we must apply. Willing is not enough; we must do"

Goethe

WHAT IS HIGH-RELIABILITY MULTIDISCIPLINARY PERFORMANCE?

Multidisciplinary performance is anchored in Mitroff's (1993) concept of 'expertise'. Mitroff claims that expertise provides a set of patterns about a subject and these in turn together construct a schemata. This schemata provides both intuition and learned opinion. For example, it is not uncommon for trained organisational consultants to walk into an organisation and talk to the receptionist to suspect that there may be something wrong with that organisation. Some people are able to offer a 'learned opinion' rather than just an 'opinion'. Judges offer 'learned opinions' based on their knowledge of the law and previous cases.

Perrow (1999) suggests a disconfirming line of reasoning when he reminds us that experts make errors and suggests that experts are people who 'abjure intuitions'. However, he applies a concept somewhat equivalent to Mitroff's schemata, in considering 'heuristics', which he suggests are 'regularised, checked out intuitions'. He suggests that heuristics prevent a paralysis of decision making and the 'costs of search', the collection, prioritising and ranking of all possible choices. This is salient when considered in light of Mintzberg's (1973 and 1989) claim that managers' activities are varied, typically of short duration – less than half an hour - and often interrupted and little time was spent reading or reflecting or in solitary activity.

Multidisciplinary performance can be illustrated in the example given by Reason (2000) who illustrates the point in the case of a Boeing 767 that, after a series of blunders, ran out of fuel on a domestic flight in Canada. Without power, the plane lost use of its flaps for a controlled descent. The captain, a skilled glider pilot, used a manoeuvre known as a sideslip. He lost height quickly without going into a dive, then kicked the tail back into normal position for landing. The plane landed safely, although it was certainly never included in any Boeing procedure manual. Reason calls this phenomena, 'resilience'. Call it schemata, heuristics or resilience, it still amounts to an example of multidisciplinary performance and it relies on expertise in other than the prime field of concern, such as the use of skills from diverse domains of knowledge, training and previous involvement in life and work.

Singer (1959) proposed that every act performed by humans was complex and had within it a complex series of other actions, which themselves could be modified by 'ideas swept in'. This critical concept of non-separability and interconnectedness forms the basis of the 'systems approach' and is the basis of this competency, which asserts that skills from different and complementary domains must be utilised with expertise in a connected way to prevent accidents. This competency is the one most obviously lacking in the examples of systemic failure in this section, suggesting that there is a failure to exercise the previous nine competencies at the same time. This is usually a consequence of the crisis at hand and a propensity for ignoring the enabling lessons of experience to address unfamiliar and unanticipated events. This may be due to a failure of training to translate skills into practical responses or simply because these competencies are not current and relevant to the specific situation, even though they may be relevant in other situations.

HyperRESEARCH disclosed several descriptors closely associated with multidisciplinary performance listed in the panel below. The cases revealed that the primary critical performance indicator expressed is a failing to exercise competent responsibility for the welfare of others by those who purport to have such responsibility (dominant management coalitions such as directors and individual managers).

Dominant coalitions have a final organisational moral responsibility for the consequences of the impacts the organisation has on stakeholders; hence, 'the problem of systems improvement is the problem of the 'ethics of the whole system' (Churchman 1968a:4). The implications are clear. Dominant coalitions in high-reliability organisations have a clear-cut responsibility to safeguard stakeholders, where unanticipated factors are in play, and require a multidisciplinary competency set to do it effectively. The various Commissions if Enquiry found that responsible managers failed to exercise the competencies they had and that many did not maintain their competencies. Cases, such as Longford, also made it clear that there were significant failures of training across many levels of management. This competency tends to capture the capabilities developed in each of the other competencies developed in this book and its failure can most be said to be a failure of competence.

HyperRESEARCH Multidisciplinary Performance Descriptors

critical performance indicators, currency of competence, failure of training, failure to exercise competencies, unanticipated factors

MULTIDISCIPLINARY PERFORMANCE, ETHOS, OTHER COMPETENCIES

If organisations learned from events, near misses and other incidents then, conceivably, such lessons would be incorporated into an organisation's systems. Ethos based team skills such as feedback, cooperation, team orientation, coordination, leadership, and backup behaviour influence a team's effectiveness. The literature supports this view and the direct linkages with other competencies discussed earlier. For example, Mitroff and Linstone (1993:91) state: 'The logic for choosing a particular way of modelling or representing a problem is not governed by considerations of conventional logic and rationality (orthodox management). It may also involve considerations of justice and fairness as perceived by various social groups and by considerations of personal ethics and morality as perceived by distinct persons.' Mitroff and Linstone's observation establishes relationships with all of the previously described competencies.

The relationship between the competencies developed in this book is organic. An absence of any of the first nine competencies will render the final one difficult. Ideally, each competency would build on the next.

A stark case of a multidisciplinary failure caused by a failure of ethics, vigilance and foresight and the other competencies were the attacks on the World Trade Centre and other US targets on September the 11th, 2001. For at least 12 minutes after the Federal Aviation Administration (FAA) warned the military's air defence command that a hijacked airliner appeared to be headed toward Washington (9:25am), the federal government failed to make any move to evacuate the White House, Capitol, State Department or the Pentagon, which was the eventual target of the attack. Only after the 9:38 a.m. impact into the side of the Pentagon were other government buildings evacuated, including the White House and the Capitol. CNN (16/9/2001) reported that officials at the Pentagon said that no mechanism existed within the U.S. government to notify various departments and agencies under such circumstances. A failure of multidisciplinary competencies in government makes catastrophic systemic failures of judgement inevitable.

IDEAS ABOUT MULTIDISCIPLINARY PERFORMANCE

This problem of multidisciplinary competence is addressed by Turner's theory of 'prior knowledge' (Turner, 1976: 78, 97). Mitroff (1993:98) suggests that a 'multiple perspective' [multidisciplinary] approach enables the use of technical, organisational and personal information to ensure that underlying assumptions and values are considered in dealing with problems. Mitroff identifies 'risky positions' taken by groups and the difficulties of measuring human reaction times in systems. Dunphy (1981:163) argues that job redesign for sociotechnical organisations must reverse the traditional principles of job design on several key dimensions. He points to the need for multiskilling and autonomy and participation in decision making applied to complex tasks, quality control, inspection and work environments. This principle can be translated to high-reliability organisations such as those studied in this book.

Dunphy and Griffiths (1998:53) define sociotechnical systems as having certain characteristics:

•*metaphor,* organised as an organic open system;

•*diagnostic,* systems combined with participant redesign and work practices;

•*ideal state,* representative democratic community composed of semiautonomous work groups with the ability to continuously learn through participative action book;

•*intervention strategies,* comprised of participative action book and workplace redesign around socio-technical principles.

. . .

Stace and Dunphy (1994:190) demonstrate a multidisciplinary 'star' concept using these principles that was developed at Alcan, Granville, NSW. It transfers new tasks and responsibilities to teams that are structured to bring a variety of competencies to a project and at the same time relieve the burden of new tasks on the team leader.

The model illustrates roles allocated to team members. Each member has a primary and an alternate role. The director stands in for the team leader and is responsible for utilisation of idle time. The personnel and safety role carries out accident investigations, reports on safety issues and conducts regular safety training events such as talks. Production and quality team members represent the team at meetings and keep production records. Administration deals with orders, supplies from store and maintains holiday and overtime schedules; while the equipment team members sets maintenance priorities and records equipment performance. This team profile may be adaptable with minor modification to high-reliability organisations. the model is based on orthodox management values and would need to be modified to take account of ethics, ethos building, vigilance and foresight systems along with training and cyclical retraining and succession. These competencies develop values and give guidance and motivation in situations where manuals cease to be effective.

This simple model can be adapted to specific situations and provides a large measure of multidisciplinary performance assurance. Had this system been employed at Longford and Moura it may well have obviated the accidents at those places. Such a model also has the benefit that it encourages job rotation, multiskilling, collaborative work practices and continuous improvement, in key areas of an organisation's activities such as safety, customer service, productivity, quality and equipment performance and maintenance and process engineering. If applied the model confers the benefits of technical, supervisory and managerial multiskilling and use of skills from different domains.

Mitroff and Linstone (1993: 90-110) argue that, '...the widest possible array of disciplines, professions, and branches of knowledge -

capturing distinctly different paradigms of thought - must be consciously brought to bear on our problems.' More recently Whittingham (2003) also examined the linkage between human error and accidents and identified failures of performance such as slips and lapses among error types. He also considered human reliability, task complexity and the problem of expert judgement and task decomposition among other task shaping factors. If this is framed by Eraut's (1994) perspective that people need to meet the requirements of a particular job to be considered competent it is possible to argue that the competency mix appears to become more complex as the literature reveals more recent and sophisticated insights.

The capacity to consistently engage in correct error modelling, or being in possession of a relevant site-specific taxonomy of error types is being revealed over time as a managerial competency requiring extraordinary breadth and depth of general and specific skills almost beyond the scale and scope of abilities of a single person to master. The problem is further amplified because as Mitroff and Linstone (1993:91) claim, 'everything interacts with everything'.

Mol (2004) also suggests a multidisciplinary strategic approach for hazardous industries that ties safety and production together. Her contribution requires managers and multidisciplinary teams to consider risk models, organisational decision making, systems change processes, technologies, physical environments, human resources, risk quantification, managerial behavioural change (suggesting leadership and management training and behavioural audits) as well as formulating a safety management plan as a method of enhancing management performance using an achievement cycle.

However, multidisciplinary teams bring with them their own approaches and some problems that need to be actively managed. Kraut et al (1988) in a collaboration study in science stressed the importance of communication and the social component of successful collaborations and found that virtually all of the social and most of the task activities were performed informally face-to-face and they found no case in which collaborators used formal management techniques or technologies. Collaborators used division of labour to reduce demands on communication. Also, institutional, disciplinary, and professional norms (that the collaborators shared in common) resolved many problems of how to proceed.

High-reliability organisations should understand that systems are evolving to fit with the information sharing practices of different industries and professions (see, for instance, Lodahl & Gordon, 1972; Hargens, 1975; Garvey, 1979; Whitley, 1984) that reflect disciplinary norms of information ownership and communication and help collaborators to learn the norms of other disciplines. These emerging adaptive systems themselves require special competencies to manage them. For example, there are different issues among co-located teams and teams experiencing geographic and functional distance between members (Krackhardt, 1992). In addition, when teams are distributed, membership is often transitory, and representation varies over time, then new problems in coordination arise including members' incomplete understanding of others' group identity, questions about information ownership, secrecy, and proprietary products, and socialization of newcomers. Compounding these problems is a "misinformation effect" (Reder, 1998) whereby interaction in a group and discussion of ideas distort the real sources of ideas, which may obscure early warning signals.

CASES OF FAILURE OF HIGH-RELIABILITY MULTIDISCIPLINARY PERFORMANCE

Creating and evaluating systems for members of multidisciplinary groups, as for individuals, requires managers to understand non-managerial concepts such as advice networks, professional weak ties, and social filters (whereby certain important traits are actively selected and others are not) and their effects on collaboration, shared knowledge and access to multidisciplinary competencies (Hill, et al, 1995; Resnick & Varian, 1997; Terveen & Hill, 1997). While experts tend to solve problems faster and better than non-experts they may also redefine problems to suit their schemata and hence solve the wrong problems. Many of these issues are addressed or implied in the following data extracted from the cases using HyperRESEARCH.

Both the Moura and the Lake Illawarra cases illustrate the process of failing to exercise multidisciplinary competencies. The Moura Enquiry (Queensland Warden's Court, c1996) found the explanation for the accident was management neglect and the wrong assumptions made.

Moura

[failure to exercise competencies] The complex of competencies which must come together in a crisis is critical to steering a safe path through a hazardous situation. For example, the Coronial Enquiry's ultimate explanation for what had caused the fatal accident at Moura No. 2 Underground Mine on Sunday, 7 August 1994, was 'management neglect':

"It is the opinion of the Enquiry that events at Moura surrounding assumptions as to the state of knowledge of the night shift on 7 August and the safety of those at the mine represents a passage of management neglect and non-decision which must never be repeated in the coal mining industry. Mineworkers place their trust in management and have the right to expect management to take responsible decisions in respect to their safety. They also have the right to expect management to keep them informed on any matter likely to affect their safety and welfare (Windridge 1996:412)."

The Lake Illawarra case found that a failure to exercise several competencies contributed to the accident. The findings against Captain Pelc seem somewhat unjust if one contemplates that his 'expertise' or mental map of Hobart harbour and all its eddies and tidal swirls around the bridge failed him due to the production pressures that may have been on him to turn his ship around. The word, 'precautions' in the data extract point to a failure of schemata. Had he had a higher level of 'expertise' he may well have asked for a pilot. More to the point, the Harbour Master should have insisted on it if he had the more recent and comprehensive 'expertise' of Hobart harbour.

Illawarra

Ordinarily, when incidents which happened on an isolated occasion are in question, the Court will be considering whether there was careless navigation on the part of a competent Master or Officer. "Careless navigation" in this context, therefore, connotes a failure to navigate with such care and skill' as a competent Master or Officer would reasonably be expected to exercise in the circumstances.

There is little if any difference, in our opinion, between "careless navigation" and "negligent navigation". That view is supported by the definition of a shipmaster's duty of care given by Isaacs and Rich JJ. in Spain v. Union Steamship Co. of New Zealand Ltd. (1923) 33 C.L.R. 555, at p. 569:

". . . the legal standard of the Captain's duty was that he should take whatever precautions a hypothetical prudent and skilled navigator would reasonably be expected to take in the actual circumstances."

The Longford Royal Commission, (1999:13.134-5) found that the evidence before it indicated that critical performance indicator data that was recorded by the Bailey system and also stored in the PIDAS database (PIDAS provided a continuous record of process information) were not used as effectively as they might have been and that their ineffective use played a part in the occurrence of the accident on 25 September 1998. This was mostly due to a loss of expertise when the plant engineers were transferred to Melbourne. This effectively mitigated 'learning' because the essential records for surveillance purposes and for accident investigation and analysis were thrown away.

Longford 13.134 The consequence of the relocation of plant engineers to Melbourne was that the important task of continuous monitoring of process conditions within the Longford facility was diminished. Moreover, what was done was no longer carried out by plant engineers.

Instead, it was undertaken almost exclusively by operators and plant supervisors whose surveillance work was focused on immediate production requirements rather than trend analysis or the analysis of recurring process problems.

13.135 The lack of plant surveillance activity in GPI was demonstrated by the lack of use made of process information. Electronically generated process information was automatically retained in the PIDAS database. However, it would seem that it was rarely, if ever, looked at, let alone subjected to any trend analysis. The remaining 70% of process information for GP1 was to be found on chart recordings and was also not subjected to any trend analysis. This is apparent because there was no system in place for preserving such records either for surveillance purposes or for accident investigation and analysis. The evidence was that charts, once used, were discarded by operators. They were not stored or retained. Thus, historical process information covering some 70% of GPI operations was never reviewed by engineers for surveillance purposes, but simply thrown away. Charts were not even date stamped at their beginning and end to make analysis easier.

DIAGNOSTIC TOOLS TO IMPROVE HIGH-RELIABILITY MULTIDISCIPLINARY PERFORMANCE

The loss of expertise points to the need for a system of developing and enriching the available schemata of dominant coalitions in high-reliability organisations. It should include a focus of concern on each of the competencies elaborated in this book and be seen as something needed in addition to individual expertise. A multidisciplinary competency approach such a this should be informed by the work of authors such as Dunphy and Griffiths (1998), Stace and Dunphy (1994), Mitroff (1993), Whittingham (2003), and Mol (2004).

THINKING ABOUT JUDGEMENT

There is a difference between knowledge held by the system and knowledge held by the dominant coalition (those who make decisions). It seems that in many cases the dominant coalition makes wrong assumptions about safety and passes off its responsibility to OH&S or other departments while it is focused on concerns other than safety, such as profit, or acts deliberately in a straightforward criminal way and ignores safety in spite of signals warning of hazards (Longford/Esso). Hopkins (1999:57-8) observes that the normal practice at Moura No. 2 was to go underground to work elsewhere when a recently sealed panel was going through the explosive stage. In contrast, at the adjacent Moura No. 4 mine, the practice had been for panels to be sealed on a Friday and for the men to stay out of the mine over the weekend while the panel went through the explosive stage. Both were BHP mines. However, there was no head office safety policy and the site-specific result was that the Moura No. 4 miners simply refused to go underground while a panel was explosive. At Moura No. 2, a different workforce had not taken similar collective action.

It appeared to be a BHP policy that the miners at both mines could decide and implement policy for themselves. Individual middle-level managers imposed variants of policy to focus on performance for their own personal ends. There seemed to be considerable bullying by individual managers and it was a simmering industrial issue. The Commission found that one deputy had raised the issue repeatedly with management. In response, he was told it was a ploy by workers to get time off. The deputy had been suspended twice for arguing the safety case with management. This is a clear case of a particular site developing a different culture and set of working conditions because of different site-specific managerial values and could not have happened if there had been multidisciplinary teams in place such as the Alcan 'Star Model'.

The cases and literature when considered together point to the need for critical performance benchmarks supported by cyclical retraining for dominant coalitions to ensure currency of competencies - if necessary, required by the regulator. Multidisciplinary collaboration in business organisations in the 1980s (Sproull & Kiesler, 1991) provided a better understanding of how multidisciplinary groups can effectively use the new technologies available to them. These multi-disciplinary capabilities are viewed as essential in the more recent literature, such as that of Whittingham (2003), who examined a range of cases and identified different detectable and preventable errors confirming Turner's thesis of prior knowledge that underpins this book.

Whittingham's examples included:

••organisational and management errors (Flixborough, Herald of Free Enterprise, railway privatisation);

••design errors (BP Grangemouth explosion, Estonia ferry sinking, Abbeystead explosion);

••maintenance errors (Royal Flight engine failure, Hatfield and Potters Bar rail crashes);

••active errors in railway operation;

••active errors in aviation;

••violations (Chernobyl, Mulhouse A320 crash);

••incidence response errors (Swissair flight SR111, Channel tunnel fire);

Most, if not these, could have been prevented if early intervention had occurred through these errors being signified as critical by multidisciplinary capable individuals or teams. The prior knowledge was available in each case but was not converted into intervention by those responsible.

HIGH-RELIABILITY DIAGNOSTIC QUESTIONS

Questions that assess mental schemata as suggested by Perrow (1999), Reason (2000), and Mitroff (1997) should reveal an existing rigidity and inflexibility in specific situations where diagnostic skills arising from expertise and intuitive approaches may be better suited. These questions should also go to the heart of learning failures, and issues related acquiring expertise, such as:

••To what extent do organisations learn from the lessons of accidents?

••Does the depth (within the multidisciplinary skill set - team or individual) and breadth (across the team and each individual's skill set) enable integration of knowledge to support decisions?

••Is there a measurable difference in team orientation, related to power, in communication skills, leadership and hazard reduction between female and male team members?

••What consequences might flow if a team or individual responsible for safety decisions becomes dysfunctional?

••How might dysfunctional behaviour be mitigated?

••What factors enable or inhibit team problem solving?

••What is the nature and impact of successful multidisciplinary collaborations, and the role of technology in these collaborations?

Mostly these are questions for postdoctoral investigation, however, this book attempts to address some of them, where expertise and integration are concerned. Finally, as Perrow (1999) suggests, we should also ask, 'What risks should we run to promote the private profits of a few?'

Evidence from the cases examined in this book revealed that prior knowledge could have prevented the Moura and Longford accidents if it had been acted on. Moura No 2 was the third explosion in a BHP coal mine in fifteen years. There seemed to be a loss of corporate memory. The Esso oil platform fire in Bass strait in 1989 was found by the Victorian coroner to be almost identical to the Piper Alpha fire in the North Sea only nine months before. Kletz (1999:21-2) suggests that because of this loss of corporate memory managers at the highest level need to undergo regular refresher courses on the kinds of things that can go wrong in their own organisations. The Enquiry found that Moura No. 2 was a result of 'management neglect and non-decision that must never be repeated.' It was entirely foreseeable and could have been avoided.

Dominant coalitions in high-reliability organisations have a clear cut responsibility to safeguard stakeholders (Windridge 1996:412; Lord Denning, 1975; Turnbull 2002; Gunningham and Johnstone, 1999:308-340), especially where complex systems govern safety, and they require a multidisciplinary competency set to do it effectively. The acquisition of such skills should be performed voluntarily or insisted on by statutory mandate. The principle focus of concern appears to be ethics, ethos building and competency enhancement.

A multidisciplinary competency program would enable the use of skills from diverse domains of knowledge, training and previous involvement in life and work. to ensure that managers understand that every act performed by humans is complex and has within it a complex series of other actions. Critical concepts of non-seperability and interconnectedness underpin the insights sought from such a program and is the basis of this competency which asserts that skills from different and complementary domains must be utilised to prevent accidents. Managers need to understand that decisions made 'on the run', outside their own areas of expertise, may be based on faulty schemata and often relying on a mix of hubris and poor information as a consequence of the crisis at hand, will demonstrate a propensity for ignoring the lessons of experience, in unfamiliar and unanticipated events. Of most concern to stakeholders appears to be a willingness by managers to trade-off the welfare of others for profit. This propensity should be curbed by a punitive regulatory and compliance regime.

21.COMPLIANCE ISSUES: HIGH-RELIABILITY COMPLIANCE

THIS CHAPTER EXAMINES THE COMPETENCIES CONSIDERED MOST relevant to the requirement imposed on managers of high-reliability organisations to ensure compliance with the regulatory regimes that govern their enterprises.

'A company may, in many ways, be likened to a human body. It has a brain and nervous centre which controls what it does. It also has hands which hold the tools and act in accordance with directions from the centre. Some of the people in the company are mere servants and agents who are nothing more than hands to do the work and cannot be said to represent the mind or will. Others are directors and managers who represent the directing mind and will of the company.'

Lord Denning, 1975.

WHAT IS HIGH-RELIABILITY COMPLIANCE?

As in the three previous chapters this chapter adopts the framework of the modified grounded theory approach set out in sections 4.2 and 4.3 of the Data Analysis chapter: interpretation of the concept as it is used in this book followed by a consideration of the relationships between the competency under consideration and the other key competencies. The chapter then poses a set of generative questions and a review of the literature salient to the concept. An elaboration of the insights revealed to theory is attempted and other data from the book is then used to ground the theory. Finally a hypothesis based on the issues revealed by the book is suggested.

When the other competencies fail and an accident occurs it becomes necessary to determine to what extent the organisation complied with safety policies, laws and guidelines. Ensuring compliance is an ongoing managerial task or competency. Compliance failure is managerial failure. Compliance is a competency differentiated from the other competencies in this book by its 'end game' status. Rather than a concern with eleven key competencies the book addresses ten competencies plus compliance to establish that this is a competency in a special relationship with the others. It is both a process of ensuring safety on an ongoing basis and a legal requirement of management. It is knowledge based rather than behavioural. Managers must know the compliance requirements of their organisation's operations.

Compliance issues arise when an organisation fails to comply with specific laws which govern the actions of the organisation and where that law is enforced by a regulator, rendering the regulator a party to an accident. Compliance determinations also include consideration of accountability issues where, for example, the regulator is unable to enforce regulations or their regulatory independence is seriously compromised, such as where the regulator becomes dominated by the regulated organisation or industry or where the relationship between regulator and regulated is compromised by government intervention.

The law is based on precedents and, therefore, is backward looking. The legal system makes judgement about accidents that have already happened in its determinations of responsibility in such cases as are presented here. However, it also takes account of the regulations governing the ongoing conduct and commercial practices of the organisations it examines, in relation to the Acts of Parliament that govern them through their regulatory authorities, who should anticipate potential accidents and intervene in the potentiating stream of factors that lead to an accident.

Tension between the law and management, in relation to the managerial responsibilities of the dominant coalition (Lord Denning, 1975), arises partly because the law looks backward, and management looks forward. Mintzberg (1973, 1975) said that managing involves staying on track (managing continuity), staying in touch (managing boundaries), and keeping up to date (managing change). The more complex the organisation and its operations are, the more managers are duty bound to take responsibility for the complexity and safe running of it (Crainer, 1993). Managers in high-reliability organisations have a legal responsibility to anticipate how each of these might be done while at the same time ensuring they do not generate hazards.

A further complicating factor is that large organisations are legal entities in and of themselves and under Australian corporate law, directors have absolute power to manage their own conflicts of interest (Turnbull, 2000). This has direct compliance consequences because the dominant coalition of large organisations can hide behind the corporate veil, even in cases where fatal accidents are preventable or where organisations bypass safety requirements or are not carrying out the necessary interventions to stop accidents from occurring. Under the current regulatory regime, such accidents tend to be related to managerial systems or blamed on 'systemic failure' and are seen as misconduct at worst.

In sentencing the train driver after his train killed five people after going through a red light in Purley in 1989, the judge said, 'The railway passenger who gets onto a train puts himself, in a very special way, into the hands of the driver.' Crainer (1993) observes that the railway company is also responsible for the maintenance of the train, the systems surrounding its running, and the training and proficiency of its staff.

The dominant coalition, as identified in this and other book (Crainer, 1993), joins corporate directors with senior managerial staff in a fundamental deontological premise that such dominant coalitions have prime duties for safety above production and shareholder returns if they are governing the affairs of high-reliability organisations. For example, the dominant coalition has both a moral and legal responsibility to intervene where prior knowledge is available or where bypassing safety standards in favour of the priority of production may occur. This book suggests that the exercise of these responsibilities must be supported by strong legal and financial sanctions, in high-reliability organisations.

The HyperRESEARCH analysis of the text data revealed the following behavioural descriptors supporting this view.

HyperRESEARCH Regulatory and Compliance Descriptors

accountability, breach of law, bypassing safety requirements, cause real, certificate of competency withdrawn, collateral casualties, collusion, compliance with national standards, contamination of evidence, criminal offence, dominance of CEO, dominant coalition, economic factors, enforcement, failure of regulator, misconduct, regulator unable to enforce compliance, regulatory independence regulator dominated by regulated, relationship between regulator and regulated, role of government, role of regulator,

COMPLIANCE AND THE COMPETENCY SET

Compliance is a complex issue in preventing accidents. This book treats it as a core competency that relies to a large extent on mastery of specific knowledge and its application through the other core competencies, because senior managers have a responsibility to develop a competent working knowledge of their legal and ethical responsibilities (*compliance* and *ethics*), including the day-to-day running of the company (*understanding the salience of the particular situation*) while retaining sufficient independence of mind (*balance*) to enable them to reach sound decisions (*judgement*) (Crainer, 1993). They need sufficient knowledge and mastery of the systems as they are designed and as they will be used in practice (*performance in a particular setting*). They also need the ability and detachment (*foresight*) not to make too rapid decisions about changes to prevent the *last* disaster (Hall, 19891).

The problem of compliance also implies that failure of the ten core competencies cannot be excused. If the necessary competencies were established and practised there would be very few, if any, accidents which could be sheeted home to individuals (ie most accidents would be classed then as acts of God).

Ethics is perhaps the most critical of the competencies to which compliance measures should apply since it is unethical to decide to allow unsafe conditions to persist which could cost lives as a trade-off for profits or personal power. All of the compliance issues involving the other competencies flow from this.

IDEAS ABOUT COMPLIANCE

Turnbull (2002) claims that shareholders, stakeholders and the public cannot trust corporations because our system of corporate governance creates at least eight reasons why they should not be trusted:

1. Information overload that makes is impractical for directors to monitor complex and/or dynamic businesses with monthly meetings.

2. Lack of information, independent of management for directors to determine the Strengths, Weakness, Opportunities and Threats (SWOT) of management or the business.

3. Lack of systemic process for directors to discover when their trust in management might be misplaced.

4. Expropriation by dominant shareholder or management who can determine the appointment of each director and the auditor.

5. Absolute corruption from absolute power of directors to manage their own conflicts of interest.

6. Non-Executive Directors (NEDs) lacking the will to act in the best interest of the company.

7. NEDs lacking the capability to act alone in the best interests of the company.

8. Shares can be covertly traded and/or manipulated by insiders.

These elements are congruent with the findings of this book. For example, it became legislatively necessary for the *Review of the Mines Safety and Inspection Act, 1994,* in the light of recent cases that indicated managerial failure as a factor in accidents, to set out several recommendations related to managerial responsibility, and therefore compliance. For example:

R:7: It is recommended *s.12* of the *Mines Safety and Inspection Act 1994* be amended to:

• specify the duty of employers and self-employed persons to protect non-employees from adverse consequences of work so that it extends to all aspects of work including systems of work and hazards arising after direct work activity has ceased. The application of the section should be restricted to workplace-initiated safety and health matters.

Recommendations 15 and 16 suggest mine managers be required to have knowledge of the Act and certification under the Act.

R:15 It is recommended the Mines Safety and Inspection Act 1994 be amended to require Registered Mine Managers to be able to demonstrate a knowledge of the Act and associated Regulations.

R:16 It is recommended a review be undertaken of the certification requirements in Part 4 of the Mines Safety and Inspection Act 1994.

The West Australian Government set up a safety review in mid-June 2004 to run concurrently with the statutory investigations under the Mines and Safety Inspection Act 1994 to examine the underlying culture of BHP at its WA Pilbara iron ore operations mine sites and Boodarie Iron hot briquette iron plant following three deaths (The West Australian June 19, 2004:6). The State Development Minister set the terms of the review to include an examination of the cultural and behavioral factors affecting safety. The review will also try (at the time of writing) to determine the nature of issues arising from the attitude to regulations and company policies prior to the accidents. It seems that BHP has learned little from the Longford, Moura and other accidents described in this book.

The data examined in this book is suggestive that dominant coalitions should be held responsible for preventable accidents. Gunningham and Johnstone (1999:308-340) offer the most recent, elaborate and thorough exegesis of the compliance issues surrounding management responsibility as it relates to safety in an Australian legal framework. Salient to this book is their argument that there is a problem of identifying the responsible officer in large organisations. They suggest that these difficulties can be overcome by: (a) presuming that the CEO is the responsible officer; or (b) requiring the organisation to nominate a responsible officer and provide that officer with adequate training and resources.

Gunningham and Johnstone also argue a case for redesigning OHS regulation and its enforcement, so as to make it both more effective and efficient in addressing OHS problems. In doing so they identify a range of 'next generation' regulatory and enforcement instruments arguing that OHS statutes to be reformed to increase the maximum fines available (to increase the size of the stick) along with a range of sanctions for OHS breaches. They suggest these sanctions might include:

•court-ordered adverse publicity, which enables a court to require the details of the contravention and the outcome of the prosecution to be publicised through the media to enhance general deterrence, and to affect non-financial values of the organisation.

•supervisory orders and corporate probation, which include:

- internal discipline orders requiring the organisation to investigate the contravention, discipline those responsible, and return a compliance report to the court;

- organisational reform orders, which require organisations to report regularly to the court on its efforts to develop a compliance programme and to reform its OHS management system; and

- punitive injunctions, where the court requires the organisation to introduce a specific OHS management system.

•community service orders, which require the duty holder to carry out an OHS-related project using the organisation's resources, involving top management, during normal business hours.

•dissolution, where the most egregious offenders are required to cease their activities until their OHS management systems are reformed or wound up permanently if the court decides that they are incorrigible.

•equity fines, where instead of being fined, offenders are required to issue new shares to the OHS agency which can be liquidated by the agency when it chooses. This sanction might result in a dilution of the offenders shares, might increase its susceptibility to a takeover, and might decrease the value of top management's shares in the organisation.

•disqualification from tendering for government contracts. (Gunningham and Johnstone, 1999:334)

The book data would support this set of sanctions for failure to comply with OHS regulations, since the current impression is that most OHS regulations focus on management systems rather than the consequences of them.

Gunningham and Johnstone (1999:309) also examine the issue of compliance and conclude that there is a debate between specification standards (which tell duty holders how to meet a goal by requiring compliance with detailed technical requirements) and performance standards (which define the duty in terms of problems to be solved or goals to be achieved). They note a trend towards replacing specification with both performance standards and principle-based standards (for example, very general 'duty of care' provisions) while complementing these with greater reliance on codes of practice rather than regulations. They claim that their approach, in most circumstances, establishes general goals but leaves duty holders with the flexibility and discretion of finding the most effective and efficient way to achieve them and they see this as a benefit.

This book agrees but caveats their claim in that such benefits appear to rely on the competencies of dominant coalitions. These competencies cannot be assumed, based on the data at hand. They point out that recently, there has been a trend to complement performance standards with process-based standards: standards which address procedures for achieving a desired result. However, this book is suggestive that compliance with performance standards becomes compliance with minimum performance standards in practice, and that these minimum standards become defacto benchmarks that organisations set as the highest standards they are prepared to meet.

In general, Gunningham and Johnstone recognise this problem and suggest that the weight of specification standards should be substantially reduced. But where there is a high degree of risk and there are specific controls which are applicable to all circumstances where the risk occurs and which are essential to control the risk, then more rigid standards should be maintained. They suggest that small employers and subcontractors, in particular, remain a problem under this approach because they often require much more concrete direction as to what is required of them. They claim that this direction can be most appropriately given through technical guidance documents, rather than through legally binding and prescriptive specification standards.

This view assumes that the regulator is competent, which the data in this book does not support. For example, Seaview Airlines was in possession of all the technical documents it needed to avoid accidents and the regulator knew of the regulatory breaches this airline was engaging in. The regulator should have intervened and did not. It was the combination of regulator and operator incompetence which resulted in the fatal Seaview accident. The CAA, however, sought to entirely blame Seaview.

. . .

Congruent with these findings, Gunningham and Johnstone (1999:317) found that empirical scrutiny revealed that inspectors did not use a framework for an escalating enforcement response against individual employers and the enforcement response tended to be informal and unstructured. Moreover, they found that there may be little consistency across the inspectorate (regulator) about the circumstances in which the various notices are issued, or prosecutions taken. Again, the Seaview case supports their findings.

Gunningham and Johnstone also develop an argument for a lateral approach to regulation, taking advantage of the considerable leverage that large firms have over smaller trading partners. This would involve using the former as surrogate regulators, who would act if not to 'police', at least to oversee, the OHS performance of their suppliers and contractors, exercising control through the extended application of their management systems. Had the Navy overseen the manufacture of the fuel hoses installed in the Westralia, for example, it is unlikely there would have been an accident.

CASES OF FAILURES OF HIGH-RELIABILITY COMPLIANCE

This book suggests that compliance should be an issue when an organisation is in breach of common laws, such as those that consider culpable manslaughter to be a criminal act, or where there is deliberate contamination of evidence or other criminal behaviour in fatal or serious injury accidents. However, it becomes apparent on reading the various accident reports from this book and others, such as Zeebrugge and Bhopal, that senior management seems to be protected from prosecution even where culpability is established. For example, Crainer (1993) observes that British precedents demonstrated some confusion regarding the role of managers. A 1971 House of Lords case found that Tesco was not criminally liable when one of its shop managers defaulted on a payment. It decided that the manager was not sufficiently senior enough to count as the 'company'.

This decision found its way into later safety related accident cases. In reference to the Zeebrugge case (*Herald of Free Enterprise*), an article in the *Guardian* (13 Oct, 1987) by Hugo Young captured, albeit in journalistic rhetoric, the attitude to responsibility often found among senior management: 'It says something about the moral climate in which we live that a ship can sink, 188 people die, a judge report a catalogue of negligence, a coroner's jury find unlawful killing - and yet the owners can be so bold as to contend that they, of course, are not to blame.' This is in spite of the fact that Lord Brabazon said that 'The government fully accepts that a sloppy and inefficient shipowner or ship's manager can make it difficult for a master to carry out his duties.' 'Sloppy' management was used to describe the actions of Townsend Thoresen's management after the capsize of the *Herald of Free Enterprise* of Zeebrugge in the Sheen Report (1984).

Compliance is a fluid and changing legal palette on which the law is practised. Sometimes the legal brush is broad and sometimes finely nuanced. For example, judges have differed on what constitutes 'senior management'. Lord Denning in 1975 suggested that it is directors and managers who represent the directing mind and will of the company. Lord Diplock restricted the definition to directors. Lord Reid included senior officers who carry out the functions of management. Lord Dilhorne included persons in actual control of operations who in practice are not responsible for anyone else.

The report of the Court of Marine Enquiry: ss Lake Illawarra (1975) was interesting in that it went beyond management and recognised the role of the regulator, and yet went to considerable lengths to exonerate the Harbour Master. However, it seems inescapable that the conditional paragraphs below are suggestive that the role of the regulator was at best discretionary, if not borderline, and perhaps a causative factor in this accident. The accident occurred on the cusp of the altered navigation arrangements in the Port of Hobart and it is quite clear the Captain Pelc should have been piloted through the port since he had not previously entered the port under the new navigation regulations.

. . .

ILLAWARRA

[role of regulator]

The evidence given by Captain Pelc makes two matters clear:

a.there was no doubt in his mind about his ability to navigate his vessel into the Port of Hobart without the aid of a pilot (1041); and,

b.his purpose in sending a telegram (before entering the port of Hobart) was to check whether his Pilotage Exemption Certificate remained valid in accordance with the Regulations (1040).

The Master's Pilotage Exemption Certificate remained valid in accordance with Regulation 8, and that there was no reason to exercise the discretion which the Harbour Master believed (759) he had under Regulation 10 (2) to prevent Captain Pelc exercising his right as an Exempt Master to enter the Port. We believe their decision as to the validity of Captain Pelc's Pilotage Exemption Certificate was correct.

We do not stay to consider closely the nature of the Harbour Master's discretion under Regulation 10 (2), or the circumstances in which it might be exercised. (Court of Marine Enquiry: ss Lake Illawarra, 1975:7)

The next paragraph suggests that it was unfortunate that the Port of Hobart did not act consistently with its altered policy. This is congruent with a propensity to exonerate the regulating authority and to blame the frontline operator.

However, we think it appropriate to observe, in light of what has occurred, that it is unfortunate that when the Marine Board in 1971 introduced the two-year pilotage rule for the Zones of the Port of Hobart it did not act consistently with its altered policy by making that rule applicable, not only to future Exemption Certificates, but also to those issued before the division of the Port into Zones. We desire to recommend that the Regulations be altered so as to make it clear that an Exempt Master must navigate the waters of a Zone of the Port of Hobart within two years if his Exemption Certificate is to remain valid in respect of that Zone. (Court of Marine Enquiry: ss Lake Illawarra, 1975:7)

The Lake Illawarra case is one of the first cases in Australian law to offer a finding which to some extent engaged with the role of the regulator.

Later cases such as the Seaview/CAA, Westralia, and Longford cases had much better theoretical and case precedent information to work with and were critical of the role of the regulator and used the evolving language and insights from work such as that of Reason (1982, 1987, 1994, 1995, 2000) and Turner (1976, 1997). The Longford case also seems to have relied to some extent on the analysis of the Moura case by Hopkins (1999). The Longford Royal Commission Report (1999) illustrates the relationship between prior knowledge and responsibility for handover, or accountability - failures that played a part in the cause of the accident.

Longford

13.101 At the commencement of the day shift on 25 September 1998, the outgoing GP1 panel operator had an obligation to tell the relieving operator, not only about the cold temperatures in Absorber

B, but about the off-scale levels of condensate in that vessel. Both of these conditions had existed for some time (prior knowledge). Olsson should at least have told Ward about the almost constant occurrence of the Absorber B high level alarm and the TC913 alarm and the fact that such alarms were still active at changeover (accountability). Indeed, the purpose of the handover procedure as a communication tool was to ensure that important process information was passed on. In the same way, Olsson's log book entries at the conclusion of his shift could have been, and should have been, more informative. They should also have made reference to these matters.

13.128 However, the evidence before the Commission indicates that such records were not used as effectively as they might have been in GPL Indeed it is possible that their ineffective use played a part in the occurrence of the accident (cause real) on 25 September 1998. (The Longford Royal Commission Report, 1999:13.101)

The Longford Royal Commission Report (1999) also made it clear that in order to provide a safe working environment there was an obligation to provide appropriate operating procedures to deal with the loss of lean oil circulation, cold temperatures and the shutdown and start up of the plant. Furthermore, the operators and supervisors could and should have known of and understood the real hazards confronting them on the day. Esso failed to take measures that were plainly practicable. Bypassing safety requirements this way also affects the organisation's capacity to learn from reported anomalies.

13.144 The SMM definitions of 'incident' and 'near miss' were wide enough to require operations personnel to report as an incident any serious process upset that occurred during the operation of the Longford plant, in practice, however, the obligation to report incidents was construed by Esso management and by operations personnel. Process upsets were rarely, if ever, the subject of an incident report, unless they were accompanied by injury to persons or damage to property.

13.145 The consequence of this practice was that process upsets which may well have signified to qualified and experienced personnel, defective equipment, or inappropriate operating conditions or unsafe operating practices, were not brought to their attention. Thus, valuable opportunities to learn from process upsets were lost. (The Longford Royal Commission Report, 1999:13.144-5)

The cases examined revealed many examples of a failure of accountability leading to safety requirements being bypassed or overlooked. Since this can be a real cause of an accident it is a serious breach of regulations or failure of compliance. Each commission and coronial Enquiry have placed more or less weight on these failures of accountability. In any case, they serve to point to a human competency failing in understanding the actual cause of accidents.

Reason (1995, 2000) is right in that a tight system should have prevented the failing; however, these are failures of individual accountability and are sufficiently important to be considered more grievous than mere oversights, or to be excused as 'systemic failures in organisations where they have occurred time and again (such as BHP). Turner's (1997) observation that prior knowledge was ignored has more traction. This is heartening since it more accurately points to the critical and often failed intervention role of the regulator in cases where management orthodoxy has not prevented and accident or where negligence or management incompetence or criminal behaviour has been a factor.

The Longford Commission pointed out that regulations promulgated under the Commonwealth Petroleum (Submerged Lands) Act 1967 (Cwlth) required the consent of the Designated Authority to construct or install a facility and to use a facility offshore. Obtaining consent entails the submission and acceptance of a safety case. The Gas Safety Act and the Gas Safety (Safety Case) Regulations 1999 require a gas company to submit a safety case to the Office of Gas Safety. The safety case must be in writing and comply with the regulations.

If managerial competencies had ensured that compliance with this process had occurred, BHP would have submitted a safety case that, in turn, would have identified the hazards that caused the accident.

Longford

14.33 The regulatory regime covering Esso's operations at Longford was less stringent than for its facilities upstream from Longford and for the gas transmission and distribution facilities downstream from Longford. Had Esso been required to submit a safety case with respect to its facilities at Longford before 25 September 1998, it is likely that it would have identified the very hazards which were in evidence on that day, hazards which a proper HAZOP study of GP1 would also have identified.

14.34 The Commission notes that the Dangerous Goods (Storage & Handling) Regulations 1989 were amended in 1997 to enable operators of MHFs to obtain exemptions from certain prescriptive provisions contained in the regulations if they could demonstrate compliance with the national standard. There is no evidence that Esso ever sought such an exemption. Failure to hold such a license was an offence under s.21(2) of the Dangerous Goods Act. The license held by Esso expired on 26 August 1998 - exactly one month before the accident. (The Longford Royal Commission Report, (1999:14.34)

However, the Longford Royal Commission Report (1999) observed that Esso/BHP's failure to secure a current license effective at the time of the accident was 'technical'. It sets this observation against the legislative framework which gave rise to the Occupational Health and Safety Act and the Dangerous Goods Act. It unequivocally stated that it is a continuous legal and social responsibility of all those who have control over the conditions and circumstances under which work is performed.

Longford

14.16 Until 1985, the legislative scheme in Victoria dealing with occupational health and safety was prescriptive. That is to say, it laid down specific requirements, compliance with which was supervised by government agencies. For example, there was legislation dealing separately with disparate matters such as pressure vessels, hazardous substances, scaffolding and lifts and cranes. Following the 1972 Robens Report in the United Kingdom, a decision was made to change, at least in part, from a prescriptive system to one that was performance based, that is to say, one which enunciated the basic and over-riding responsibilities of employers and employees. The report (Paragraph 130) explained that system as follows:

"A positive declaration of the over-riding duties, carrying the stamp of parliamentary approval, would establish in the minds of all concerned that the preservation of safety and health at work is a continuous legal and social responsibility of all those who have control over the conditions and circumstances under which work is performed. It would make clear that this is an all-embracing responsibility, covering all workpeople and working circumstances unless excluded."

The Longford Royal Commission Report, (1999:14.16)

As in the BHP/Esso case, there seemed to be a persistent permissive cultural attitude to regulations in the CAA (Staunton, J. H., 1996). The Enquiry identified process steps which are in themselves compliance audit competencies. The regulator should, as a matter of course, have these capabilities in place. It should pursue them to prosecution if clear breaches occur.

CAA

It is accepted that the aviation industry has a responsibility to comply with regulations and that the CAA, not being able to monitor every aspect of every operation, must place a degree of trust in operators. However, there should be limits to the degree of trust. CAA officers should not assume the accuracy of what they are told. The information should be received sceptically. It should be tested more than occasionally for its accuracy, either by inspection or by random ramp checks.

When inaccuracies are uncovered the CAA should become more probing. It must do so in order to determine the truth about the level of compliance in an operation. If that truth reveals criminal offences, consideration should be given to prosecution or other enforcement action-just as all regulators are obliged to consider such possibilities when a breach of the law is uncovered. (Executive Summary p7)

This is also salient in that the CAA case observes a regulator must to some extent trust an operator to provide proper levels of health and safety, but is still clear that the responsibility to ensure compliance is on the regulator. 'Responsibility' also embraces its duty of care or deontological interpretation under the Act that governs its role and responsibilities as a regulator, to those who may suffer as a consequence of operator negligence or incompetence.

In 1985 the Victorian Occupational Health and Safety Act and the Dangerous Goods Act were enacted. Section 21 of the Occupational Health and Safety Act is one of the two sections (the other being s.22) which imposed the primary obligation upon an employer to provide and maintain a safe workplace and working environment, leaving it to the employer to identify the specific steps required for the carrying out of that obligation.

This does not exonerate the regulator. Both regulator and organisation are bound in law to comply with specific Acts governing safety in Australia, each regulator under its establishment Act, and each organisation under various Occupational Health and Safety Acts.

DIAGNOSTIC TOOLS TO IMPROVE HIGH-RELIABILITY COMPLIANCE

Both the organisation and the regulator should be held accountable for fatal accidents. The book revealed many instances of criminal behaviour, negligence and sheer incompetence which resulted in fatal accidents. These acts and behaviours go well beyond 'systemic failure'. For example, in the CAA case, the CEO of Seaview lied, falsified maintenance reports and records, behaved like a schoolyard bully, engaged in a long record of duplicitous conduct and showed continuing contempt for critical safety regulations and the regulator.

Clearly, the Enquiry into the fatal Seaview crash could not contemplate allowing this incompetent person (he appeared to possess none of the competencies suggested in this book) to hide behind the veil of the corporate entity. Paradoxically, the regulator failed to intervene and deal with this dangerous situation even though it was aware such a potentially hazardous situation existed. Had the CAA at the time intervened, doubtless the fatal crash would not have occurred. However, its senior officers also hid behind the corporate veil and received little more than admonishment for the lives lost. One is compelled therefore to ask to what extent the lax regulator is complicit in the crash. This suggests that prosecutions ought to be brought against individuals in organisations, and their regulators, where criminal offences can be established.

THINKING ABOUT COMPLIANCE

Gunningham and Johnston (1999:333) suggest that higher monetary fines, and the possibility of imprisonment for culpable corporate officers, are required to provide a greater general and specific deterrent to Occupational Health and Safety (OHS) duty holders to ensure that the perceived costs of OHS contraventions exceed the likely benefits of ignoring or side-stepping statutory OHS obligations. Sanctions should also signal to OHS duty holders that, where they fail to introduce appropriate OHS management systems, courts will order them to do so. The Longford case demonstrated this more recent trend.

The Westralia case illustrated the effect of non-compliance with Naval regulations that insists that fuel hoses meet certain technical specifications. This non-compliance was found to be the direct cause of the Westralia accident. The West Australian Coroner, Alistair Hope, said that "gross mistakes" were made in not assessing flexible fuel hoses that had been fitted prior to the fire. Mr Hope's findings concluded that a 'series of mistakes and systemic deficiencies' had led to the fuel hoses being changed from solid metal to a flexible type. 'The mistakes were very serious mistakes as the hoses were to be installed close to the indicator cocks which were known to be extremely hot and a possible ignition source. The use of flexible fuel hoses to replace pipes in the close vicinity of an exposed heat source capable of igniting diesel without any engineering assessment of their fitness for the purpose was an outrageously bad error.'

He said the tragedy could have been avoided.

In certain cases, such as fatalities, regulatory acts may be insufficient to both render justice and to uncover serious failure of duty of care. At best the Navy has been admonished and perhaps the Commonwealth will have to pay fines as consequences flow from a compliance failure.

Solicitor, Bernard Collaery (West Australian Dec 20, 2003), said he intended to file civil suits on behalf of the families of the four sailors killed in the accident, despite the expiration of the 12-month statute of limitations. Mr Collaery said, 'We are going to be filing civil processes against the Commonwealth, and we suspect that they will not oppose those writs being filed past the 12-month limitation period.' He said the coroner's findings vindicated the family's quest for an inquest. 'The persistent opposition by the Navy to an inquest, claiming that the Naval Board of Inquiry had answered all the questions, has been found to have been the smokescreen it was. The system of outsourcing used amounted to nothing short of abdication by the Commonwealth of its responsibilities to maintain defence assets in proper operational order.'

The Beechcraft Super Twin Air 200 incident is significant because it succinctly illustrates many of the research findings that show how compliance issues such as the failure of regulators to act on prior knowledge often goes together with managerial hubris and failure of judgement and demonstrates the relationship of compliance to several core competencies.

On Monday, September 4, 2000, nine people died when their flight from Perth to Leonora overflew its destination by more than 2,300 km and crashed in northern Queensland near the outback town of Burketown, northeast of Mt. Isa. The aircraft appeared to have lost pressurisation and flew at around 34,000 feet on autopilot until it crashed. The depressurisation warning system failed to alert the pilot. The problem is that if depressurisation occurs slowly people on board can lose consciousness and not be aware of what is happening. The system installed on the Beechcraft is a small flashing light above the pilot's head. The issue here is that the Bureau of Air Safety advised the Civil Aviation Safety Authority over a year previously that the flashing light ought to be accompanied by an audible alarm, but CASA did not act on the advice and no audible alarms were installed on Beechcraft Super Twin Air 200's in Australia. This aircraft was normally used as a flying doctor aircraft.

. . .

The strange paradox of this accident is that Tom Ballantyne's article in The Bulletin of the 5th of September (the same day the accident was reported in headlines around the country) carried a picture of the CEO of the Civil Aviation Safety Authority, Mick Toller, on its cover with the lead story of that issue entitled, *'Zero Tolerance, Taking the Fear out of Flying'*. The article has the CEO arguing that safety fears have been 'overblown'. It was a response to the premise that air safety regulation in Australia is in turmoil and following the resignation of Dr Rob Lee, the head of the Bureau of Air Safety Investigation (BASI) , which insiders report was due to his belief that organisational changes (BASI being incorporated into the Australian Transport Safety Bureau (ATSB) and funding cuts undermined the work of the air accident branch's ability to do its job. Again, Turner's (1997) argument is established (that prior information was known which could have prevented the accident, but it was not heeded by the dominant coalition).

In each of these accident scenarios we see 'scientific' insights failing to prevent future accidents and, in each case, the dominant coalition could have acted to prevent the accident but did not. This failure to act on previously known information is central to this book. It raises concerns about the preoccupations and state of mind of managers. The Western Australian Coroner, Mr Alistair Hope reported that his attempts to conduct an inquest into the Beechcraft accident were 'bedevilled from the start'. Counsel Assisting, Mr. Dominic Mulligan, echoed this view when he said that a lack of cooperation between various government bodies did not justify a high level of public confidence.

The accident report eventually presented revealed that ATSB investigators did not include interviews, nor did they take notes and their sources of information remained confidential. During the hearing an ATSB investigator said he was instructed not to bring the bureau's files to court. Similarly, a doctor, called to give evidence was told that his files were not available for release. The inquest ended in acrimony when Mr Hope ordered the ATSB to provide him with the engineers' report on the plane. Mr Mulligan accused CASA of taking no active part in any meaningful form of investigation. He had written to CASA on February 15 and March 1 seeking their current attitude to the fitting of audible alarms on aircraft to alert pilots of pressurisation problems. Neither letter had been acknowledged or answered until after the start of the inquest.

Neither the ATSB nor Air Services Australia would provide the Coroner with a copy of the final conversations between the doomed flight and ground control. Air Services' advised the Coroner that: 'As long as Air Services receives written confirmation that there is no potential adverse involvement for Air Services, we are more than happy to cooperate with the Coroner.' The Queensland police finally forwarded their report to the Coroner on February 27, but only after repeated requests and telephone calls. The evidence demonstrates the hubris of senior management and confirms that as the pressure increases the stronger is the tendency to autopoiesis.

Gunningham and Johnston (1999:333) hold that corporate liability should be attributed to the acts of upper and middle management. This is congruent with the evidence from each of the cases examined in this book which revealed that erroneous thinking by senior personnel was at the centre of accident causes. For example, in the case of Moura No.2, considerable financial incentives were paid for production but none for the conscientious management of catastrophic risk (Hopkins, 1999:134). The research suggests that each party should be held accountable for failures which could have been prevented where breaches of governing acts and criminal law occur.

The Review of the Mines Safety and Inspection Act 1994 made several recommendations related to managerial responsibility and therefore compliance, for example,

R:7: It is recommended *s.12* of the *Mines Safety and Inspection Act 1994* be amended to:

• specify the duty of employers and self-employed persons to protect non-employees from adverse consequences of work so that it extends to all aspects of work including systems of work and hazards arising after direct work activity has ceased.

It then goes on to limit the effect stating, 'The application of the section should be restricted to workplace-initiated safety and health matters.'

HIGH-RELIABILITY DIAGNOSTIC QUESTIONS

Several questions arise from consideration of sources such as Turnbull (2000), Gunningham and Johnstone (1999), and the body of this book. these include:

•In what circumstances does managerial failure and neglect become a criminal offence?

•Should incompetent, negligent and criminal behaviours in individuals, organisations and their regulators attract legal consequences for the key individuals involved?

•Should these individuals be allowed to hide behind the veil of the corporate entity?

•What consequences should flow from the contamination of evidence and the failure to comply with safety standards?

•What is the effect on stakeholders of ensuring a high-reliability entity is governed by a statutory act while its senior managers face only misconduct charges for preventable fatal accidents?

If benighted managers in positions of responsibility in high-reliability organisations, or people in the appropriate regulatory authority, are negligent or incompetent, or their actions can be construed to be criminal and this results in fatal accidents, then those people ought not to be able to hide behind the corporate veil. At the very least, if the corporate entity is considered to be a legal entity in law for which they purport responsibility, then they should be found individually complicit in accidents in which there is a failure of responsibility of the corporate identity.

There should be a presumption that the CEO is the responsible officer, or the organisation should be required to nominate a responsible officer. Mainstream criminal law (for example, manslaughter and related crimes) should allow enforcement officials to initiate prosecutions for manslaughter and causing serious injury over and above statutory OHS acts governing such organisations. Most OHS statutes appear to be inadequate in dealing with attributing criminal cause in fatalities and currently portray contraventions in terms of inadequate OHS management systems. These should be rewritten to reflect criminal law or be tied to criminal law in cases of fatalities or serious injury so that the Rule of Law applies equally to all legal subjects including corporate entities in matters of safety.

1. Professor A.R. Hall, of the Safety Science Group at Delft University made this observation regarding making rapid decisions to prevent the last disaster while presenting a paper at the Disaster Prevention and Limitation Conference, Bradford University, December, 1989.

2. Daniel Clery reporting in the West Australian, Tuesday Sept 5 2000. He stated that the pilot was heard gasping and breathing heavily before air traffic controllers lost touch with him soon after take-off. A similar event occurred in the United States in 1999 on October 25 when golfer Payne Stewart's private Learjet 35 flew 2240 km on autopilot before crashing after decompression caused the six people on board to lose consciousness.

3. The West Australian Saturday, March 16, 2002 (p36)

4. The bodies referred to are the Australian Transport Safety Bureau, The Civil Aviation Safety Authority, Air Services Australia, and the Queensland Police Department. The ATSB said that the Coroner and

the victim's families were not 'interested parties' and they were not made aware of a draft of the ATSB report. When the ATSB were told that the Coroner would hand down an adverse report that the ATSB were not competent to investigate air crashes, the report was fast tracked. Eleven counsel representing the various parties turned up for the inquest.

22. CONCLUSIONS AND RECOMMENDATIONS

PUTTING IT ALL TOGETHER

"Power is the ability not to have to learn anything."

Karl Deutsch: MIT political scientist.

Premise

This book began with the critical Turner (1978) premise that information needed to prevent accidents was already available and known to organisational personnel and others before an accident. It also established that critical competencies, such as *ethics, foresight, vigilance* and *judgement,* require specific training, because if they are left to ordinary humans who have not incorporated them into operational schemata, then when extraordinary circumstances arise they are unlikely to spontaneously do so, and this may well result in unreliable and inaccurate organisational memes rather than educated responses to dangerous situations.

Or:

Like fish in a fish tank, culture is the water the organisation swims in. An organisation's culture is all around them and it is invisible - but it contains the oxygen (values) everyone in the organisation breathes all the time.

If safety is not valued in the water the organisation swims in, then it will not be there when it's needed. You have a safety culture or you don't.

The investigation was guided by the following questions:

Principal Question

What significant underpinning capacities, organisational factors, and performance capacities are revealed in accident reports, and what competencies flow from these to enable dominant coalitions in high-reliability organisations to effectively engage in accident prevention?

The competencies developed in this investigation in response to this question are:

Underpinning Capacities:

•**ethics** (organisational and individual manager's values and behaviour as they influence the determination of right from wrong in decisions concerning safety)

•**foresight** (attitudinal 'stance' and 'intelligent looking ahead' as factors in decisions concerning safety)

•**vigilance** (hazard perception and awareness and an alert 'way of seeing' are necessary to signal detection)

•**judgement** (weighing up, trading off, and deciding - often in circumstances that make little sense or meaning, are factors in all competencies)

•**balance** (psychological tenor, courage and persistence are essential in safety versus financial decisions)

Organisational Factors:

•**organisational ethos** (open or closed [autopoietic] organisational cultures shape hazard management capabilities)

•**constructing a culture of safet**y ('intention' to establish a culture of safety, 'ways of seeing', and persistent personal or organisational ideas - 'memes' influence the systemic capacities for managing safety)

Capacity to Perform:

•**understanding the salience of the particular situation and its context** (awareness of organisational and incident factors peculiar to particular hazardous environments)

•**performance in a particular setting** (managerial capacity to deal with stress, conflict, and unfolding disaster in particular hazardous environments)

•**multidisciplinary performance** (bringing together skills from different and complementary domains to manage a particular hazard)

Subsidiary Question

What significant factors are revealed in accident reports and key literature as being required by dominant coalitions in high-reliability organisations to effectively enable compliance with accident prevention regulations and appropriate intervention strategies in unfolding accident scenarios?

The competency developed in this investigation in response to this question is:

Regulatory Compliance and Intervention

•**compliance** (compliance and regulatory factors, legal and other punitive responses to managerial failure)

The two book questions directed the book activity to the discovery of eleven managerial competencies, which together constitute a core set of high-reliability competencies considered essential for the prevention of preventable accidents. They also suggested the need for training and cyclical refresher training for dominant coalitions in high reliability organisations, in the capabilities needed to create and maintain a safety aware habitus.

The research also indicated serious implications for corporate governance and the role of government policy and corporate alliances in the construction of organisational capabilities needed to attend to risk.

Finally, two questions suggested directions for further research.

The Case for Competency Training

Values may have a variety of manifestations, including, arrogance demonstrated by those in power, hasty propagation of unsound ideas, inhibition of individuals' capacity for judgement, an inward and defensive outlook, work systems that do not convey crucial information or allow accountability, masking of critical signals concerning potential hazards, and a tendency for decisions to be based on false consensus, assumptions or group-think, and for management to blame operational staff for accidents (Mitroff & Pauchant, 1990; Mitroff & Linstone, 1993).

. . .

This proposition revealed that even though the organisations concerned espoused compliance with current safety regulations and standards, and the dominant coalition sustained an official model of competent understanding of the responsibilities for which they purported to be responsible, whereas, where accidents occurred that resulted in fatalities or serious injury, it could be established that they were not competent. The task of the research, therefore, was to discover evidence of this failure of competence and to identify in that evidence the competencies that were lacking. This research was carried out and framed by an examination of the seminal literature and representative case evidence. The method adopted to examine the case evidence and elicit the core competencies was a modified form of grounded theory.

The case evidence suggested that skilled use of 'prior knowledge' and 'managerial competencies' culminating in an operational schemata based on 'expertise' are needed to limit fatal accidents in high-reliability organisations.

It emerged from the case evidence that most, if not all, accidents occur in spite of a recognition somewhere in the organisation that just such an accident could occur (bearing in mind, that paradoxically, an accident is an unanticipated event and is a surprise to those involved). This supports Turner's accident foresight theory, in which he and his co-author, Pidgeon, suggest that there is an incubation period, during which the factors that contribute to an accident are known to various people (Taylor & Pidgeon, 1997:68).

This emphasis on 'prior knowledge' in the data is premised on the reasoning that when an accident occurs it is too late to start planning for it, therefore focus must be placed on the managerial competencies of members of the dominant coalition and their deontological capacity to exert influence to eliminate or mitigate the likelihood of fatal accidents.

The problem of training is complicated by the certain knowledge that some CEOs and other senior members of the dominant coalition may be clinically assessable as psychopathic. Such people are not amenable to normal training techniques and some programs may make them worse, or at least better-functioning psychopaths.

Hare (2004) suggests that programs that are emotion-based and appeal to one's sense of right and wrong or depend upon the presence of a conscience or the ability to understand emotionally what other people are going through, will not work for psychopaths.

Professor Hare suggests that programs based on enlightened self-interest may have some effect on psychopaths. Programs for corporate psychopaths would indicate or convince them that there are ways in which they can get what they want and need without harming other people.

Self-interest and emotional detachment appeal to corporate psychopaths.

Real world implications for corporate governance in high-reliability organisations through the application of the research findings

The concern for a pattern of dovetailing competencies highlights the key failures of assumptions and communications made by managers. Mitroff (1993:69-81 & 136-150) identifies the critical need to surface safety related assumptions. The case evidence is suggestive that members of the dominant coalition subscribe to faulty assumptions and ignore the knowledge and advice available from those at the interface of potential accidents, especially when the 'bottom line' is at stake.

This takes us full circle to the central argument of this book that the core competencies, which enhance the responsibility to manage safety and put safety before other factors, are essential in high-reliability organisations. Also critical is the motivation to employ these competencies, either by encouragement or coercion, through managers knowing there will be a personal 'cost' for negligence in the form of a strong compliance regime.

This aspirational view must be set firmly against real world observations such as those made by Cyert and March (1963), who claim that goals (and therefore, decisions) are largely set by a negotiation process among members of dominant coalitions in the pursuit of certain interests related to production.

Punitive compliance measures are necessary because evidence shows that safety goals are inclined to be influenced by the interests of 'managerial' individuals and groups as they engage in "horse trading" and build self-interested alliances. These potentially dangerous activities are, in effect, supported by Australian corporate law, which allows directors the absolute power to manage their own conflicts of interest (Turnbull, 2000).

There is strong evidentiary support for a compliance regime because the research shows that in each case where accidents occurred there was an amplified concern for 'the bottom line' and 'stakeholder returns' and a range of other 'production' or 'corporation-first' related pressures, rather than safety.

Competency Training for Dominant coalitions and Compliance

The accident reports make it clear that the competencies or capabilities identified were lacking or not employed in the accidents studied at the points of intervention required by the circumstances. One is inclined to the view that these key managerial competencies failed or were overwhelmed when financial or production pressures took precedence over deontological requirements. If managers have acquired the competencies described, through experience and training, and use them to intervene in unfolding accident sequences then accidents will be less likely to occur. This line of reasoning is suggestive of the need for mandatory training and retraining and a powerful supporting compliance regime to ensure that such pressures do not prevail over the competencies needed to ensure safety. Gunningham (1999) suggests the need for significant sanctions against managers for managerial and organisational lapses, where fatalities occur in preventable accidents.

Points of intervention

Clear points of intervention are possible. For example, at the operator interface, the managerial decision that put the operator in harm's way, senior management and boards that escalate the risk attached to managerial decisions regarding safety, and the influence of stakeholders such as shareholders and governments that impose cost cutting and profit imposts on boards and senior managers, have all been identified.

Government Policy and Industry Alliances

There is a continuing role for government policy directions and industry alliances to urge, if not insist on, individual organisations to set innovative directions and capabilities in safety systems management. As international trading alliances, treaties, conventions and agreements are implemented it will fall to governments, through policy directions, to reconcile the private rights of individuals and corporations and the public interest for safe goods, services and workplaces. Such policy settings should be supported by strong regulation and compliance regimes.

For example, the common law concept of negligence, shared by Australia with its trading partners, through international law, includes 'duty of care', 'right to know', and 'duty to warn'. In this book, the Seaview case showed negligence attributable to the CEO and the Regulator where each of these failed. In future, governments will be compelled to ensure such acts of negligence are mitigated through adequate compliance requirements.

For example, when California enacted the Safe Drinking Water and Toxic Enforcement Act of 1986, it combined a 'duty to warn' requirement along with the demand to advertise the safety levels of known carcinogens.

In 1992 the Australian Prime Minister announced the establishment of a National Pollution Inventory to ensure the Community's right to know their exposure to hazardous materials. It should prove relatively simple to adapt this 'duty to warn' model to Corporate and Occupational Health and Safety laws.

If organisations fail to protect their stakeholders, then the law should be up the task of serving the public interest. Companies in Australia should not be able to treat their responsibilities with impunity, due diligence responsibilities in safety matters. Their directors should not be able to hide behind the corporate veil and escape liability for the harmful consequences of their actions and inactions and their greed and negligence.

Attending to Risk

Greed, inadequate training, bypassing regulations and failure of the regulator to adequately insist on safety standards should be unacceptable when set against a managerial schemata and organisational habitus that espouses a responsibility for ensuring an appropriate priority on safety. A number of principles emerge from this book about how to get organisations to attend to risk.

Dominant coalitions must be made legally accountable for what goes wrong in their organisations and financial incentives should reward them for attending conscientiously to the control of catastrophic risks. Organisations that are concerned to be seen must also be seen to be concerned. Legal accountability is also necessary because of the potential for dominant coalitions to be populated by psychopaths (Babiak and Hare, 2000).

Decision-making must be structured so that the 'do nothing' option is removed. This involves the development of comprehensive, site-specific schemata and plans for the management of known major hazards. These plans must specify information gathering processes, signal recognition, possible trigger events, what must be done when these trigger events occur, and who is responsible for carrying out these actions.

There should be rigorous ongoing auditing to ensure that the protocols are working as intended. Within sensible boundaries, auditors must find ways of 'pulling the triggers' to see if what is intended to happen really does happen. Moreover, someone must audit the auditors to ensure that they are doing their job thoroughly. Regulators must also be willing to enforce the requirements of safety management plans and be prepared to prosecute when they find serious cases of non-compliance with plans that are supposed to be in operation.

The Significance of a Safety Aware Habitus

Differences in the way managers see a 'particular' situation and the events that pertain to it construct their decisions and therefore outcomes. Therefore, it is essential that dominant coalitions are able to manage the 'salient' psychological space. This leads to a requirement for a capacity to then manage the 'particular' background and the 'salient' physical factors. Managing the physical space is a different task for each operational site and depends on the capacity to manage the psychological space. These capacities are necessary to constructing the habitus needed to ensure high reliability.

A significant part of managing the psychological space is to manage the climate of power relations inside the organisation so that talented individuals are able to feel confident that they can safely pass important insights up the chain of command. The literature that signifies the psychopathologies also points to issues related to 'harassment', 'bullying', 'mobbing', victimisation and 'whistleblowing'.

Almost all of the literature suggests that individuals who are bullied, mobbed, harassed and victimised are subject to preventable poor human resource management practices that often result in qualified and capable staff leaving or being 'expelled' from their positions because they display qualities such as enthusiasm, integrity, and commitment that challenge the status quo or dominant culture. They are easy targets for passive-aggressive and abusive behaviours, including constant criticism, fault-finding, gossip and slander, and false accusations (Shalcross, 2003). People subject to these behaviours lose the motivation to prioritise safety.

The following cautionary quotation from Tom Wolfe (2000), connects the suggestion that both a 'corporate community' or habitus (ethos and culture) and competency 'training' (for understanding and schemata building, not just performance) are salient, as is the idea of not training for failure through 'the primitive stupidities of bureaucratism' ('ways of seeing', 'stance', ideas about management [memes]) and the influence on work practices imposed by others, such as management and unions (systemic factors).

Fairchild was rather enlightened, for an Eastern corporation, but truth was, there was no one back East who understood how to run a corporation in the United States in the second half of the twentieth century. Back East they had never progressed beyond the year 1940. Consequently, they were still hobbled by all the primitive stupidities of bureaucratism and labour-management battles. They didn't have the foggiest comprehension of the Silicon Valley idea of a corporate community. The brightest young businessmen in the East were trained– most notably at Harvard Business School– to be little Machiavellian princes. Greed and strategy were all that mattered. They were trained for failure.

If the core managerial competencies were present and had been applied, they may well have prevented 'preventable' fatal accidents from occurring. It also suggested that dominant coalitions both shaped and at the same time were influenced by certain key situational factors, such as the role played in decision making about safety by the mental schemata of managers and the heuristics they employ, by ethical practices considered central to an organisation's operations, their compliance with regulations, and stakeholder and stockholder pressures for profit. Training that addresses issues such as power and responsibility, language and sense making, ethics and priorities is critical in most organisations and essential in high-reliability organisations.

Limitations and constraints

The limitations of the book are related to the constraints of methodology and issues of scope and scale. Five cases may be too small a sample, even though the literature on small 'n' case studies suggests it is adequate. The inability to see inside the unfolding accident process limits accuracy, even though if that were possible, many cases would need to be studied to have any confidence in generalising from specific cases. It is not possible to interview accident victims, even for data triangulation purposes, which limits the verification of some assumptions.

This short section might be useful if you are applying Grounded Theory approaches in your own Research

Issues emerging as important for further research include addressing questions related to the ten competencies and compliance, and might focus on integrative aspects relating to management and organisations, such as organisational identity (culture, memes, ethos), change (as it relates to loss of ethics and corporate and individual responsibility), and the priority of production as it stands against responsibility for other than fiscal drivers (such as judgement, safety, and the management of a wide range of systemic factors particular to each organisation).

If the phenomena under study are amenable to surveying techniques it may be useful to 'quantify' each of the key codes and its dimensions (perhaps using a Likert scale). This is revealing if done in selected and related groupings and for each case.

Code Dimensions of the Key Code

Competencies: Advanced <----> Naive

Vigilance: Active intelligence capturing <----> Ignores signals

Ethics: Permeates organisation <----> Absent

Foresight: Scenario and contingency planning <----> SCP not done

Compliance: Self-imposed <----> Statutory imposition

Judgement: Jurisprudential <----> Impetuous

It would be feasible, using survey and questionnaire techniques, to establish baseline level competency assessments among experts along the following lines. The application of such information may be to apply baseline studies to particular high-reliability settings in a range of industries.

For example,

Competencies for high-reliability managers questionnaire:

Please rate the baseline level of competency (ie., before placement) you would expect of graduating managers from a Certificate IV of PG1 Diploma Degree on placement in your organisation in a role where responsibility for safety is a requirement; where:

1. = not necessary for the position

2. = somewhat necessary

3. = moderately necessary

4. = necessary

5. = essential

Competencies Codes Rating (1-5)

Ethics: (organisational influence is a factor as well as individual manager's values and behaviour)

Foresight: ('stance' is a factor here as well as 'intelligent looking ahead')

Vigilance: ('way of seeing' is necessary to 'alertness', signal detection)

Judgement: (weighing up, trading off, and deciding - often in circumstances that make little sense or meaning)

Balance: (psychological tenor, courage, persistence)

Organisational ethos: (open or closed [autopoiesis])

Constructing a culture of safety: ('ways of seeing' and persistent personal or organisational ideas - 'memes', enduring 'intention' to establish a culture of safety)

. . .

Understanding the salience of the particular situation and its context: (insight into the real and potential organisation and incident factors)

Performance in a particular setting: (stress, conflict, unfolding disaster, capacity for action)

Multidisciplinary performance: (using skills from different and complementary domains)

The investigation of correlational coefficients between key variables such as prior knowledge and systemic failure, vigilance and judgement, accident rates and compliance, ethics and foresight, autopoiesis and meme frequency may also be a worthwhile postdoctoral project.

In Conclusion

- The book hypothesises that incidents of organisational failure frequently happen with the information needed to prevent them actually available in the organisation before the incident occurs.

- This book suggests that incidents are scenarios of a rapidly converging confluence of events, none of which would individually cause an accident, and in which management does not seem to understand the forces it makes decisions about.

- This book suggests that if the managers who make cost cutting decisions could foresee their consequences, then they may reverse those decisions or not make them at all.

- This book found that managers who misuse power and control resources in favour of production interfere with the capacity for vigilance for critical accident avoiding information.

• This book showed that cultures favour satisficing, and that satisficing may compromise foresight and judgement and mitigate against a habitus of safety.

• This book considered the 'memetic' perspective and found that dysfunctional memes subverted critical communications, promoted autopoiesis and a dysfunctional habitus, which then became the cultural background to information, vigilance and decision making.

• This book contends that managers use selective and often unreliable heuristics, patterns, ways of seeing and schemata to construct models of reality, models they socially construct among themselves and share with each other.

• The book shows that a confluence of factors incubating in the organisation along with a limited stochastic attention span for essential information by managers results in critical information not being discovered

• The research suggests that it could be argued, if the manager failed to foresee an incident and did not exercise a level of judgement needed to organise the resources needed to avoid a disaster, then the regulatory regime governing that industry and the appropriate criminal law should be considered. Senior executives can not expect to hide behind the corporate veil.

• Each of the competencies identified should become part of a training and cyclical refresher training requirement aimed at building the schemata necessary to intervene in and manage accidents, for the dominant coalitions of high-reliability organisations.

Finally, an observation central to the assumptions underpinning this entire book, but which did not form part of the discovery process, is the impression gained by the booker that members of dominant coalitions are consumed with 'doing' and 'acquiring'. The outcome of many accident scenarios would be very different if they at least balanced this drive with some concern for 'being' and 'giving'. This returns us to Hiedegger's quest to understand 'being', introduced in the Introduction (chapter 1) as Eeyore's metaphysical engagement with ontology and phenomenology (Heidegger and Krell, 1993; Heidegger, 1927).

'I'm not saying there won't be an Accident now, mind you. They're funny things, Accidents. You never have them till you're having them.'

A.A. Milne, The House at Pooh Corner.

The issue developed in this book is that they *are* preventable, you have them BEFORE you have them. They are in train long before they happen.

The task for regulators, through policy and intervention, seems to require them to ensure that the members of the dominant coalition of high-reliability organisations act with a measure of diligence and altruism toward others.

However, this may not be possible in the light of the findings that significant numbers of people in dominant coalitions have personality disorders that are sufficiently serious to be formally diagnosed as having narcissistic, antisocial, or psychopathic personalities. The need for regulatory control over high-reliability organisations, therefore, should incorporate the notion that managerial psychopaths must *not* be allowed to act out their impulses simply because those impulses arise in them.

Perhaps Shakespeare sums it up best:

> *The world is still deceived with ornament.*
>
> *In law, what plea so tainted and corrupt,*

But, being seasoned with a gracious voice,
Obscures the show of evil? ...
What damned error, but some sober brow
Will bless it, and approve it with a text,
Hiding the grossness with fair ornament?
There is no vice so simple, but assumes
Some mark of virtue on his outward parts.
Merchant of Venice, Act 3, Sc 2.

Finally, is there a way of ensuring high-reliability safety?

The French solved the problem over 200 years ago. They passed a law requiring the explosives manufacturer to live on the explosives storage premises, *with his family*.

PART II

PART TWO: HIGH-RELIABILITY MANAGEMENT: A STUDY GUIDE

ACCIDENT PREVENTION: A HOLISTIC APPROACH

This section summarizes the key findings and implications of the research, offering a comprehensive framework for understanding and preventing accidents in high-reliability organisations. It reiterates the importance of developing the identified managerial competencies and fostering a proactive, vigilant, and ethically-grounded approach to safety management.

The Foundation of Accident Prevention: A Holistic Approach

The sources offer a multifaceted perspective on accident prevention, going beyond simplistic notions of "human error" to present a more nuanced understanding of the complex factors at play, especially within HROs. A central theme is the need for a comprehensive approach that incorporates robust safety systems, proactive risk management, and a deeply ingrained safety culture.

Moving Beyond "Human Error": A Systems-Based Perspective

While individuals bear responsibility for their actions, attributing accidents solely to "human error" is often inadequate and can hinder efforts to prevent future incidents. As discussed in the previous turn of our conversation, Reason's "Swiss cheese" model, mentioned in the sources, illustrates the concept of systemic failure, where multiple, seemingly minor weaknesses can align to create pathways for accidents to occur. The sources argue that a more effective approach involves examining the context in which individuals operate, identifying underlying vulnerabilities within systems, and implementing safeguards to mitigate those weaknesses.

For instance, the sources cite instances where inadequate log books and shift handover procedures contributed to accidents. This highlights how systemic failures can create conditions that increase the likelihood of human error, rather than simply blaming individuals for mistakes.

Harnessing "Prior Knowledge": A Proactive Approach to Accident Prevention

The sources underscore the crucial role of "prior knowledge" in shaping effective accident prevention strategies. This concept, championed by Turner's accident foresight theory, emphasises that information about potential hazards often exists within an organisation long before an accident occurs. This knowledge might be found in:

- Past incident reports: Even seemingly minor incidents or "near misses" can hold valuable insights into potential vulnerabilities within systems.

- Employee feedback: Frontline workers often have a keen understanding of risks associated with their work and can provide valuable observations about potential hazards.

- Hazard and Operability (HAZOP) studies: These structured analyses can help identify potential hazards and recommend safeguards to mitigate those hazards.

- Scenario planning: By considering a range of potential events, organisations can develop proactive strategies to prevent accidents and prepare for a variety of contingencies.

The sources argue that actively seeking out, analysing, and acting upon prior knowledge is essential for cultivating foresight and building a robust safety culture.

Cultivating a Safety Culture: A Collective Responsibility

A recurring theme within the sources is the vital importance of a strong safety culture, which they define as an environment where safety is genuinely valued and prioritised at all levels of the organisation. This goes beyond mere compliance with regulations and instead involves fostering a mindset where:

- Safety is seen as an investment, not a cost: The sources caution against the dangers of prioritising production or financial considerations over safety.

- Open communication about safety concerns is encouraged: Employees at all levels should feel comfortable reporting potential hazards without fear of reprisal.

- Continuous learning and improvement are embraced: Organisations should actively seek to learn from incidents, near misses, and best practices from other organisations.

- Dominant coalitions (senior management) are held accountable for fostering a safe work environment: The sources repeatedly stress the responsibility of leadership in setting the tone for safety culture.

Key Takeaways: Building a Multi-Layered Approach to Accident Prevention

The sources emphasise that accident prevention is an ongoing process that requires a multi-layered approach, incorporating:

- Robust safety systems: Identifying and mitigating hazards through thorough risk assessments, clear procedures, and well-maintained equipment.

- Proactive risk management: Actively seeking out and addressing potential hazards before they lead to incidents.

- A deeply ingrained safety culture: Fostering a collective mindset where safety is truly valued and prioritized.

- A strong compliance regime: Holding individuals and organisations accountable for meeting safety standards and regulations.

By embracing these principles, Organisations can move beyond reactive responses to accidents and create environments where safety is woven into the very fabric of their operations.

STUDY GUIDE : HIGH-RELIABILITY MANAGEMENT

Quiz

Answer the following questions in 2-3 sentences each.

1 What is the primary argument put forth by Kets de Vries regarding decision-making and organisational outcomes?

2 Explain the significance of habitus in the context of managerial competencies and organisational culture.

3 According to Boyatzis, what defines a competency?

4 Describe the characteristics of an "Antisocial Personality" as outlined in the DSMIV.

5 How does "resilience," as described by Reason, contribute to safety in high-reliability organisations?

6 What are the five stages a psychopath typically goes through in an organisation, according to Babiak?

7 Explain the difference between "foresight" and "vigilance" as high-reliability competencies.

8 What is the core distinction between "judgement" and "decision-making" in the context of high-reliability management?

9 Describe the concept of "salience" and its importance in managing hazardous environments.

10 What is "multidisciplinary performance" and how does it contribute to high-reliability operations?

Answer Key

1 Kets de Vries argues that unconscious psychological forces significantly influence decision-making and other key organisational processes, leading to irrational and dysfunctional outcomes, particularly in high-reliability organisations.

2 Habitus, a socially constituted set of understandings, shapes individual and group perceptions, influencing organisational behaviours and actions. It is transferable across domains and contributes to forming a specific organisational culture, impacting the effectiveness of managerial competencies.

3 Boyatzis defines competency as an inherent characteristic of an individual that leads to effective or superior performance in a specific job role.

4 The DSMIV describes "Antisocial Personality" as a pervasive pattern of disregard for and violation of the rights of others, often accompanied by a lack of remorse, impulsivity, aggression, and deceitfulness.

5 Resilience refers to the ability of individuals and systems to adapt and overcome errors, particularly in unexpected or high-pressure situations. It is crucial for maintaining safety in high-reliability organisations as it allows for flexible responses to unforeseen challenges, preventing potential accidents.

6 According to Babiak, a psychopath typically navigates an organisation through five stages: entry, assessment, manipulation, confrontation, and ascension. This progression involves charming colleagues,

building an influence network, eliminating those deemed useless, and ultimately seizing a position of power.

7 While both are crucial for high-reliability management, foresight involves proactively expecting potential hazards and planning for them. Vigilance focuses on actively monitoring the environment for emerging danger signals and responding promptly.

8 Judgement, a broader concept than decision-making, encompasses the entire process of weighing up options, considering ethical implications, and understanding the wider context before reaching a decision. Decision-making is the final act of choosing a specific course of action.

9 Salience refers to the ability to understand the specific and unique aspects of a hazardous situation, recognise its potential dangers and tailor appropriate responses. This competency is crucial for effectively managing risk as it moves beyond generic approaches and focuses on the nuanced details of each specific context.

10 Multidisciplinary performance involves drawing on skills and knowledge from diverse domains to address complex challenges. This competency is essential for high-reliability operations as it allows for a holistic understanding of interconnected systems and facilitates innovative solutions to unforeseen problems.

Essay Questions

1 Critically analyse the impact of "habitus" on the development and effectiveness of high-reliability competencies within organisations. Discuss how this concept influences organisational culture and safety outcomes.

2 Explore the potential dangers posed by individuals with psychopathic traits in high-reliability organisations. Drawing on examples from the source material, discuss how such individuals can exploit organisational structures and what measures can be taken to mitigate these risks.

3 Compare and contrast the high-reliability competencies of "foresight" and "vigilance." Explain how these competencies contribute to safety management, and discuss the challenges associated with developing and maintaining them within an organisation.

4 Discuss the ethical considerations that are central to high-reliability management. Using examples from the source material, analyse how ethical failures can contribute to accidents and what role a robust compliance regime plays in fostering a culture of responsibility.

5 Critically evaluate the argument that multidisciplinary performance is essential for achieving high reliability in hazardous environments. How does this approach differ from traditional, compartmentalised methods of operation, and what are the key benefits and challenges associated with fostering multidisciplinary collaboration?

Glossary of Key Terms

• Antisocial Personality Disorder: A personality disorder characterised by a pervasive pattern of disregard for and violation of the rights of others.

• Competency: An underlying characteristic of an individual that results in effective or superior performance in a job.

• Compliance: Adherence to rules, regulations, and standards relevant to high-reliability operations.

• Corporate Psychopath: An individual in a leadership position exhibiting psychopathic traits, potentially manipulating others and causing harm to the organisation.

• Ethics: Moral principles that guide decision-making, particularly concerning right and wrong safety-related actions.

• Ethos: An organisation's prevailing character or spirit, influencing its values and behaviours.

- Foresight: The ability to anticipate potential hazards and proactively plan for them to prevent accidents.

- Habitus: A socially constituted set of understandings, perceptions, and dispositions that guide individual and group behaviours within a specific context.

- High-reliability organisation (HRO): An organisation that operates in hazardous environments while maintaining consistently low accident rates.

- Judgement: The cognitive process of weighing up options, considering ethical implications, and understanding the broader context before deciding.

- Multidisciplinary Performance: The ability to draw on skills and knowledge from diverse domains to solve complex problems and make effective decisions.

- Psychopathy: A personality disorder characterised by a lack of empathy, remorse, and conscience, often accompanied by manipulative and deceitful behaviours.

- Resilience: The capacity of individuals and systems to adapt and overcome errors, particularly in unexpected or high-pressure situations.

- Salience: The ability to recognise and understand a hazardous situation's specific and unique aspects, tailoring appropriate responses to its particular characteristics.

- Signal Detection: Identifying and interpreting warning signs or indicators of potential hazards.

- Vigilance: The ability to actively monitor the environment for any emerging signals of danger and respond promptly.

ORGANISATIONAL ETHOS: THE FOUNDATION OF SAFETY CULTURE

Organisational Ethos: The Foundation of Safety Culture

The sources posit that organisational ethos acts as the bedrock of safety culture in high-reliability organisations (HROs), profoundly influencing how safety is perceived, valued, and integrated into daily operations. It is conceptualised as the invisible yet pervasive "water" in which the organisation "swims," shaping behaviours, decisions, and ultimately, safety outcomes. Going beyond a mere collection of rules and procedures, organisational ethos embodies the deeply ingrained values, beliefs, and assumptions that underpin an organisation's approach to safety.

The Morphogenic Power of Ethos

The sources draw on the concept of morphogenesis to illuminate how organisational ethos acts as an organising force, shaping the "form" and trajectory of an HRO. Likening an organisation to a living organism, they suggest that ethos acts like a guiding principle, akin to the inherent organising power of a tree seed to grow into a tree. It directs the development of the organisation, influencing its structure, systems, and ultimately, its capacity to function safely and reliably.

Dysfunctional Ethos and Autopoiesis: Threats to Safety

The sources warn against the dangers of a dysfunctional ethos, particularly its tendency towards autopoiesis. Autopoiesis is described as an inward focus, where organisations become self-referential, resistant to change, and closed off from external feedback. They prioritise self-preservation over safety, often exhibiting behaviours such as:

- Ignoring warnings and denying problems: A culture of denial takes root, suppressing valuable information that could prevent accidents.

- Blaming individuals for systemic failures: Responsibility is deflected from the dominant coalition, allowing flawed systems and practices to persist.

- Creating a culture of fear and silence: Individuals hesitate to raise concerns, hindering open communication and impeding the identification and mitigation of risks.

- Resisting external scrutiny and intervention: Input from stakeholders is disregarded, perpetuating a cycle of isolation and self-justification.

The CAA, as depicted in the sources, serves as a prime example of an autopoietic organisation. Its inward focus, resistance to change, and defensive response to criticism ultimately eroded public trust and hindered its ability to fulfil its safety mandate.

The Contagion of Dysfunctional Memes

The sources introduce the concept of memes as cultural replicators that can profoundly influence organisational ethos. These "persistent ideas" and "ways of seeing" act like viruses, spreading through communication channels and shaping how individuals perceive and respond to safety issues. Dysfunctional memes, such as "prioritising production over safety" or "that's how we do things here," can become deeply embedded in an organisation's culture, hindering the development of a safety-conscious ethos and impeding efforts to learn from past mistakes.

Cultivating a Safety-Focused Ethos

The sources advocate for a proactive approach to shaping a positive organisational ethos that prioritises safety and fosters a culture of learning and continuous improvement. They propose strategies to achieve this, including:

- Assumption Surfacing and Verification: Encouraging critical examination of the often-unconscious assumptions that drive behaviours and decisions, particularly those related to safety.

- Open Communication and Feedback: Creating a safe space for individuals to voice concerns, offer feedback, and challenge the status quo without fear of reprisal.

- Stakeholder Engagement: Actively seeking input from employees, customers, regulators, and other stakeholders to gain a broader perspective on safety risks and identify areas for improvement.

- Empowerment and Accountability: Giving individuals the authority and responsibility to act on safety concerns, fostering a sense of ownership and shared commitment.

- Leadership Commitment and Role Modelling: Leaders must champion safety values, demonstrate ethical behaviour, and hold themselves and others accountable for creating a safer work environment.

By fostering a culture of transparency, accountability, and continuous improvement, organisations can shift from a dysfunctional, autopoietic ethos to one that prioritises safety, embraces learning, and safeguards the well-being of all stakeholders.

MEMES AND SAFETY CULTURE

Memes and Safety Culture

Discuss the role of "memes" in the creation and maintenance of a culture of safety within high-reliability organisations.

The sources discuss the role of "memes" in the creation and maintenance of a culture of safety within high-reliability organisations (HROs). They argue that persistent ideas and "ways of seeing," which can be understood as memes, play a crucial role in shaping an organisation's safety culture.

• Memes are cultural units of information that replicate like viruses, spreading through communication networks. For instance, common phrases like, "That's how we do things here," can function as powerful memes, discouraging the examination of core assumptions and reinforcing potentially dangerous practices.

• The sources emphasise the danger of dysfunctional memes, which can hinder safety efforts in several ways. For instance, they can:

• Subvert critical communications by promoting a culture of denial or by encouraging reliance on outdated or flawed procedures.

- Foster autopoiesis, a phenomenon where organisations close themselves off from external feedback and become resistant to change. This can prevent HROs from learning from mistakes and implementing necessary safety improvements.

- Shape an organisation's "way of seeing," blinding insiders to potential hazards and creating a false sense of security.

- The sources highlight the importance of "meme management" for fostering a strong safety culture.

- Leaders, as the dominant coalition, play a key role in shaping an organisation's memetic landscape. Their actions, communications, and attitudes towards safety all contribute to the spread of certain memes.

- Dominant coalitions need to actively promote positive safety memes and challenge or eliminate dysfunctional ones. They can achieve this by:

- Modeling safe behaviours.

- Encouraging open communication and feedback.

- Challenging the status quo and encouraging the examination of potentially dangerous assumptions.

- Implementing training programs that focus on safety and risk management.

- Recognising the influence of memes is crucial for understanding the complex interplay of factors that contribute to safety culture. By analysing an organisation's communication patterns and identifying prevalent memes, safety professionals can gain insights into the underlying values and beliefs that shape behaviours and practices.

- The sources contend that simply changing organisational structures is not enough to improve safety; rather, a deliberate and focused effort is needed to cultivate a positive "safety habitus." This involves instilling a shared understanding of safety as a core value and promoting behaviours and practices that support this value.

In general, the sources promote a detailed view of safety culture that acknowledges the significant impact of memes. By proactively shaping the memetic environment within their organisations, leaders can cultivate a “safety conscious culture” that helps prevent accidents and incidents in high-reliability settings.

FREQUENTLY ASKED QUESTIONS ABOUT HIGH-RELIABILITY MANAGEMENT

Frequently Asked Questions About High-Reliability Management

What is high-reliability management?

High-reliability management is a set of practices and competencies that help Organisations operating in high-hazard environments maintain a low risk of accidents. These Organisations recognise the inherent risks associated with their operations and actively work to minimise them, even in complex and challenging circumstances.

What are the key competencies of a high-reliability manager?

There are ten core competencies crucial for effective high-reliability management:

Underpinning Capacities:

1 Ethics: Strong Organisational and individual ethics that guide decision-making, ensuring safety is prioritised and actions are morally sound.

2 Foresight: An attitude of proactive and "intelligent looking ahead" to anticipate potential hazards and develop strategies to mitigate them.

3 Vigilance: Maintaining a heightened awareness of risks, actively monitoring for signals and anomalies, and responding effectively.

4 Judgement: The ability to weigh options carefully, consider various factors and potential consequences, and make sound decisions, especially in ambiguous situations.

5 Balance: Achieving equilibrium between various Organisational pressures, such as production demands and safety protocols, without compromising either.

Capacities to Perform:

1 Habitus: Cultivating an Organisational culture that prioritises safety and embeds high-reliability practices into everyday operations.

2 Ethos: Fostering an atmosphere where safety is a shared value and concern, encouraging open communication to get ahead of hazard identification.

3 Salience and Context: Understanding the specific factors and nuances of each situation and adapting approaches to hazard management accordingly.

4 Performance in a Particular Situation: Possessing the necessary technical and human skills to respond to challenges and hazards within a specific context effectively.

5 Multidisciplinary Performance: Integrating knowledge and skills from diverse domains to address complex safety challenges that require a multifaceted approach.

What is the role of compliance in high-reliability Organisations?

Compliance with regulatory regimes and industry standards is essential for high-reliability Organisations. It involves adhering to established rules and procedures designed to minimize risks. Effective compliance requires:

- A clear understanding of relevant regulations and standards.
- Robust systems and processes for monitoring and enforcing compliance.
- A culture where compliance is valued and actively promoted.
- Holding individuals accountable for non-compliance, regardless of position or influence.

However, compliance alone is not sufficient. High-reliability Organisations go beyond mere adherence to rules and cultivate a proactive safety culture where continuous improvement and learning are paramount.

How does "habitus" contribute to high-reliability management?

Habitus refers to the ingrained habits, dispositions, and values that shape an Organisation's culture and influence individual behaviour. In a high-reliability context, habitus promotes a shared commitment to safety, where individuals instinctively prioritise risk mitigation and follow established procedures without constant reminders or enforcement. This ingrained safety culture is crucial for consistently maintaining a low risk of accidents.

Why is understanding "salience and context" important for high-reliability managers?

Every situation is unique, with specific factors and nuances that influence hazard potential. High-reliability managers understand that a generic, one-size-fits-all approach is insufficient. They recognise the importance of:

- Analysing each situation carefully to identify the salient features and specific risks involved.
- Adapting hazard management strategies to suit the particular context and address the unique challenges presented.

• Avoiding the trap of applying pre-determined solutions without considering the specific circumstances.

This context-specific approach allows for more effective risk mitigation and a more robust safety culture.

What are the dangers of psychopathic personalities in high-reliability Organisations?

Psychopathic individuals, with their manipulative tendencies, lack of empathy, and disregard for consequences, pose a significant threat to high-reliability Organisations. Their actions can undermine safety culture and lead to disastrous consequences. Organisations should implement measures to:

• Screen potential employees for psychopathic traits during the hiring process.

• Create a culture that discourages manipulative behaviour and promotes accountability.

• Implement robust whistleblowing systems to encourage reporting of unethical actions.

• Be vigilant in identifying and addressing the actions of individuals who exhibit psychopathic tendencies.

How can Organisations promote multidisciplinary performance?

High-reliability Organisations encourage multidisciplinary performance by:

• Fostering collaboration and communication between individuals from diverse backgrounds and areas of expertise.

• Valuing diverse perspectives and insights when addressing complex safety challenges.

• Providing opportunities for cross-training and knowledge sharing.

- Creating a culture that recognises the value of integrating different skill sets.

This collaborative approach allows for a more comprehensive understanding of risks and more innovative solutions for hazard mitigation.

How can an Organisation ensure high-reliability safety?

Achieving high-reliability safety requires a multifaceted approach that goes beyond implementing regulations and procedures. Organisations must foster a culture where:

- Safety is a shared value and responsibility at all levels.
- Open communication and reporting of hazards are encouraged.
- Individual accountability for actions is emphasised.
- Continuous learning and improvement are prioritised.

Leadership commitment, effective communication, and a genuine commitment to safety are essential for creating this high-reliability culture.

IS MANAGING HRO'S FOR YOU

A no-nonsense look inside at terms used in some chapters to help you decide if Managing HROs is a reference that should be on your management bookshelf.

This list of terms provides a quick overview of some of the key issues focusing on managerial competencies crucial for safety in high-reliability Organisations.

1. RELEVANT TAXONOMIES

• INTRODUCTION: INTRODUCES KEY CONCEPTS AND THE CURRENT STATE of knowledge in accident analysis, emphasising the need for a robust compliance regime that holds individuals accountable for errors.

• Limitations of Formal Decision-Making Models: Critiques idealised decision-making models like Bayesian Theory, arguing they fail to account for the complexities and pressures of real-world situations.

• Underpinning Capacities: Identifies five core managerial competencies vital for safety: ethics, foresight, vigilance, judgment, and balance.

• Habitus and its Influence: Explores the concept of 'habitus' as a system of ingrained dispositions shaping perceptions and actions, highlighting its relevance to understanding individual and Organisational behaviour in high-reliability settings.

• High-Reliability Competencies: Introduces high-reliability theory, suggesting that some Organisations foster a culture of failure tolerance, leading to inadequate managerial competencies and hazardous conditions.

• Defining Competencies: Explores the concept of 'competency' and its various dimensions, including roles, skills, attitudes, and emotional responses to situations.

• Psychopathological Personality Styles: Delves into the influence of personality disorders, particularly Antisocial Personality Disorder, on managerial behaviour and safety outcomes.

• Identifying Psychopathic Traits: Presents tools like the Hare Psychopathy Checklist and the "B-Scan 360" to identify potentially destructive personality traits in managers.

• Psychopath's Rise in Organisations: Outlines the five stages through which a psychopath typically ascends to a position of power within an Organisation.

• Countering Dysfunctional Behaviour: Proposes strategies to mitigate the risks posed by dysfunctional individuals and groupthink, including encouraging open communication, examining hidden assumptions, and promoting psychological balance.

• Reflective Practice for Enhanced Safety: Highlights Donald Schön's concept of reflective practice as a method for improving safety by focusing on system interconnections.

• Corporate Culture's Impact: Examines how certain corporate cultures might inadvertently foster psychopathic behaviour by prioritising manipulation and profit over ethical considerations.

• Historical Anecdotes: Uses anecdotes, like the Space Shuttle booster design constrained by a horse's rump width, to illustrate the unexpected factors influencing complex systems.

• Memes and their Impact: Introduces the concept of 'memes' as cultural units of information that replicate and influence behaviour, emphasising their potential impact on Organisational culture and safety.

• Managerial Networks and Idea Propagation: Explores how

managers' extensive social networks contribute to the spread of ideas, both positive and negative, within Organisations.

2. WHAT ARE HIGH-RELIABILITY ETHICS?

• DEFINING HIGH-RELIABILITY ETHICS: EXAMINES DIFFERENT ETHICAL systems and their implications for decision-making in high-reliability Organisations.

• Ethical Frameworks: Explores deontological ethics and the concept of 'duty of care', emphasising compliance with regulations, codes of conduct, and professional standards.

• Ethical Systems and Decision-Making: Discusses the role of consequences, laws, community norms, and personal conscience in ethical decision-making.

• WD Ross's Duties: Outlines WD Ross's framework of ethical duties, including fidelity, reparation, gratitude, and justice.

• Kant's Categorical Imperative: Explains Kant's concept of the 'categorical imperative', advocating for actions that could be universally applied as moral laws.

• Case Study: HMAS Westralia: analyses the Westralia fire incident, highlighting responsibility failures and the importance of forensic examination to uncover individual accountability and prevent future accidents.

• Case Study: Civil Aviation Authority: Examines a case involving a CAA officer's misconduct, emphasising the need for distance between regulators and the regulated to avoid conflicts of interest.

• Solomon's Social Responsibility Audit: Presents Solomon's framework for auditing social responsibility, prompting managers to consider the wider impact of their decisions on stakeholders and communities.

• Formulating High-Reliability Diagnostic Questions: Encourages the development of specific questions to assess ethical behaviour and decision-making within high-reliability Organisations.

3. COMPETENCY 3: VIGILANCE

• Defining High-Reliability Vigilance: Defines vigilance as the ability to attend to safety-critical information and maintain a low threshold for detecting potential hazards.

• Human Limitations and Information Processing: Acknowledges human limitations in information processing and the risks of task overload, highlighting the need for systems that support vigilance.

• Vigilance Descriptors: Lists key characteristics of vigilance, including attention to risk, auditing systems, debriefing practices, and recognising discrepancies in reporting.

• The Interplay of Vigilance, Foresight, Ethos, and Culture: Explores how Organisational culture and ethos can influence vigilance and create barriers to effective hazard identification.

• Psychological Underpinnings of Vigilance: Discusses the psychological processes involved in vigilance, including perception, stimulus detection, recognition, and pattern recognition.

• Case Study: Seaview Air: analyses a case involving a Seaview Air pilot, demonstrating how Organisational dominance and pressure to prioritise production can compromise vigilance.

• Case Study: HMAS Westralia: Revisits the Westralia incident, showcasing how Organisational ethos and cultural norms can interfere with debriefing processes and hinder the identification of contributing factors.

• Training and Maintaining Vigilance: Raises questions about the effectiveness of training methods for maintaining vigilance, considering factors like skill decay, site specificity, and individual differences in learning.

This timeline focuses on the Seaview Air case and the actions of Mr. Paull and Mr. Green.

Before March 7, 1994:

• Mr. Green, proprietor of Seaview Air, routinely offers wages and conditions to his pilots that are considerably less advantageous than those provided by the Pilots (General Aviation) Award. Pilots accept these conditions due to job scarcity.

• Mr. Green pressures pilots to break or bend aviation rules for his financial benefit.

• Mr. Paull, a Civil Aviation Authority (CAA) officer, engages in a close relationship with Seaview Air and Solitary Island Helicopter Service, compromising his ability to act as an impartial regulator.

• Mr. Paull uses training allowances to have the CAA pay for private excursions and accepts paid positions with operators he supervises, demonstrating a lack of integrity.

March 7, 1994:

• Mr. Matthews, the chief pilot of Seaview Air, is dismissed by Mr. Green and replaced by Mr. Mclver with CAA approval.

March 10, 1994:

• Mr. Matthews writes to Mr. Paull, warning him that Seaview Air is "a disaster waiting to happen" due to Mr. Green's negative and dangerous attitude and disregard for safety regulations.

After March 10, 1994:

• Mr. Macionis, prompted by Mr. Matthew's letter, requests an independent audit of Seaview Air.

• Mr. Abberton, Acting Regional Manager, thwarts the inquiry by simply soliciting a denial from Mr. Paull, neglecting an independent investigation.

Unknown Dates:

• Mr. Green acquires an aircraft, later discovered to have a cracked cylinder. Despite being informed of the issue, he halts the inspection and makes his own arrangements for repair.

• Melissa Munday, a former RAN marine technician, is instructed by a senior officer to lie to the Board of Inquiry about attempts made by crew members to fix leaking fuel lines on HMAS Westralia.

March 16, 2002:

• A news article in The West Australian reports on the above incident involving Melissa Munday and the HMAS Westralia.

February 27, 2004:

• The WA Court Of Petty Sessions holds a hearing on the HMAS Westralia case.

Undisclosed Dates:

• Multiple incidents and investigations occur, including those involving HMAS Westralia, Esso/BHP Longford, and Lake Illawarra, highlighting failures in safety management, compliance, and regulation within various Organisations.

Cast of Characters

Dr Maher: Argues for specific managerial competencies for high-reliability Organisations.

Marcus Aurelius, Roman emperor and Stoic philosopher, is quoted in the book to emphasise the influence of "invisible" psychological forces on organisational outcomes.

Sir Isaac Newton: Quoted to acknowledge the contributions of previous thinkers to the field of accident analysis.

Herbert Simon: Economist and political scientist whose description of the "ideal formal machine of decision making" is discussed in the book.

Pierre Bourdieu: French sociologist whose concept of "habitus" is central to the book's framework for understanding Organisational culture and individual behaviour.

Richard Boyatzis: Psychologist known for his pioneering work on competencies, whose definition of competencies is cited in the book.

Robert Hare: Criminal psychologist known for his work on psychopathy, particularly the development of the Hare Psychopathy Checklist. His work is used in the book to analyse the role of psychopathic individuals in Organisations.

Paul Babiak: Industrial and Organisational psychologist known for his work with Robert Hare on corporate psychopathy. The book outlines Babiak's five stages of a psychopath's movement through an Organisation.

Ian Walker: The interviewer in a discussion with Robert Hare about corporate psychopathy.

Daniel Dennett: Philosopher and cognitive scientist whose ideas about memes are discussed in the book as a potential framework for understanding the spread of dysfunctional Organisational cultures.

James Reason: Psychologist known for his work on human error and Organisational accidents. His concept of "resilience" is discussed as an example of multidisciplinary performance.

Ian Mitroff: Professor known for his work on crisis management and stakeholder theory. His concept of a four-dimensional perspective on problems is used to analyse failures of high-reliability salience.

Charles Perrow: Sociologist known for his work on Organisational accidents, particularly his Normal Accidents Theory. His analysis of the maritime system's contribution to errors is mentioned in the book.

Rupert Sheldrake: Biologist and author known for his controversial theory of morphic resonance. His concept of organizing fields is used as an analogy to visualize the influence of Organisational ethos.

Mr. Macionis: Individual who initiated an inquiry into Seaview Air based on concerns raised by Mr. Matthews.

Mr. Abberton: Acting Regional Manager who thwarted the inquiry into Seaview Air by accepting Mr. Paull's denial without further investigation.

Mr. Matthews: Former chief pilot of Seaview Air who warned the CAA about Mr. Green's disregard for safety regulations.

Mr. Mclver: Pilot who replaced Mr. Matthews as chief pilot of Seaview Air.

Mr. Green: Proprietor of Seaview Air whose dominant personality, disregard for regulations, and pressure on pilots contributed to safety concerns.

Melissa Munday: Former RAN marine technician who was instructed to lie to the Board of Inquiry about attempts to fix fuel leaks on HMAS Westralia.

Captain Pelc: Master of the ss Lake Illawarra who was found to have navigated carelessly, contributing to the accident.

Lord Denning: British judge whose definition of negligence is cited in the book.

Several other figures are mentioned in passing, including individuals involved in specific incidents, authors of relevant literature, and experts in various fields. The book utilises their contributions to develop its framework for understanding high-reliability Organisations.

4. COMPETENCY 4: JUDGEMENT

• Defining High-Reliability Judgement: Defines judgement as the complex process of weighing options, considering various factors, and making informed decisions, particularly in ambiguous and high-pressure situations.

• Distinguishing Judgement from Decision-Making: Differentiates judgement from the act of making a decision, emphasising judgement's broader scope encompassing ethical considerations, context, and potential consequences.

• Factors Influencing Judgement: Highlights the diverse factors influencing judgement, including cost analysis, discretion, stakeholder interests, impact assessment, ethical codes, and social responsibilities.

• Decision Styles and Their Impact: Explores different managerial decision-making styles and their potential influence on judgement, such as results-oriented, people-focused, analytical, and creative approaches.

• Kant's Perspective on Judgement: Relates Kant's ethical framework to the concept of judgement, emphasising respect for individuals and the intrinsic worth of all people.

- Case Study: HMAS Westralia: Revisits the Westralia incident, highlighting the role of misplaced trust in external agencies and the failure to adequately assess risks associated with subcontracted work.

- Cognitive Biases and Judgement: Discusses the limitations of self-insight and the influence of cognitive biases on judgement, acknowledging that additional information can sometimes hinder rather than improve decision-making.

5. COMPETENCY 5: BALANCE

• Defining High-Reliability Balance: Explores the concept of 'balance' as a state of equilibrium within an individual and an Organisation, enabling adaptable responses to dynamic situations.

• Bourdieu's Concept of Habitus: Connects balance to Bourdieu's concept of habitus, arguing that socially constructed understandings shape our perceptions, motivations, and behaviors.

• Aristotle's Notion of Hexis: Links balance to Aristotle's concept of 'hexis', referring to an ingrained moral character that guides our feelings and actions in different situations.

• Open and Closed Organisational Cultures: Discusses how Organisational cultures, categorized as open or closed (autopoietic), influence the ability to maintain balance and adapt to changing circumstances.

6. COMPETENCY 8: SALIENCE AND CONTEXT

• Defining High-Reliability Salience: Defines salience as the ability to understand the specific context and critical factors of a hazardous situation, moving beyond generic risk management approaches.

• The Importance of Site-Specific Understanding: Stresses the need for localized knowledge and expertise to effectively manage hazards, recognising that each situation presents unique challenges.

• Critiques of Orthodox Risk Management: Criticizes the limitations of traditional risk assessment models that prioritize frequency counts and financial implications over the broader impact on stakeholders and victims.

• Mitroff's Multi-Dimensional Problem-Solving: Introduces Mitroff's framework for analyzing problems from scientific, existential, inter-personal, and systemic perspectives, advocating for a holistic approach to safety management.

• Case Studies: Maritime and Mining Industries: Uses examples from the maritime and mining industries to illustrate the importance of understanding site-specific factors and the dangers of prioritising production over safety.

7. COMPETENCY 10: MULTIDISCIPLINARY PERFORMANCE

• DEFINING HIGH-RELIABILITY MULTIDISCIPLINARY PERFORMANCE: Defines multidisciplinary performance as the ability to integrate skills and knowledge from diverse domains to effectively manage complex situations.

• Mitroff's Concept of Expertise: Links multidisciplinary performance to Mitroff's concept of 'expertise', highlighting the role of experience, intuition, and learned opinion in problem-solving.

• Case Study: Boeing 767 Fuel Emergency: Illustrates multidisciplinary performance through the example of a pilot using glider skills to land a fuel-depleted aircraft, demonstrating the value of drawing upon diverse knowledge bases.

• Error Modelling and System Complexity: Emphasises the importance of understanding error models and the interconnectedness of systems, acknowledging the limitations of single individuals to master all aspects of complex environments.

• Mol's Multidisciplinary Strategic Approach: Presents Mol's framework for integrating safety and production in hazardous industries, advocating for a multidisciplinary approach to risk management, Organisational change, and human behaviour.

• Case Study: ss Lake Illawarra: analyses the Lake Illawarra incident, highlighting the importance of clear regulatory frameworks, well-defined responsibilities, and the dangers of inconsistency in applying safety procedures.

• The Need for a Multidisciplinary Competency Program: Advocates for the development of comprehensive training programs that equip managers with a diverse range of skills and knowledge necessary for high-reliability performance.

8. COMPETENCY 11: COMPLIANCE

• DEFINING HIGH-RELIABILITY COMPLIANCE: EXPLORES THE CRUCIAL role of compliance with regulatory frameworks and the ethical responsibility of managers to ensure adherence to safety standards.

• Case Study: ss Lake Illawarra: Reexamines the Lake Illawarra incident, focusing on the role of the regulator and the need for consistent enforcement of safety rules and exemption certificates.

• Case Study: Civil Aviation Authority: Revisits the CAA case, highlighting the importance of scepticism, independent audits, and verification processes to ensure compliance within Organisations.

• Permissive Cultural Attitudes and Compliance: Discusses the dangers of permissive attitudes towards regulations, emphasising the need for robust enforcement mechanisms and accountability measures.

9. CONCLUSION: SOME ANSWERS AND SOME QUESTIONS

• Reiterating Core Competencies: Summarises the eleven core competencies identified as essential for effective management in high-reliability Organisations.

• Quantitative Assessment of Competencies: Suggests the potential for quantifying and assessing competency levels using survey techniques and Likert scales, enabling baseline comparisons and targeted development initiatives.

• Competency Questionnaire for High-Reliability Managers: Proposes a sample questionnaire to assess the perceived importance of different competencies for specific roles in high-reliability settings.

• The Importance of Ethical Leadership: Reiterates the paramount importance of ethical leadership and behaviour in fostering a culture of safety and accountability.

• The French Solution: Concludes with an anecdote highlighting the need for personal accountability and a stark reminder of the potential consequences of safety failures.

PART III

BRIEFING DOC: HIGH-RELIABILITY MANAGEMENT

HIGH-RELIABILITY MANAGEMENT

High-Reliability Management

Dr Maher's emphasis on managerial competencies, the cultivation of a "high-reliability habitus," and the need for robust compliance regimes offers a practical framework for improving safety in organisations operating in high-risk environments. His analysis focuses on ten core managerial competencies identified as crucial for maintaining safety in high-reliability organisations (HROs).

Central Argument: Dr Maher argues that despite operating in high-risk environments, certain organisations fail to cultivate a "high-reliability habitus" – a culture that prioritises safety and learns from past mistakes. He attributes this failure to managerial incompetence, particularly in relation to the ten core competencies.

Methodology: Dr Maher utilised a modified grounded theory approach, drawing upon diverse sources, including accident reports, legal proceedings, psychological literature, and philosophical concepts. This multidisciplinary approach allows for a comprehensive analysis of factors influencing HRO safety. It reports in forensic detail on failed systems but does not put lives or systems at risk as would happen in double blind trials.

1. Ten Core Competencies:

Dr Maher identifies ten core managerial competencies essential for high-reliability management, which can be categorised as follows:

Underpinning Capacities:

• Ethics: Aligning individual and organisational values with ethical decision-making in safety matters.

• Foresight: Adopting a proactive stance and anticipating potential hazards through scenario planning and risk assessment.

• Vigilance: Maintaining a heightened awareness of risk, actively seeking out potential hazards, and effectively interpreting warning signals.

• Judgement: Carefully weighing trade-offs, considering diverse factors, and making well-informed decisions, particularly in ambiguous situations.

• Balance: Cultivating a psychologically balanced approach to decision-making, avoiding neurotic or psychopathic tendencies.

Capacities to Perform:

• Salience and Context: Understanding the unique characteristics of each situation and tailoring safety measures to the specific context.

• Performance in a Particular Situation: Effectively applying skills and knowledge in real-time, adapting to changing circumstances, and utilizing intuition when necessary.

• Multidisciplinary Performance: Drawing upon expertise from diverse fields and collaborating effectively with specialists to address complex challenges.

• Error Modelling: Accurately identifying and analysing potential errors, understanding their root causes, and implementing preventative measures.

• Compliance: Ensuring strict adherence to regulatory regimes and proactively engaging with relevant authorities.

2. The High-Reliability Habitus:

Inspired by Bourdieu's concept of "habitus," Dr Maher emphasises the importance of cultivating a safety-oriented culture within HROs. This involves instilling values, practices, and systems that prioritise safety and facilitate continuous learning from past incidents.

Quote: "Habitus informs this book as a principle of sociation and individuation: sociation because our categories of judgment and action, coming from society, are shared by all those who were subjected to similar social conditions and conditionings (thus one can speak of a high-reliability habitus)."

3. The Role of Psychopathy:

Dr Maher expresses concern regarding the presence of individuals with psychopathic tendencies in management positions within HROs. He argues that their manipulative, remorseless, and self-serving behaviours can undermine safety efforts and create hazardous conditions.

Quote: "Perhaps most frightening, [psychopaths] often seem completely normal to unsuspecting targets. Babiak and Hare (2000) argue that the corporate psychopath's cold-blooded ability to manipulate others without remorse, coupled with a veneer of charm and high energy, can make them successful in many walks of life."

4. The Importance of Salience:

Dr Maher stresses the need for managers to understand the specific context of each situation and tailor their actions accordingly. He criticises the generic, "off-the-shelf" approach often adopted in risk management, arguing that it fails to account for the unique nuances of each situation.

Quote: "Salience is a psychological way of seeing a 'particular' situation and the events that pertain to it. It is necessary, therefore, for managers cultivate the skill to manage the 'salient' psychological space. This leads to a requirement for a capacity to manage the 'particular' background and the 'salient' physical factors."

5. Systemic Failures and Compliance:

Dr Maher argues that systemic failures often contribute to accidents in HROs. He highlights the importance of robust compliance regimes, holding both individuals and organisations accountable for safety breaches.

Quote: "The Westralia incident was another example of how several factors can work together to subvert vigilance. What should have been a vigilance - foresight building opportunity was contaminated by Navy ethos issues."

6. Practical Implications:

Dr Maher's work offers practical guidance for enhancing safety in HROs. He recommends:

- Implementing competency-based training programs for managers, focusing on the ten core competencies.

- Establishing clear ethical guidelines and fostering a culture of accountability.

- Developing robust risk assessment and scenario planning processes.

- Encouraging multidisciplinary collaboration and knowledge sharing.

- Implementing rigorous compliance and auditing systems.
- Screening potential employees for psychopathic tendencies.

ABOUT THE AUTHOR

Dr Patrick S Maher holds three undergraduate degrees, four postgraduate degrees, two master's degrees, and the University Prize for Doctoral-level Research and Outstanding Scholarship.

After early studies in medicine he gained post-graduate academic qualifications and real-world practical experience in management, management psychology, organisational psychology, applied science, ethics, marketing and education.

He holds two MBAs and a prize-winning PhD in Management Psychology.

He is a qualified teacher and has taught at all university undergraduate and postgraduate levels in a wide range of disciplines.

He was a senior consultant to the Australian Civil Aviation Authority and a senior compliance consultant to the Western Australian Public Sector Standards Commission.

Dr Maher is a Golden Key National Honour Society member for outstanding scholastic achievement and excellence. He is a member of the Australian College of Educators and a member of the Australian New Zealand Academy of Management.